This book must be returned immed-
iately it is asked for by the Librarian,
and in any case by the last date
stamped below.

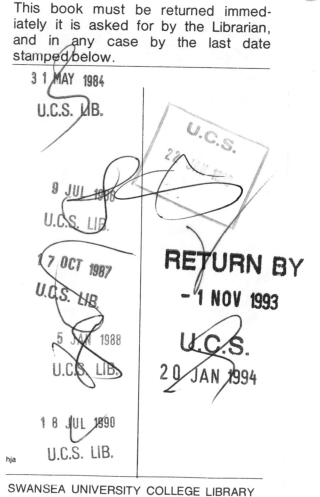

SWANSEA UNIVERSITY COLLEGE LIBRARY

THE EC'S GENERALIZED SYSTEM OF PREFERENCES

THE EC'S GENERALIZED SYSTEM OF PREFERENCES

by

Axel Borrmann
Christine Borrmann
Manfred Stegger

1981

MARTINUS NIJHOFF PUBLISHERS

THE HAGUE / BOSTON / LONDON

Distributors:

for the United States and Canada

Kluwer Boston, Inc.
190 Old Derby Street
Hingham, MA 02043
USA

for all other countries

Kluwer Academic Publishers Group
Distribution Center
P.O. Box 322
3300 AH Dordrecht
The Netherlands

Library of Congress Catalog Card Number: 81-50358

ISBN 90-247-2547-X

A publication of the
HWWA-Institut für Wirtschaftsforschung - Hamburg

PREFACE

The developing countries have long been complaining that the protectionism of the industrialized countries represented an obstacle to their export-oriented growth and industrialization endeavours. Free access to the markets of the industrialized countries is indeed vital to the developing countries, the more so as south-south trade is still relatively slight. From the point of view of the developing countries, therefore, the trade policy of the EC, by far their most important market, is of particular significance.

The EC was the first group of industrialized countries to introduce, with the enactment of the Generalized System of Tariff Preferences on 1 July 1971, a comprehensive preferential treatment of the developing countries, designed to help increase export earnings in those countries, promote industrialization and accelerate economic growth. The example of the EC was followed by the other industrialized countries, sometimes with a considerable delay.

Until recently there was widespread vagueness, both among scholars and politicians, about the actual efficacy of the Generalized System of Preferences, mainly because basic statistical data were lacking or were inaccessible. The HWWA-Institute, which, within the framework of its research programme, has long been concerned with problems of trade and development policy as well as with problems concerning the EC, was very pleased therefore to accept a commission from the German Federal Minister of Economic Affairs to subject the EC's Generalized System of Preferences to an analysis. The present study is the result of that research project which was finished in October 1979.

The main brief of the study was

— to create a data base providing for a detailed evaluation of the EC's system of preferences,
— to ascertain the effect of various factors upon the impact of the system of preferences,
— to explore the question of trade stimulating effects of the preferences and
— to establish the ranking of the EC's Generalized System of Preferences within the pattern of preferential trade relations between industrialized and developing countries.

In the course of their investigations the authors greatly benefited from the client's readiness to supply lacking information, also of a non-statistical character, and to discuss general and special problems of the EC's system of preferences. The HWWA-Institute owes a great debt of gratitude to the EC Commission in Brussels and to the Statistical Office of the EC in Luxembourg. The broadly-based empirical approach to the investigation would have been impossible without the provision of the necessary basic data on preferential trade or without the numerous individual items of information and suggestions from the two EC institutions. Thanks are due also to the Central Office for Tariff Quotas in Düsseldorf. The extensive data processing as well as the numerous analytical transformations were carried out at the computer centre of the University of Hamburg.

Hamburg   Armin Gutowski

TABLE OF CONTENTS

CONTENTS IN DETAIL

LIST OF TABLES AND DIAGRAMS

14

16

LIST OF ANNEXES

LIST OF ANNEX TABLES

LIST OF ABBREVIATIONS

ACP	African, Caribbean and Pacific countries
ASEAN	Association of South-East Asian Nations
BTN	Brussels Tariff Nomenclature
CARICOM	Caribbean Community
CCT	Common Customs Tariff of the EC
COM	Commission of the European Communities
CPG	Product code of the GSP
DIE	Deutsches Institut für Entwicklungspolitik
DIW	Deutsches Institut für Wirtschaftsforschung
EC	European Communities
EC-6	Community of the Six
EC-9	Community of the Nine
ECSC	European Coal and Steel Community
EDP	Electronic Data Processing
EEC	European Economic Community
EFTA	European Free Trade Association
EUA	European Unit of Account on a product basket basis at parities with only limited fluctuations
EUROSTAT	Statistics of the European Communities
GATT	General Agreement on Tariffs and Trade
GDP	Gross domestic product
GNP	Gross national product
GSP	Generalized System of Preferences
HYBR	Hybrid GSP products
IMF	International Monetary Fund
LAFTA	Latin American Free Trade Association
LDC	Less Developed Countries
LLDC	Least Developed Countries

MCCA	Mercado Comun Centro Americano (Central American Common Market)
MSAC	Most Seriously Affected Countries
NfA	Nachrichten für Aussenhandel
NIMEXE	Product list for the statistics on the EC's foreign trade and on trade between EC Member States
NSEN	Non-sensitive GSP products
OCT	Overseas Countries and Territories
OECD	Organization of Economic Co-operation and Development
OPEC	Organization of Petroleum Exporting Countries
SEN	Sensitive GSP products
SITC	Standard International Trade Classification
SOEC	Statistical Office of the European Communities
SSEN	Semi-sensitive GSP products
UA	European Unit of Account on gold basis at fixed parities
UNCTAD	United Nations Conference on Trade and Development

24

Chapter 1

THE DESIGN OF THE EC'S GENERALIZED SYSTEM OF PREFERENCES (GSP)

§ 1. Objectives of the GSP

The concept of generalized, non-reciprocal and non-discriminatory tariff preferences granted by the industrialized countries to developing countries reflects a change in development strategy: the traditional emphasis on "aid policy" is henceforth to be replaced by "trade policy" as one of the principal measures for the advancement of the poorer countries of the world.

The demand for the introduction of a preferential system was first raised in a wider forum at the First United Nations Conference on Trade and Development (UNCTAD) in Geneva in 1964. However, considerable conflicts of interests were revealed: the industrialized countries—in particular the USA—rejected a breach of the most-favoured-nation principle, and even in the camp of the developing countries those which—as members of the Commonwealth or as former French colonies—were already enjoying tariff preferences and feared a diminution of their privileged position reacted coolly to the idea of a generalized preferential system.[1] In consequence no agreement was reached in 1964, and another four years were to pass before industrialized and developing countries agreed in principle on the introduction of tariff preferences at the Second UNCTAD Conference in New Delhi under Resolution 21 (II). However, no such details as scale and duration of preferences, range of eligible countries and pro-

1. For the debate at the First UNCTAD Conference see H. Johann, *Zollpräferenzen zugunsten von unterentwickelten Ländern*, Hamburg 1969, p. 11 ff., and T. Murray, *Trade Preferences for Developing Countries*, London and Basingstoke 1977, p. 14 ff.

duct coverage, safeguard clauses, etc., were laid down in New Delhi. On 14 November 1969, eventually, a formal offer was lodged for the establishment of a preferential system by those industrialized countries which were members of the OECD, within the framework of UNCTAD, whereby they undertook to grant to the developing countries generalized non-reciprocal and non-discriminatory preferences. It was by then becoming obvious that the original hope of achieving a uniform preferential system of all industrialized countries with a uniform list of countries and products would not be fulfilled because of the divergent economic and political interests of the industrialized countries. On 1 July 1971, therefore, the EC, as the first group of industrialized countries, put its GSP into effect.[2] The other industrialized countries followed suit with preferential systems of their own: the first to grant preferences to the developing countries were Japan and Norway on 1 August and 1 October, respectively, of the same year; on 1 January 1972 Finland, Sweden, New Zealand, Great Britain, Ireland and Denmark joined the list, followed by Switzerland and Austria on 1 March and 1 April 1972, respectively. At the beginning of January 1974 Australia reformed and extended its already existing preferential scheme, and in July of that year the Canadian preferential system came into force. The USA took over six years before, on 1 January 1976, it implemented its offer of granting preferences lodged in 1969. Following the enlargement of the EC and the taking over of the EC's GSP by the new Member States there now exist eleven different generalized preferential systems alongside each other in the Western world. Several socialist countries such as Hungary, Czechoslovakia, Bulgaria, Poland and the Soviet Union likewise grant tariff concessions to the developing coun-

---

2. Strictly speaking, Australia was the first country, as early as 1966, to introduce a generalized preferential system in response to the demands of the developing countries; this, however, comprised only a rather limited list of 160 different products. See R. Pickel, *Handelspräferenzen als Mittel der Entwicklungspolitik unter besonderer Berücksichtigung des EWG- und des neuen australischen Präferenzsystems*, Diss. Cologne 1969, p. 170 ff.

tries. The different structures of the various systems will be examined later.

The developing countries had hoped that the introduction of a generalized system of tariff preferences would, as a first step, result in an increase of their export earnings from semi-finished and finished products. Opportunities to increase exports are not only provided by the direct effects on prices, which might, given certain prerequisites, lead to trade creation, trade expansion and trade diversion, but they are further intensified if account is taken of the specific tariff structure of the industrialized countries. Owing to the fact that the products at the beginning of the production chain are, on average, charged at a lower rate than semi-finished or finished products—i.e. the nominal tariff rate rises with the degree of processing—effective tariff protection in the industrialized countries is greater than the nominal rate suggests. In specific terms this means[3] that producers in an industrialized country can incur greater expenditure on their value added than is expressed in the nominal tariff rate without thereby losing their competitiveness as against the manufacturers in a developing country. The nominal tariff rate cannot therefore provide the sole basis for assessing the export opportunities of developing countries under preferential conditions; another decisive factor is the existing tariff structure of the industrialized countries.

Rising export earnings are the prerequisite of the elimination of the traditional chronic balance of payment deficits of most developing countries and of the widening of the freedom of action with regard to imports which is necessary for the development of the economy. At the First UNCTAD Conference the concept of the "trade gap", represented chiefly by Prebisch, played a central part in the developing countries' demand for

3. On the concept of effective tariff protection see W. M. Corden, *The Theory of Protection*, Oxford 1971. H. Hiemenz, L. Hoffmann and K. von Rabeneau, "Die Theorie der effektiven Protektion", in: *Weltwirtschaftliches Archiv*, Vol. 107, Part II, Tübingen 1971, p. 191 ff. For the empirical application of the proposition see B. Balassa, "Tariff Protection in Industrial Countries: An Evaluation", in: *Journal of Political Economy*, Vol. 73 (1965), No. 6, p. 573 ff.

trade preferences. Prebisch had forecast that the export volume of the developing countries would not, other things being equal, be sufficient to cover the import requirements of an average annual growth rate of 5%.[4]

In addition, the trade preferences are expected to help widen the (so far very limited) domestic market for sellers from the developing countries by the creation of additional foreign demand, and thereby to provide incentives for the extension of export capacities—i.e. growth-promoting investments—while at the same time rendering possible the realization of potential external and internal economies, designed in the longer term to promote the competitiveness of the developing countries vis-à-vis sellers from the industrialized countries.[5]

UNCTAD Resolution 21 (II) summed up the objectives of trade preferences for developing countries as follows:

— increase in export earnings;
— promotion of industrialization and
— acceleration of economic growth of the developing countries.

Non-reciprocal preferential systems vis-à-vis a limited circle of countries constitute a violation of the most-favoured-nation clause enshrined in Article I of GATT. However, the objection —made initially by the USA in particular—that the international trade system was being undermined has to be somewhat qualified, considering that customs unions and free trade areas, as well as the granting of so-called "waivers", had long ago led to a de facto breach of the principle of treating all countries alike. The question, moreover, arises of whether the idea of the most-favoured-nation treatment can altogether, in view of the differ-

---

4. See R. Prebisch: *Towards a New Trade Policy for Development: Report by the Secretary-General of the United Nations Conference on Trade and Development*, New York 1964.

5. See M. Feldsieper: *Zollpräferenzen für Entwicklungsländer, Bochumer Schriften zur Entwicklungsforschung und Entwicklungspolitik*, Vol. 20, Tübingen and Basle 1975, p. 54 ff.

ent commercial strength of industrialized and developing countries, still be regarded as either rational or fair.

§ 2. Structure of the GSP

A. Beneficiaries

The economic definition of the concept of "developing countries" has always been controversial; to this day there exists no unambiguous operational distinction criterion between industrialized and developing countries. The offer of the OECD countries to establish a generalized system of preferences took account of this difficulty by proceeding from the principle of "self-election", i.e. the countries concerned were free to decide for themselves whether they wished to be included in the group of developing countries and thereby become entitled to participation in GSP. The industrial countries, admittedly, reserved the right to reduce or enlarge the circle of beneficiaries in individual cases on economic or political grounds.

The EC, for its part, in selecting the beneficiaries proceeded from the "Group of 77", which in 1971 comprised 91 countries. In addition, a number of dependent countries and territories were included in GSP. As Table 1 shows, the list of beneficiaries was considerably enlarged between 1971 and 1978; the reduction shown for 1977 and 1978 is solely due to re-definition and to the combination of individual countries and territories.

Because the Group of 77 includes countries of very disparate states of development (e.g. Yugoslavia and Burundi), and hence also of very different competitiveness, the EC decided in favour of a differentiated treatment of the beneficiaries. Whereas in the agricultural sphere and in respect of most manufactures not affecting domestic production all beneficiaries are entitled to preferential imports, other products are subject to a multitude of special regulations. This applies above all to Romania and Yugoslavia, but also to the entire group of dependent countries and territories (among them, in particular, Hong Kong and Macao) which, until 1976 inclusive, were not entitled to import any kind of textiles or—until 1975—footwear. Altogether, duty-free imports of cotton textiles and goods enjoying equal customs consideration was permitted, until 1976 inclusive, only to the signatories of the Long-term Arrangement Regarding Trade in Cotton Textiles and to a few other developing countries which had undertaken appropriate obligations vis-à-vis the EC. From 1977 onwards, following the coming into effect of the Multi-Fibre Agreement, the various regulations on preferential imports of textiles were brought together, resulting in the non-discriminatory enjoyment of preferences by all independent developing countries. The dependent countries and territories, however, continue to be excluded from preferential imports of sensitive textile manufactures.

The lists of beneficiaries appended in the GSP to the various regulations do not, however, provide reliable information on the range of actual GSP beneficiaries. The prerequisite of duty-free importation is, as a matter of principle, that certificates of origin have been issued by certain governmental authorities notified to the EC Commission. Notification consists of the individual developing countries specifying to the EC Commission the customs authorities entitled to issue certificates of origin and depositing their stamp imprints and signatures. Initially the developing countries were exceedingly slow in meeting the requirements of formal notification: as recently as 1974 only 96 independent and dependent countries had fulfilled these preconditions of preferential imports; by 23 September 1977 their number had increased to 98 only. During the initial phase of GSP the customs authorities were instructed to adopt a liberal practice on the notification problem. Since 1975 fulfilment of this formal requirement has been enforced more strictly.

A particular role among beneficiaries of GSP is played by those countries which enjoy equivalent or even more favourable tariff advantages with their EC imports under special preferential agreements. Of the 147 beneficiary developing countries in 1977 this applied to as many as 70. These countries are able to choose between their special and the generalized system of preferences, which in fact means that an economically rational decision will as a rule go in favour of the special preferential agreement; these countries, therefore, may be viewed as purely "nominal" beneficiaries under the GSP.[6]

Table 1. *Beneficiaries under GSP[a] from 1971 to 1978*

	Independent countries	Dependent countries and territories	Total
1971	91	41	132
1972	91	41	132
1973	103	38	141
1974	104	44	148
1975	105	43	148
1976	109	39	148
1977	114	33	147
1978	115	27	142

[a] See the extensive list of countries in Annex 1.

Source: Own calculations based on *Official Journal of the European Communities*, various years.

B. Product Coverage

The objective of the GSP is the promotion of exports of semi-finished and finished products from developing countries by granting them suspension or reduction of duties. Raw materials and base metals up to the ingot stage, which are otherwise not subject to any or only to very low customs duties, are not, with few exceptions—also in respect of the associated developing countries—included in the GSP lists of products. The main emphasis in the granting of preferences is on semi-finished and finished industrial products, covered by chapters 25-99 of the Common Customs Tariff nomenclature. Among these products only a few are excepted from the granting of preferences. These are predominantly processed agricultural products.[7] Since some de-

6. For a more detailed examination of the problem of overlapping between GSP and special preferential agreements see § 9.

7. Not eligible, among others, are headings 29.04 C II, III; 35.02 A II; 35.05; 38.12 a I.

veloping countries have virtually no export opportunities for industrial products the EC increasingly also permits preferential imports of selected agricultural products. Table 2 shows the number of eligible agricultural products as well as the so-called "preference offer"[8] since the coming into existence of the GSP.

Table 2. *Preference Offer for Processed Agricultural Products*

Year	Number of products[a]	Preference offer in million UA[b]
1971	147	22
1972	147	45
1973	147	65
1974	187	450
1975	220	600
1976	241	1,000
1977	296	1,235
1978	307	1,300

[a] Number of tariff headings.

[b] Volume of imports during the preceding year.

Source: "Report drawn up on behalf of the Committee for Development and Co-operation on the proposals from the Commission of the European Communities to the Council (Doc. 245/77) concerning regulations relating to the application for the year 1978 of the generalized tariff preferences of the European Community", in: *European Parliament: Working Documents 1977/1978*, Doc. 302/77, 10 October 1977.

C. Depth of Tariff Cuts

The manufactured products of chapters 25-29 of the CCT, covered by the GSP, may without exception be imported duty-free. It should be noted that on principle only such products have been included in the system of preferences as are dutiable under most-favoured-nations terms or whose rate of duty was suspended for a short period only. Among the few exceptions to this rule are, for instance, heading numbers 31.03 A II; 31.05 A III a; 32.07 A VI a; 33.01 A II b and 70.01 A.

8. The "preference offer" for eligible agricultural products equals the volume of imports during the preceding year.

By contrast, preference in the case of agricultural products is predominantly confined to a reduction of tariffs. When the system was introduced the preferential margin was four percentage points, i.e. the average rate of duty was reduced from 16% to 12%. Over the years, admittedly, the EC made increasingly far-reaching tariff concessions also in respect of agricultural products: by 1976 as many as 61 of the altogether 241 eligible products could be imported duty-free.

After 1974 up to four different preferential tariffs existed for a number of agricultural products. The reason for that was in the differences between the external tariffs of the Community of the Six and the new Member States. For processed agricultural products the tariffs of the new Member States were, on average, substantially lower than those of the Community, and adoption of the preferential rates of duty would have resulted in exceedingly low preferential margins for certain products. In order to avoid this a lower preferential rate of duty was laid down for the new Member States, one which ensured the same preferential margin as in the other EC countries. As a result of the progressive adjustment of external tariffs of the Community of the Nine —accompanied by appropriate annual assimilation of preferential tariffs—uniformity of preferential rates of duty was achieved by the middle of 1977.

D. Import Potential under the GSP

1. The role of a-priori limitations

When they introduced the generalized system of preferences the industrialized countries reserved for themselves the right to lay down quantitative limitations on preferential imports whenever their economic interests demanded such action. To that end the GSP was furnished, in the industrial area, with a number of instruments designed to affect the volume, the origin and the allocation of preferential imports. These are:

1. Ceilings or Community tariff quotas representing the upper

limit of duty-free imports for each separate manufactured product,

2. Member State shares, regulating, in respect of a number of products, the allocation to the EC countries of total imports under Community customs quotas and

3. Ceilings or maximum country amounts specifying the maximum import volume from each individual developing country.

The strictness of application of these a-priori limitations depends on the nature of the products. Three main groups of preferences for manufactured products have come into being, graduated according to degree of competition with domestic products:

— sensitive,
— semi-sensitive and
— non-sensitive products.

These differ clearly in liberality of preferential treatment. The way in which quantitative a-priori limitations are calculated and applied is to be examined more closely in the following section.

2. Quantitative a-priori limitations

a. Quotas and ceilings

For all three groups of preferential industrial products the principle applies that duty-free imports are admitted only up to the level of the ceilings—known for sensitive products as the duty-free Community tariff quota. Admittedly, strictness of surveillance of these import ceilings—as will be demonstrated later —still varies a good deal.

Ceilings are laid down anew for each year and for each product. A ceiling consists of a basic amount to the level of imports from beneficiary countries[9] and a supplementary amount comprising 5% of imports from all other countries. The year of calculation of the basic amount as a rule remains unchanged for three years at a time, while the period of reference for the supplementary amount is intended to be as up-to-date as possible

9. Except countries with special preferential agreements.

34

according to the availability of statistical data. Table 3 shows the reference years for the calculation of ceilings and Community tariff quotas throughout the period of validity of the GSP so far.

It is true that, out of consideration for domestic competitors, there has been an increasing deviation from the general calculation formula, more especially if the reference year was one of extremely large imports. Thus in 1977, compared with the preceding year, no increase of preferences of any kind was allowed in respect of footwear or coal, iron and steel products, while for petroleum products and textiles the maximum import increment was only 5%. A similar picture emerged in 1978: for textiles, footwear, products of the European Coal and Steel Community (ECSC) and petroleum products the ceiling of the preceding year remained in force, while for semi-sensitive products the raising of the ceiling was limited to a maximum of 50%.

Table 3. *Reference Years for the Calculation of Duty-free Community Tariff Quotas and Ceilings in the GSP 1971 to 1979*

GSP in years	Basic amount	Supplementary amount
1971	1968	1968
1972	1968	1969
1973	1968	1970
1974	1971	1971
1975	1971	1972
1976	—a	—a
1977	1974	1974
1978	1974	1975
1979	1974	1976

a Because of inadequate statistical information the method of calculation was set aside in 1976 and the ceiling increased instead by a flat rate of 15% (5% for textiles and 5% also for hot-rolled ECSC products).

Source: Own calculations based on *Official Journal of the European Communities*, various years.

Generally speaking it should be noted that the method of calculating ceilings and Community quotas often severely restricts the developing countries' opportunities for expanding their trade.

Especially in the case of products in which the developing countries traditionally occupy a strong market position the time lag of three to five years for the calculation of the basic amount is a major factor. If additionally—in order to protect domestic producers—the supplementary amount is discarded[10] imports are virtually kept down to the level of the reference year. This applies in particular to sensitive products which are subject to strict surveillance of imported quantities and to which, as soon as the Community quota is reached, the most-favoured-nation tariff is applied. For semi-sensitive products such an automatic procedure is not mandatory; for them the Commission, when the import maximum is reached, may, upon application and following consultation with the Member States, reintroduce the normal duty. Non-sensitive products enjoy the most liberal treatment: in principle GSP imports of this group of products are admitted on an unlimited scale. For them there is no provision for regular surveillance of preferential imports, and reintroduction of the duty has so far been practised only in a few exceptional cases.

b. Member State shares

For sensitive products the instrument of Member State shares has been created in addition to the Community customs quotas; this provides for the Community customs quotas to be shared out among the Member States in accordance with a definite proportional formula. This formula (see Table 4) was laid down on a largely uniform basis for all groups of products[11] on the basis of general economic criteria such as share of foreign trade, gross national product and population total. The problematic aspects

10. According to calculations by the Deutsches Institut für Wirtschaftsforschung in 1974 no supplementary amount, or only a reduced supplementary amount, was fixed for manufactured products (excluding textiles) in respect of 35% of the quotas; for textiles (excluding cotton textiles) and footwear this state of affairs applied to just under 20% and for cotton textiles to as much as 85% of the quotas. See U. Möbius, "Gemeinschaftskontingente für gewerbliche Produkte aus Entwicklungsländern", in: *DIW-Wochenbericht*, Vol. 41 (1974), No. 29, p. 254 f.

11. A slightly amended formula is applied to textiles (see Table 4) and special arrangements also exist for certain products in cases where a Member State is particularly dependent on imports.

of this instrument—originally conceived as a temporary feature
—is obvious; it is unable to take account of traditional product-
specific trade flows and therefore results in a reduced utilization
of the Community tariff quota, apart from running counter to the
idea of the EC as a uniform customs area. The persistent criticism of Member State shares—criticism voiced also by the Commission—has since 1975 resulted in an increasing scale in the
creation of what are known as Community reserves. For sensitive
products subject to the Community reserve 80% of the Community quota is initially shared out among the individual EC
countries. Whenever a Member State share is exhausted the EC
country concerned must draw additional shares from the Community reserve to an amount of up to 40% of its initial share and
thus admit further preferential imports. Similarly the countries
will return to the reserve any unused portion of their shares. By
1978 nine industrial and four out of five agricultural sensitive
products were subject to the reserve arrangement. At the same
time the number of sensitive products (excluding textiles) in the
industrial sphere was reduced from 44 in 1971 to 13 in 1978. The
quotas operate at national level.

Table 4. *Formula for the Share-out of Community Tariff Quotas among Individual EC Countries (as a Percentage)*

Country	Until 1973	Since 1974	
		Textiles	Other sensitive products
Federal Republic of Germany	37.5	27.0	27.5
Benelux countries	15.1	10.0	10.5
France	27.1	19.0	19.0
Italy	20.3	14.0	15.0
Denmark	—	7.0	5.0
Ireland	—	1.0	1.0
United Kingdom	—	22.0	22.0

Source. *Official Journal of the European Communities*, various years.

c. Maximum amounts

It is a principle that, for sensitive as well as for semi-sensitive and non-sensitive products, an individual supplier country must not exceed a definite import maximum. This maximum amount as a rule is about 50%, though for the majority of semi-sensitive and especially for sensitive products it is often far from being attained. These maximum amounts, in contrast to the quotas, operate at Community level. Whenever a maximum amount is exhausted the most-favoured-nation tariff may be reintroduced for the supplier country concerned; all other countries may continue to export to the EC duty-free until the Community quota—or, in the case of sensitive products, the individual Member State share—is reached.

Strictness of surveillance is graduated also for the maximum amounts according to the degree of sensitivity. For sensitive products reintroduction of the tariff rate is automatic and immediate as soon as the maximum amount is reached; for semi-sensitive products the Member States' maximum amount may often be considerably exceeded, and for non-sensitive goods the GSP trade of individual supplying countries comes under surveillance and regulation only in exceptional cases.

The purpose of the maximum amount regulation is to allow for the differential commercial strength of developing countries and to prevent particularly competitive countries from exhausting the Community quota on their own. Needless to say, the interests of domestic producers also were a factor in the institutionalization of maximum amounts.

The extent to which such a limitation of imports from individual supplier countries is in fact designed to promote the export opportunities of the less developed countries and to spread the benefits of the GSP more evenly among all beneficiaries will be examined more closely in the analytical section.

d. Special maximum amounts

A certain special position is occupied by the special maximum amounts applied to hybrid products as well as, since 1977, to textiles because here the instrument of maximum amounts has been differentiated and refined, as well as being more or less closely linked to the establishment of Member State shares.

In the group of so-called hybrid products, which has existed since 1976—"hybrid" because they exhibit the characteristics of both semi-sensitive and of sensitive products—differential maximum amounts were first introduced for one individual product. This differentiation—or even discrimination—was introduced in order to restrict more effectively than in the past the export opportunities of the more highly developed countries. A developing country must expect its normal maximum amounts to be reduced to 15% whenever

— that beneficiary country or territory either attained the maximum amount for a given product during two successive years or
— it supplies the Community with at least 40% of its imports of the product in question from the beneficiary countries and territories as a whole.

The limit will not be applied in the case of those developing countries

— which have a very low per capita national product or
— which for a given product have charged against the preferences an amount representing at least 10% of their deliveries to the Community of industrial manufactured products eligible for the Community preference scheme.

Another rule is that the value of the special maximum amounts must not be generally lower than that of the Member State share since 1974.

For certain hybrid products a uniform distribution of reduced maximum amounts among the EC Member States is ensured by the fact that each Member State is able, at national level, to reintroduce the normal customs tariff with regard to a developing country covered by a special maximum amount whenever its GSP imports from that developing country have reached 50% of the special maximum amount. Whenever in an individual EC Member State preferential imports are found to have reached the level of the overall special maximum amount, the national customs authority is also entitled to reintroduce immediately the most-favoured-nation tariff. We have here therefore a combination of national and Community operation of the special maximum amounts.

The special maximum amounts created since 1977 in the textile sphere also exhibit a number of additional peculiarities. When, following the conclusion of the Multi-Fibre Agreement, the previous limitation of beneficiaries to the signatories of the Arrangement Regarding Trade in Cotton Textiles, and to countries which had undertaken commitments vis-à-vis the Community similar to those existing under that arrangement, was no longer justified, there seemed to be a need for special measures designed to protect both domestic producers and minor sellers from the developing countries against competitive pressure from particularly competitive developing countries. The instrument, in this case again, was the imposition of a special maximum amount reduced by up to 10% upon those developing countries which were supplying the Community with more than 6% of its imports from beneficiary countries and territories as a whole, provided that their per capita gross national product in 1972 did not exceed US $275. The distinction criterion between competitive and less developed beneficiaries is therefore somewhat different from that applying to hybrid products. For 12 of the altogether 33 textile products with divided maximum amounts the special maximum amounts operate at national level, with 30% of the Community tariff ceiling being allocated to the more competitive developing countries which are explicitly listed in respect of each product. Under the so-called "cumulative special maximum amount" the share of the special maximum amount due to each EC country may also be taken up unevenly; the share of the developing countries in the reduced maximum amounts is not subsequently laid down. The remaining 70% of the ceiling operates at the Community level in accordance with the rules for semi-sensitive products with Member States shares of 50% across the board.

Since 1977 the arrangement in the textile sphere has been further complicated by the fact that the special maximum amount is broken down into Member State shares also for sensitive textile products so that the national authorities have to supervise both their own national share of the special maximum amount vis-à-vis one or several most competitive suppliers and the "normal" maximum amount vis-à-vis the other developing countries.

e. Special treatment of least developed countries

In recent years the problem of the different starting points of the developing countries and the particular problems of the least developed countries among them has been increasingly to the fore in discussions at UNCTAD and GATT conferences. Under the existing structure of the GSP the group of 28 developing countries with a particularly low per capita income had been able to increase their exports to the Community to but a very limited extent. The EC therefore—largely in response to pressure from the Federal Republic of Germany—decided to take additional measures in favour of the least developed countries. As a first step the maximum amount regulation for semi-sensitive and non-sensitive products was suspended for this group of countries in 1977. However, the practical significance of this import easement remained limited since none of the countries affected had by then approached the maximum amount import limits. In 1978 the EC therefore logically abolished the ceiling limitation for semi-sensitive and non-sensitive products (except textiles) so that the least developed countries were able to rely on unlimited duty-free import opportunities for these products in the long run. In actual fact, however, only eight countries are affected by this liberalization of trade; the remaining 20 have already, since 1975, been enjoying unlimited exemption from tariffs under the Lomé Convention.

f. A-priori limitations for agricultural products

Agricultural products generally are subject neither to ceilings nor to Member State shares or maximum amounts, nor are these products classified according to degree of sensitivity. There are, however, a few exceptions to this basic rule—out of consideration for the ACP countries: five groups of products, including soluble coffee, cocoa butter and several types of tobacco, as well as preserved pineapples are subject to import restrictions. With the exception of unprocessed tobacco these products are treated as sensitive goods, although the possibilities of fully utilizing the Community tariff quota have been improved by the establishment of a Community reserve.

For the overwhelming majority of agricultural products the only a-priori limitation is the so-called "escape clause" which permits the EC to revoke the granting of preferences either totally or partially in order to remedy unfavourable situations which might arise in associated countries as a consequence of the GSP or in order to avoid serious disturbance in any of the economic sectors of the Community. This "escape clause" has never yet been applied.

3. Formal a-priori limitations

Acknowledgment of imports as preferential products is subject to formal conditions designed to prevent abuse of the GSP. Regardless of a product's degree of sensitivity every product must be accompanied by a valid certificate of origin. Originating products of beneficiary countries under the GSP are goods which are either wholly obtained in the beneficiary country or—if foreign (including EC-originating) preliminary products have been used in their manufacture—have undergone sufficient working or processing in the developing exporting country. The yardstick for sufficient processing as a rule is the so-called change in tariff classification, i.e. the product receives a classification under a four-figure tariff heading in the Brussels Tariff Nomenclature (BTN) other than that covering each of the third country products worked or processed. Here, too, there are a large number of exceptions.

A further prerequisite of the granting of preferences is that the goods are consigned directly from the beneficiary country to the EC unless temporary storage in another country is indispensable for geographical or technical reasons; in the latter case they must remain under the control of the customs authorities.

A liberalization of the GSP rules of origin—which, by comparison with the Lomé Convention, for instance, are fairly restrictive—took place in 1975, when cumulative origin was recognized for three regional groupings of developing countries (ASEAN, MCCA and the Andean group). Goods from any one Member State of these regional groupings are considered as originating products even if they are worked or processed in another country of that region and are subsequently exported to the EC. Goods from third countries not belonging to the region [12] may be used in production provided their value does not exceed 5% of the value of the final product. As a general principle evidence of origin requires use of the prescribed Form "A" certificate which must be issued by the competent customs authorities in the developing countries. Reference has already been made to the formal requirement that the customs authorities issuing such certificates of origin must be communicated to the EC and their specimen signatures and stamps transmitted to the Commission (Notification requirement).[13]

The European Community's offer of a Generalized System of Preferences was initially limited to a period of ten years.[14] In March 1975 the EC Council decided to apply the GSP, which had by then become a fundamental instrument for co-operation in development matters, beyond the year 1980. The areas in which the GSP of the 1980s might be revised and improved in order to serve more effectively the objectives aimed at—increase of export earnings, promotion of industrialization and acceleration of growth in the developing countries—are to be revealed by the following analysis of its effects to date.

12. Including preliminary products from the EC; the principle of so-called "bilateral cumulation" does not therefore apply.

13. See § 2 A.

14. The GATT "waiver" is valid until 25 June 1981.

Chapter 2

EVALUATION OF THE EC's GSP AND ITS EFFECT ON IMPORTS

§ 3. Methods

A. Scope of Analysis

The objectives and structure of the GSP having been set out in the preceding chapter, the time has now come to evaluate the GSP and its effects on imports. By way of introduction the problems of data processing and estimation arising in this study will be described (§ 3 B).

In § 4 are presented the statistical findings and calculations for the period under review 1973-1976; they are to throw light on the scope, structure and development of GSP imports. This is followed by a comparison of the GSP with the EC's overall trade (§ 5). The aim is the determination of the potential volume of preferential imports as it arises from the product-specific and country-specific limitations of the GSP. This GSP potential is next compared with actual GSP imports. The discrepancy between GSP potential and actual GSP imports is then traced to its causes (§ 6). Particular attention is given in this connection to the part played by a-priori limitations.

A tariff-analytical consideration of the GSP is presented in § 7. This deals not only with tariff structure and with tariff revenues foregone owing to GSP but also with the problems of tariff incidence.

Finally, § 8 examines the stimulation effect of tariffs. This is a root problem of this study: the question of whether—and, if so, to what extent—the GSP is succeeding in providing *additional* growth impulses to the EC's import trade with beneficiary developing countries. In a reduced procedure the increase in trade during the period under review is traced back to its individual determinants, such as product effects and country effects, so that an adjusted GSP effect is eventually isolated.

B. Data Processing and Problems of Estimation

Like all other industrialized countries granting general tariff preferences the EC so far has had only very scanty and fragmentary statistical information on the scope and structure of its preferential trade with developing countries. One of the principal tasks of the investigation, therefore, was to gain, for the first time, a substantially more complete and more detailed view of the EC's GSP and its performance over the longest possible span of time.

The empirical part of the study is based on data made available in the form of magnetic tape by the German Federal Ministry of Economic Affairs and the Statistical Office of the EC (SOEC). In addition, use was made of generally accessible data from official publications. All necessary calculations were performed by electronic data processing.

As is probably inevitable whenever such large quantities of data are involved, accurate analysis and, more particularly, the confrontation of data from different sources revealed a considerable number of data errors. The errors thus discovered were, whenever possible, corrected by reference to further sources or else by considerations of plausibility. Special emphasis was laid on the elimination of incompatibilities. In cases of doubt preference was given to the statistics closest to the data surveyed.

At the SOEC the GSP trade data of all Member States are available in machine-readable form only for the years from 1975 onwards. For the earlier years the EC's general foreign trade statistics (NIMEXE) only were available. One of the main tasks of the study consisted in estimating the missing preferential trade for 1973 and 1974. This was done by proceeding from the German GSP statistics, which are available at the German Federal

46

Ministry of Economic Affairs for the period from 1973 onwards, though in a divergent form of processing. On the hypothesis that for every product the ratio between German GSP imports and total German imports, as determined from the NIMEXE statistics, was transferable also to the GSP trade of the remaining EC countries, the GSP imports of those remaining countries were estimated. This calculation had to be performed for non-sensitive goods only since in the sensitive and semi-sensitive areas the total trade volume and selected national figures were available in respect of each product from data of the customs administration of the EC Commission. The figures for the countries not specified were determined by the share of their trade in the total imports of the product concerned.

According to the GSP scale established, GSP trade is defined in terms of units of account (UA), kg or m^3. In order to achieve horizontal comparability of the data all data were uniformly converted into UA. From the NIMEXE statistics, which lists both the import volume and the import value in respect of each product heading, supplier-country-specific average import values were calculated for each product and the necessary transformations were then performed by means of these. Since GSP trade, wherever it is defined in terms of value, was recorded and supervised in UA—which means that the EC Commission accepted the risk that preservation of the UA/national currency parities, as they became obsolete in later years, would lead to certain distortions of trade—the UA has been used as a yardstick in the present study.[1]

There are two other reasons why a warning should be uttered here against any excessively precise interpretation or, more particularly, any excessive extrapolation of the data. First, the period of time since the implementation of the GSP in mid-1971 has been rather short; during the initial phase in particular, certain untypical trends are bound to occur, and more detailed investigation results have only been established for the even shorter three-year period from 1973 to 1976. Secondly, the period

1. The UA problem will be dealt with in greater detail below. See § 4 B.

under review has been marked by a large number of international economic upheavals, of which the worldwide recession, the oil price crisis and the worldwide boom in raw materials are only a few. These factors also change the relations between industrialized and developing countries and are bound to affect the findings of this study.

§ 4. Volume and Structure of GSP Trade

A. GSP Trade by Products

1. Product coverage of the GSP

a. NIMEXE items

The most detailed system of product classification is the NIMEXE code. The EC's official foreign trade statistics are based on this 6-digit code. With very few exceptions the assignment of a product to a particular code number remains fixed over the years. Longitudinal section investigations based on the NIMEXE code can therefore claim a higher degree of significance than, for instance, those based on the frequently changing CPG code.[2]

Table 5 compares, for each year under review, the number of different GSP products with the number of all products imported into the EC in the year concerned. By relating these two sets of figures to each other we obtain the percentage of relevant products covered in any form whatsoever by the GSP.

If assessment is based solely on product categories then the GSP's coverage is fairly high at over 75%. As, throughout four years, the growth of eligible products, at 10.3%, was greater than the growth of all products traded, at 6.5%, the degree of coverage also exhibited a rising trend.

From a development policy point of view the mere number of products included in the GSP is of only slight importance. What matters is whether the developing countries were at all capable of

2. For the CPG code see § 4, A.1.b. below and Annex 2.

Table 5. *Number of Products Imported into the EC and Number of Eligible Products by NIMEXE classification, 1973 to 1976*

Year	Products imported into the EC (1)	Eligible products (2)	Coverage in % (2/1)
1973	6,396	4,833	75.6
1974	6,505	5,081	78.1
1975	6,657	5,238	78.7
1976	6,809	5,331	78.3
Increase 1973-1976	+ 6.5%	+ 10.3%	

Source: Own calculations based on SOEC and German Federal Ministry of Economic Affairs data.

supplying the individual products. Table 6 therefore additionally lists those products in respect of which imports from the eligible developing countries were in fact recorded in each year concerned.

Table 6. *Number of Eligible Products and of Products in Respect of which the Eligible Developing Countries were Capable of Delivery, by NIMEXE Classification, 1973, 1974 and 1976*

Year	Number of GSP products		Coverage in % (2/1)
	Total (1)	Which the developing countries were able to supply (2)	
1973	4,833	3,354	69.4
1974	5,081	3,889	76.5
1976	5,331	4,102	76.9
Increase 1973, 1974 and 1976	+ 10.3%	+ 22.3%	

Source: Own calculations based on SOEC and German Federal Ministry of Economic Affairs data.

It emerges from Table 6 that in 1976 only about 77% of all products represented in the GSP were in fact capable of being supplied by eligible developing countries. Yet this 77% coverage does not in fact indicate the number of products in respect of which actual GSP imports were recorded. That number would certainly be lower still since granting of preferences is subject to a number of formal requirements. Admittedly the number of GSP products in respect of which the developing countries were capable of making deliveries rose twice as fast as the number of GSP products generally. This level of coverage, therefore, is rising. A significant increase was brought about by the enlargement of the EC in 1974.

By rule of thumb the situation may be summed up as follows: about three-quarters of all products traded have found access into the GSP in some form or other. Yet this relatively high degree of coverage is subject to correction as only three-quarters of the GSP products were in fact supplied by developing countries. The percentage of actually suppliable GSP products of the total merchandise ranged from 52.4% in 1973 to 60.2% in 1976. It has a rising trend.

b. CPG items

The GSP itself describes the products not in terms of NIMEXE classification but as CPG headings.[3] At the same time the CPG code is largely based on the NIMEXE code. It takes over its first four digits and, for further information, adds the regulation under which the product concerned falls, so that degree of sensitivity and range of beneficiary countries are thereby determined. As a rule several NIMEXE items identical to four digits are grouped together as a new CPG item. The reverse case also arises: in the textiles field, in particular, products identical under NIMEXE may be assigned to different regulations according to country of origin and hence also to different CPG heading numbers.

Allocation of NIMEXE-defined products to individual CPG

---

3. For a detailed survey of the CPG code see Annex 2.

headings in many instances changes from year to year, so that meaningful longitudinal section investigation is virtually impossible at a very refined CPG level. At a higher aggregate level, on the other hand, an analysis of CPG products can be meaningful. Table 7 lists the CPG products by degree of sensitivity. The special Regulations 18 and 28 for Yugoslavia and 29 for Romania only contain products which crop up again in other regulations. They were therefore not included here.

Table 7. *Number of CPG Products by Degree of Sensitivity, 1973 to 1976 (excluding Regulations 18, 28, 29)*

Year	Degree of sensitivity			Total	Proportion of NSEN in %
	SEN	SSEN	NSEN		
1973	92	105	829	1,026	82.4
1974	85	80	919	1,084	84.8
1975	50	124[a]	967	1,141	84.8
1976	51	129[a]	947	1,127	84.0

[a] Including hybrid GSP products.

Source: Own calculations based on SOEC and German Federal Ministry of Economic Affairs data.

As under the NIMEXE classification, a slight increase in the number of products generally is observed here too. This increase is almost entirely accounted for by the non-sensitive sphere which comprises 84% of all products. The number of sensitive and semi-sensitive products together, on the other hand, showed scarcely any change. Admittedly a certain liberalization effect may be observed here: the number of particularly strictly regulated sensitive products is continually declining. By 1976 only 4.5% of all products came under this category.[4]

Of the 947 non-sensitive products existing in 1976 233 (i.e. 25%) registered no GSP trade at all (see Table 8). That the

4. Although the formerly sensitive products are no longer subject to Member State share arrangements, many of them have been categorized as hybrid products subject to an intensified maximum amount arrangement.

developing countries were in fact incapable of making deliveries in respect of a large proportion of these items is proved by the figure of 111 non-sensitive products in respect of which most-favoured-nation trade was not recorded either. The remaining products predominantly registered very small import quantities. These unused preference opportunities are spread over the entire products spectrum.

Table 8. *GSP Products without GSP Imports, by Degree of Sensitivity, 1976*

	Number of products	
	Without GSP imports	Of these without imports under most-favoured-nation terms
SEN	2	—
SSEN	29	12
NSEN	233	111
Total	264	123

Source: Own calculations based on SOEC and German Federal Ministry of Economic Affairs data.

While it might be argued in the case of non-sensitive products that such pronounced non-utilization gaps are entirely reasonable—after all, the developing countries are to be encouraged to make investments in the very areas in which they have not so far been capable of delivery—the extent of zero imports of sensitive and semi-sensitive products is nevertheless surprising. In these groups, too, 31 CPG products did not register any preferential imports at all. The major part of 28 products here comes under the special regulations for Yugoslavia and Romania. In theory imports of certain products from these two countries are regarded as so problematical that they are categorized one sensitivity class more severely than imports from other developing countries. In practice, however, this harsh treatment often does not seem justified. More than one-half of all semi-sensitive Romanian products registers no GSP trade at all, and one-fifth not even most-favoured-nation trade. Things are similar under Regulation 28 for Yugoslavia: eight out of 20 items show no GSP trade at all, and six of these no most-favoured-nation trade either.

2. Trade performance by products and product groups

a. Introductory note

An analysis of the GSP based solely on the number of types of products can provide no more than an approximate idea of the significance of individual categories, as more important and less important products are listed alongside one another as equals. A more differentiated examination, making allowance for the actual volume of individual GSP products, requires the conversion of all trade flows into a uniform dimension.

In its original form the GSP trade was available partly in terms of value and partly in terms of quantities. Another part had to be determined from scratch altogether. From the EC's overall trade, which allows both for the quantitative and the value dimension, it was possible to calculate average EC-country-specific import values for each CPG heading. With the aid of these average values the given quantitative data were then converted into the required value dimension.

The extraordinarily large amount of data renders it impossible within the framework of the present publication to list complete product and country results at CPG level. Moreover, the four-digit tariff heading numbers provide an excessively detailed break-down; results at this disaggregation level can be presented here only for the most important GSP products. Complete surveys of GSP imports during 1974 to 1976 will be given in the following passages at CCT chapter and section level, as well as by definite product groups and broken down by individual EC countries.

b. GSP trade by degree of sensitivity

In line with the presentation in Table 7, Table 9 lists the entire GSP trade as available to us in official statistics or as calculated by us, arranged by degree of sensitivity. Table 10 presents the same information in relative magnitudes.

The most striking aspect is the marked growth of preferential trade over the course of a mere three years from 612 million UA to 3,036 million UA, representing an increase of 396%. Converted to an annual growth rate this is an increase of about 70% per year.[5] The growth of GSP trade as a whole is composed of very divergent growth rates in the various sensitivity groups. While sensitive trade with an increase of 333% is increasing at roughly the same order of magnitude as total trade, non-sensitive trade at 141% lies below that level and semi-sensitive trade with an increase of 1,181% vastly exceeds it.

A glance at Table 10 illustrates the consequences resulting for the structural composition of GSP trade from the divergent growth rates of the individual areas. About one-half of GSP trade is in non-sensitive products, though their proportion shows a decline over the years. The other half is made up of sensitive and semi-sensitive products. The change (mentioned in the preceding chapter) within the regulated area, manifesting itself in a shift from sensitive to semi-sensitive products, may be observed here too. The proportion of sensitive trade declined by one-half from 29% to 14.5%.[6] This shift of emphasis from sensitive to semi-sensitive trade suggests a certain liberalization in the classification system of the GSP.

5. The 1975 figure is interesting. In that year GSP trade shows a decline compared with the preceding year—a fact which does not seem very plausible and suggests a data error. At the same time certain cyclically-conditioned setbacks were recorded throughout the entire trade of the developing countries and these had a particularly marked effect in the areas of semi-finished and finished products, the typical GSP items. Moreover, in that year SOEC switched its central data collecting on GSP trade over to electronic data processing, an operation which caused a whole string of problems there. The SOEC therefore recommends that the 1975 data should only be used with great caution. They have been listed here solely for the sake of completeness.

6. It should, however, be borne in mind that this strong recession of sensitive trade was partly offset by an increase in the trade in hybrid products which in 1975 registered imports of approximately 101 million UA and in 1976 imports of approximately 141 million UA.

Table 9. *GSP Trade by Degree of Sensitivity 1973 to 1976 in 1,000 UA*

Year	Degree of sensitivity			Total[b]
	SEN	SSEN	NSEN	
1973	183,060	86,731	342,327	612,118
1974	496,257	451,785	805,170	1,753,211
1975	274,488	608,139[a]	847,319	1,729,945
1976	441,451	1,110,720[a]	1,483,681	3,035,852
Increase 1973-1976	+ 141%	+ 1,181%	+ 333%	+ 396%

[a] Including hybrid products.
[b] Slight discrepancies due to rounding errors.

Source: Own calculations based on SOEC and German Federal Ministry of Economic Affairs data.

Table 10. *GSP Trade by Degree of Sensitivity 1973 to 1976*
(as a Percentage)

Year	Degree of sensitivity			Total[b]
	SEN	SSEN	NSEN	
1973	29.9	14.2	55.9	100
1974	28.3	25.8	45.9	100
1975	15.9	35.2[a]	49.0	100
1976	14.5	36.6[a]	48.9	100

[a] Including hybrid products.
[b] Slight discrepancies due to rounding errors.

Source: Own calculations based on SOEC and German Federal Ministry of Economic Affairs data.

That, however, would be a rash conclusion. It would be entirely possible for sensitive trade to show a relative diminution only because it is being prevented from excessive growth by a highly restrictive corset of regulating import limits. The impact of these restrictions will be further examined in § 6.

Another interesting exercise is comparison with the results of

Table 7 showing the number of products. While this shows about 85% of all products coming within the non-sensitive group and while this proportion, if anything, shows a growing trend, matters appear to be reversed if, as in Table 10, the real importance of the products is taken into account. Only about half the trade is accounted for by non-sensitive products and their proportion continues to decline.

This correlation is represented once more in Table 11. The average volume of trade in sensitive and semi-sensitive products is clearly greater than that in non-sensitive products.

Table 11. *Average Volume of Trade per CPG Heading by Degree of Sensitivity, 1973 to 1976 (excluding Regulations 18, 28, 29)* (in 1,000 UA)

Year	Degree of sensitivity			Total GSP imports
	SEN	SSEN[a]	NSEN	
1973	1,990	826	413	597
1974	5,838	5,647	876	1,617
1975	5,490	4,904	876	1,516
1976	8,656	8,610	1,567	2,694

a Including hybrid products.

Source: Own calculations based on SOEC and German Federal Ministry of Economic Affairs data.

c. GSP trade by chapters and sections of the CCT

The products most accurately defined by the six-digit NIMEXE code can be grouped together in CCT chapters. In this way all products having identical first two digits under the NIMEXE code come under the same chapter of the CCT. The EC's GSP trade, shown at that level for the 99 CCT chapters, is listed in the Annex[7] for the four years under review. As a rule several CCT chapters, where they concern kindred or similar products, are grouped together under 21 CCT sections. Overall findings for these sections are likewise given in the Annex.[8]

7. See Table A 6.
8. See Table A 1. Only a few selected figures are given below.

Table 12. *GSP Trade by Selected CCT Sections, 1973 and 1976*
(in 1,000 UA and as a Percentage)

		GSP trade			
		1973		1976	
		absolute	percentage	absolute	percentage
III.	Fats and oils	769	0.1	207,740	6.8
IV.	Foodstuffs, tobacco	11,313	1.9	400,866	13.2
V.	Mineral products	16,268	2.7	570,485	18.8
VI.	Chemicals	49,230	8.0	146,256	4.8
VIII.	Hides and skins, etc.	41,005	6.7	138,097	4.5
IX.	Wood, cork	41,020	6.7	100,195	3.3
XI.	Textiles, etc.	112,620	18.4	325,492	10.7
XV.	Base metals	64,069	10.5	197,658	6.5
XVI.	Machinery, electrical equipment, etc.	101,050	16.5	302,997	10.0
XVII.	Vehicles, etc.	42,265	7.4	77,136	2.5
XVIII.	Instruments and apparatus, clocks, recorders and reproducers, etc.	20,769	3.4	120,484	4.0
Remaining 10 CCT sections		108,740	17.7	448,446	14.8
Total		612,118	100.0	3,035,405	100.0[a]

[a] Slight discrepancies due to rounding errors.

Source: Own calculations based on SOEC and German Federal Ministry of Economic Affairs data.

Table 12 lists GSP imports in the most important sections in 1973 and 1976. Even at this high aggregation level the concentration of imports on a small number of specific sections emerges clearly. The 11 sections listed account for over 80% of all GSP trade. The remaining 10 sections account for the rest. This concentration, needless to say, will continue to increase with greater disaggregation. The fact is that the granting of preferences by the EC is by no means evenly distributed among all the products of one section; besides, the developing countries were not uniformly able to deliver all products. This emerges as soon as the results are tabled by chapters.[9] Thus more than 99% of all imports under the most important section in 1976, section 5 (mineral products), was concentrated in the single CCT chapter 27 (mineral fuels).

Equally conspicuous as concentration are structural shifts. The greatest increase during the period from 1973 to 1976 was recorded by the products of section 3 (fats and oils), with a rise from an insignificant 0.1% to 6.8%, and by the products of sections 4 and 5 (foodstuffs, tobacco, and mineral products) with increases from 1.9% to 13.2% and from 2.7% to 18.8%, respectively.

In spite of an absolute growth recorded in all sections nearly all the remaining sections declined in their proportional share—most of all sections 11 (textiles) and 16 (machinery and electrical equipment) with declines from 18.4% to 10.7% and from 16.5% to 10.0%, respectively. These CCT sections include the most import-intensive GSP products which, significantly enough, also belong to the more sensitive product groups.

d. GSP trade by product groups

Alongside presentation of the product spectrum in the above form, numerous publication also tabulate products at a very high aggregation level, mainly to enable such classical problem areas as textiles and agriculture to be viewed in their entirety. For the sake of completeness they are thus set out in Table 13.

The marked increase in agricultural products, which rose more than twenty-fold over the period under review, is particularly striking. These predominantly non-sensitive agricultural products succeeded in moving up into second place, overtaking textiles which largely belong to the sensitive and semi-sensitive groups and (possibly for that very reason[10]) recorded no better than below-average growth. The main weight nevertheless con

9. See Table A 6.
10. On the trade-impeding effects of import limits see § 6.

Table 13. *GSP Trade by Product Groups, 1973 to 1976*
(in 1,000 UA)

Year	Textiles	ECSC products	Other industrial products	Agricultural products	Total[a]
1973	120,231	17,099	445,037	29,750	612,118
1974	291,042	16,745	1,180,019	265,406	1,753,211
1975	273,331	12,051	1,149,810	294,753	1,729,945
1976	325,492	28,887	1,950,003	731,471	3,035,853
Increase 1973-1976	+ 171%	+ 69%	+ 338%	+ 2,358%	+ 396%

[a] Slight discrepancies due to rounding errors.

Source: Own calculations based on SOEC and German Federal Ministry of Economic Affairs data.

tinues to lie with the rest of the industrial products whose development, in order of magnitude, was more or less in line with the average and indeed strongly influenced that average. Totally insignificant and showing only slight increases were the European Coal and Steel Community products which, admittedly, belong to the sensitive and semi-sensitive areas to over 95%, with 70% of them coming under the strictly regulated sensitive group.

This structural trend is again clearly revealed in Table 14 which shows the proportions taken up by the four categories of products. Agricultural products were the only ones to record an increasing share. At present almost one-quarter of all preferential imports is accounted for by this sector. By contrast the proportion of textiles declined by nearly one-half to only slightly above 10%. The relative importance of the other categories likewise declined.

e. Main GSP products in 1973 and 1976

In order to obtain at least a rough picture of the concentration of GSP trade and in order to identify possible structural changes at a more detailed level of products the top 10 GSP products traded have been listed in Tables 15 and 16 at the level of four-digit tariff headings.

Table 14. *GSP Trade by Product Categories, 1973 to 1976*
(as a Percentage)

Year	Textiles	ECSC products	Other industrial products	Agricultural products	Total
1973	19.6	2.8	72.7	4.9	100
1974	16.6	1.0	67.3	15.1	100
1975	15.8	0.7	66.5	17.0	100
1976	10.7	1.0	64.2	24.1	100

Source: Own calculations based on SOEC and German Federal Ministry of Economic Affairs data.

What becomes instantly obvious is a marked concentration upon these few products. These 10 items in 1973 by themselves accounted for no less than 28.6% of the total GSP trade. In 1976 their share was even greater: the 10 leading products accounted for nearly 45%. This means that well over 700 remaining products together only accounted for 55%. The exceptionally high concentration in that year is admittedly due solely to products of tariff heading numbers 27.10 (petroleum oils other than crude). If this "petroleum effect" is removed from the calculation the remaining nine products are found to account for 26.2%, a proportion which agrees well with the 1973 figure.

Alongside the increased degree of concentration, due predominantly to the marked increase in petroleum imports, other structural changes took place in the course of the three years. Five of the 10 products are found in the top group in both years, but some of them with greatly different weighting. Thus tariff heading number 58.01 (carpets, carpeting and rugs, knotted) dropped from first place in 1973 to fourth place in 1976. Agricultural products of tariff heading numbers 15.07 (fixed vegetable oils) and 21.02 (extracts, essences or concentrates, of coffee, tea or maté), which in 1973 were not among the leaders at all, in 1976 held second and third places.

Table 15. *The Ten Most Important GSP Products 1973*
(in 1,000 UA)

Heading number	GSP product	Trade	Percentage
58.01	Carpets, carpeting and rugs, knotted	53,720	8.8
87.06	Parts and accessories of motor vehicles	22,821	3.7
43.03	Articles of furskin	14,812	2.4
02.04	Other meat and edible meat offals, fresh, chilled or frozen	13,135	2.2
44.13	Wood, planed, etc.	12,400	2.0
27.10	Petroleum oils and oils obtained from bituminous minerals, other than crude	11,500	1.9
43.02	Furskins, tanned or dressed	10,724	1.7
84.52	Calculating machines	9,802	1.6
55.09	Other woven fabrics of cotton	8,111	1.3
84.06	Internal combustion piston engines	7,924	1.3
Total of first ten tariff heading numbers		164,949	26.9

Source: Own calculations based on SOEC and German Federal Ministry of Economic Affairs data.

3. Non-GSP products

In addition to importing GSP products worth 8,613 million UA the beneficiary developing countries, excluding the countries enjoying special preferences, in 1976 imported into the EC 51,500 million UA worth of products not covered by the GSP categories. Over 83% of these countries' exports therefore are non-GSP products. These are predominantly duty-free industrial products coming under chapters 25 to 99 as well as agricultural products of which, however, 80% are dutiable.

Among duty-free industrial products which, with 43,524 million UA account for nearly 85% of the non-GSP products, raw materials occupy a leading position. Duty-free imports of crude and other petroleum products alone account for 77%. Imports of dutiable industrial products, which might possibly be considered for inclusion in the GSP, with 603 million UA represent

Table 16. *The Ten Most Important GSP Products 1976*
(in 1,000 UA)

Heading number	GSP product	Trade	Percentage
27.10	Petroleum oils and oils obtained from bituminous minerals, other than crude	566,099	18.6
15.07	Fixed vegetable oils	192,234	6.3
21.02	Extracts, essences or concentrates of coffee, tea or maté; preparations thereof	171,670	5.7
58.01	Carpets, carpeting and rugs, knotted	148,864	4.9
24.01	Unmanufactured tobacco	64,772	2.1
87.06	Parts and accessories of motor vehicles	48,490	1.6
23.01	Flours and meals of meat, offals, fish, crustaceans or molluscs, unfit for human consumption	45,433	1.5
84.06	Internal combustion piston engines	42,636	1.4
16.04	Prepared or preserved fish	41,643	1.4
43.03	Articles of furskin	40,577	1.3
Total of first ten tariff heading numbers		1,362,418	44.8

Source: Own calculations based on SOEC and German Federal Ministry of Economic Affairs data.

only a fraction of 1% of EC imports from beneficiary developing countries *without* special preferences.[11]

The picture is somewhat different in the sphere of agricultural products which represent 15% of non-GSP imports. Since most of these products come within the group of dutiable products even greater scope exists in this sphere for GSP extension.

In summary, therefore, while the GSP covers nearly all relevant dutiable products in the industrial sphere, conditions are the reverse with regard to agricultural products.

11. A breakdown according to CCT sections will be found in Table A 5.

B. Origin and Destination of GSP Trade

1. GSP imports by EC countries [12]

Table 17 contains a breakdown of total GSP imports among the six and nine EC countries respectively. For the sake of comparison the result for 1976 is given not only in units of account (UA) but also in (new) European units of account (EUA).

Until 1978 the GSP was based on the dimension of the UA. Maximum amounts for imports were laid down in UA, trade was calculated and recorded in UA. That is why this study maintains the UA as its yardstick throughout. Normally this does not give rise to any problems. For the EC Member State results, however, presentation in UA—which is based on the assumption of constant currency parities—leads to considerable distortions: the UA is defined in constant ratios to the different national currencies. Thus one UA equals DM 3.66 or £0.42.[13] These ratios did not change during the four years under review. As, however, the parities between national currencies have shifted with regard to each other—sterling being devalued and the DM revalued upwards—the problem had to be faced in 1976 that a "British UA" defined in sterling was worth only half as much as a "German UA".

Two exports, identical from the point of view of an unaffected developing country, into the EC Member States Britain and Germany thus result, in EC-internal dealings, in two totally different accountancy amounts in UA.[14] Any statistics proceeding, as do the GSP statistics, from the fiction of the equivalence of the

12. Detailed EC Member State results by two-digit CCT chapters are presented in the Annex (see Table A 7). An evaluation by sensitivity groups is also given there (see Tables A3 and A4).

13. Figures rounded off.

14. So far the effect of this differential accountancy of identical imports on the system of maximum import limits for supplying and importing GSP countries has scarcely been taken note of. As a matter of principle a supply-intensive developing country which is already close to its maximum import amounts—assuming freedom of choice and rational behaviour—will always import into an EC country with a strong currency. Member State shares are also being continually increased in real terms for strong currency countries while they are being continually reduced for weak currency countries, etc.

different national units of account, will therefore invariably underestimate the shares of countries with strong currencies. Conversely the shares of countries with weak currencies will be overestimated. From 1979 onwards, however, the new European unit of account will be used for GSP import accountancy. This new unit takes into consideration the real purchasing power of Member State currencies, thereby avoiding the above-mentioned distortions in the case of semi-sensitive and non-sensitive products. As a gradual adjustment of Member State shares to the European unit of account is envisaged, the distortion persists for the time being, though in a reduced form, for sensitive products.

The extent to which the choice of dimension can affect national results is shown—even more so than in Table 17—by Table 18 which contains the relative figures. According to the official calculation yardstick of UA, Britain with 31.5% of all GSP imports in 1976 was clearly ahead of the Federal Republic of Germany with a share of just under 30%. If, however, these figures are corrected by the elimination of the distortions stemming from the UA system, and if the same data are viewed in EUA, then the Federal Republic of Germany is seen to have nearly twice as large a share of GSP trade as Britain. Italy, in third place in the UA statistics, must similarly change places with the Benelux countries. With the other countries neither order of magnitude nor ranking is affected by the conversion.

A glance at the incremental rates of GSP imports shows that the Benelux countries had the highest increases among the six original EC Member States. The Federal Republic of Germany likewise almost quadrupled its imports. By comparison the increases of the new Member States lagged greatly behind.

Another striking feature is the fact that France has altogether only very slight GSP imports. If the gross domestic product (GDP) is used as a reference scale then French imports with a 0.09% share lie far below the EC average. In detail the following ratios are found: [15]

15. See also Table A 2.

Table 17. *GSP Imports by EC Countries, 1973 to 1976*
(in Million UA) (1976 also in EUA)

EC country	in UA				in EUA	Annual increase 1973 to 1976 in %[a]	
	1973	1974	1975	1976	1976	by UA	by EUA
France	100	208	148	265	275	38	39
Benelux	94	179	183	358	426	56	63
Federal Republic of Germany	297	542	604	902	1,173	45	52
Italy	122	287	286	460	309	56	43
United Kingdom	—	451	437	956	642	46	32
Ireland	—	14	9	20	13	20	9
Denmark	—	71	63	75	83	3	7
EC total[b]	612	1,753	1,730	3,036	2,921	71	66

[a] For Britain, Ireland and Denmark 1974 to 1976.

[b] Slight discrepancies due to rounding errors.

Note: The growth rates in EUA were calculated by transforming the data for 1973 and/or 1974 respectively. These values cannot therefore be derived from the table.

Source: Own calculations based on Statistical Office of the European Communities: *Monthly Bulletin of Foreign Trade Statistics* (1978), No. 6, p. 112 and on SOEC and German Federal Ministry of Economic Affairs data.

France	0.09%
Benelux	0.31%
Federal Republic of Germany	0.29%
Italy	0.20%
United Kingdom	0.33%
Ireland	0.18%
Denmark	0.24%
EC-9	0.24%

Apart from France only Italy and Ireland have below-average rates. GSP imports into Britain accounted for the highest proportion of the GDP. At 0.33% its percentage share is almost four times as much as that of France.

The question arises as to whether the slight shares of France, Italy and Ireland are due to any structural peculiarities of these

Table 18. *GSP Imports of the EC 1973 to 1976 in UA (1976 also in EUA)* (as a Percentage)

EC country	in UA				in EUA
	1973	1974	1975	1976	1976
France	16.3	11.9	8.6	8.7	9.4
Benelux	15.3	10.2	10.6	11.8	14.6
Federal Republic of Germany	48.5	30.9	34.9	29.7	40.2
Italy	19.9	16.4	16.5	15.2	10.6
United Kingdom	—	25.7	25.3	31.5	22.0
Ireland	—	0.8	0.5	0.7	0.4
Denmark	—	4.1	3.6	2.5	2.8
Total[a]	100.0	100.0	100.0	100.0	100.0

[a] Slight discrepancies due to rounding errors.

Source: Own calculations based on SOEC and German Federal Ministry of Economic Affairs data.

EC Member States' trade with the developing countries. To answer this question Table 19 compares GSP imports with total imports of GSP products from eligible developing countries.

Table 19 clearly shows the low shares of France, Italy and Ireland. In each case only 29% of eligible imports were in fact operated in these countries under the GSP. In the Federal Republic of Germany, by way of contrast, the figure was 42%. Even if possible differences in the trade structures of the countries are taken into account, the three countries are at the bottom of the list in respect of GSP coverage.

One of the reasons for this differential degree of utilization may be found in the administrative procedure of the customs authorities concerned. Thus, while the Benelux countries operate on a "first come first served" basis (the speediest importers obtain eligibility), France operates a "prior allocation" procedure whereby permits are allocated in consultation with representatives of domestic producers. Such a market segregation by its very nature makes full utilization of the framework of

Table 19. *GSP Imports and Total Imports of GSP Products from Eligible Developing Countries, 1976*
(in Million UA)

EC country	GSP imports	Total imports	Percentage
France	265	917	29
Benelux	358	1,090	33
Federal Republic of Germany	902	2,172	42
Italy	460	1,576	29
United Kingdom	956	2,581	37
Ireland	20	70	29
Denmark	75	206	36
EC-9[a]	3,036	8,613	35

[a] Slight discrepancies due to rounding errors.

Source: Own calculations based on SOEC and German Federal Ministry of Economic Affairs data.

preferences more difficult.[16]

To sum up: the three countries France, Italy and Ireland show the following features:

— their GSP imports have low growth rates;
— their GSP imports account for a low percentage of their GDP;
— their GSP coverage is low.

If the trend of the past few years continues in the future the EC countries will increasingly fall into two categories, those "with intensive GSP trade" and those "with slight GSP trade", and these two categories will continue to drift further apart.

2. GSP trade by supplying countries

a. Main suppliers

The fact that a total of 133 different countries and territories recorded GSP imports into the EC creates the illusion of a multi-

16. See T. Murray, *Trade Preferences for Developing Countries*, loc. cit., p. 76 f.

plicity which does not in fact exist. A glance at Table 20 and Table 21 will illustrate this. The top ten suppliers listed there for the years 1973 and 1976 accounted for 86.8% and 71.3%, respectively, of all GSP imports. If the tables are extended to include the top 20 supplying countries, the picture is even further intensified: the 20 leading suppliers among the developing countries in 1973 accounted for roughly 95% and in 1976 for about 88% of all GSP imports. Some 80 other countries each year share the remaining 5% or 12%. The concentration which we have already observed elsewhere, e.g. with regard to GSP products, therefore also applies to supplying countries.

At first glance the degree of concentration would seem to have declined between 1973 and 1976. But in fact this decline is due solely to the relative drop in Yugoslav GSP imports which in 1973

Table 20. *GSP Imports and Total Imports of GSP Products from the Ten Principal Supplier Countries, 1973*
(in Million UA and as a Percentage)

Developing country	GSP imports	Percentage	Cumulated percentage	Total imports of GSP products	Percentage
Yugoslavia	208	33.9	33.9	602	33.6
South Korea	62	10.1	44.0	139	7.8
Brazil	52	8.5	52.5	109	6.1
Iran	42	6.9	59.4	178	9.9
Argentina	35	5.7	65.1	76	4.2
Hong Kong	31	5.1	70.2	165	9.2
India	30	4.9	75.1	72	4.0
Singapore	25	4.1	79.2	99	5.5
Mexico	23	3.8	83.0	52	2.9
Pakistan	23	3.8	86.8	55	3.1
Total of top ten	531	86.8	86.8	1,547	86.3
Overall total	612	100.0	100.0	1,793	100.0

Source: Own calculations based on SOEC and German Federal Ministry of Economic Affairs data.

68

still amounted to nearly one-third of all imports. Besides, more or less always the same group of countries that are greatest suppliers. Seven countries appear among the top ten both years under review. Three countries, Iran, Mexico ar. Argentina were no longer among the top ten in 1976 but in fac occupied 11th to 13th place. All countries strong in 1973 were thus able to maintain their strong position.

In addition, however, 1976 sees the first emergence of Romania, Malaysia and Venezuela. Apart from Romania—which was not even eligible in 1973, for which reason comparisons are impossible—the other two then had no substantial imports into the EC in 1973. This shows that new countries may unexpectedly come to occupy top places.

Table 21. *GSP Imports and Total Imports of GSP Products from the Ten Principal Supplier Countries, 1976*
(in Million UA and as a Percentage)

Developing country	GSP imports	Percent-age	Cumulated percent-age	Total im-ports of GSP products	Percent-age
Brazil	357	11.8	11.8	596	6.9
Yugoslavia	338	11.1	22.9	1,089	12.6
Hong Kong	250	8.2	31.1	825	9.6
Romania	233	7.7	38.8	422	4.9
South Korea	227	7.5	46.3	940	10.9
India	214	7.0	53.3	814	9.5
Malaysia	214	7.0	60.3	659	7.7
Venezuela	133	4.4	64.7	300	3.5
Pakistan	111	3.7	68.4	201	2.3
Singapore	88	2.9	71.3	469	5.4
Total of top ten	2,165	71.3	71.3	6,315	73.3
Overall total	3,036	100.0	100.0	8,613	100.0

Source: Own calculations based on SOEC and German Federal Ministry of Economic Affairs data.

The heavy concentration of preferential trade on a small number of supplier countries is not a phenomenon typical only of the GSP. Indeed an analysis of the last column of Tables 20 and 21 reveals that total trade in preferential products is just as strongly concentrated on a small number of countries. In 1973 these were the same ten countries which also held the top positions in total imports of GSP products. In 1976 nine of the ten listed countries came within that group. Only Pakistan was down to 14th place for total imports.

A glance at the two tables reveals very clearly that, at least in the top group—and this, of course, also accounts for the lion's share—GSP trade is a very exact replica of total trade.[17] The countries with the greatest supplying capacity have managed to carve out for themselves fairly accurately that share of the preferential cake which corresponds to the importance of their other imports of GSP products—in spite of the fact that the EC had hoped, by means of the maximum amount rule, to restrict the strong countries a little in order to be better able to promote the developing countries which are still small-scale suppliers. The effects of maximum country amounts will be examined in detail under § 6 below.

b. GSP trade by country groups

For 1976 the GSP trade was calculated also by selected country groups with a view to examining the question of whether a country's membership of a geographically or economically determined group has any effect on the GSP results.

Breakdown by continents (see Table 22) shows that the major part of GSP trade consists of imports from Asia. Two-thirds of all GSP imports come from that region. In second place are the (altogether only three) European countries. It is immediately obvious that the African states are greatly under-represented.

17. The thesis of the similarity between GSP trade and total trade in GSP products, which is being supported here by the figures for individual countries, may also be verified in another way. A correlation analysis performed for several years similarly revealed a high degree of correlation for product structures: a correlation coefficient ranging from $r = 0.75$ to $r = 0.85$ given a total of between 765 and 833 data points.

The reason for this is that nearly all African states are already, as ACP countries under the Lomé Convention, enjoying preferential treatment outside the scope of the GSP.

Table 22. *GSP Imports by Continents, 1976*
(in Million UA and as a Percentage)

Continent	Imports	Percentage
Europe	571	18.8
Africa	116	3.8
America	322	10.6
Asia	2,026	66.7
Oceania	1	0.0
Total	3,036	100.0

Source: Own calculations based on SOEC and German Federal Ministry of Economic Affairs data.

The large number of countries which, under special agreements, already enjoy a more extensive preferential status and therefore no longer enter consideration for treatment under the GSP also affects the results for the other groupings. Thus of the 45 MSAC countries—the countries most seriously affected by the oil price increase—27 belong to the group of ACP countries, and from the official list of 28 LLDCs—the least developed countries, the poorest of the developing countries—18 have to be deleted as ACP countries. If the share of LLDCs and MSACs in GSP trade is calculated then the very low values of 1.4% and 14.3%, respectively, are obtained.

If for the last two groups of countries we examine what proportion of the preference potential is in fact represented by GSP imports we find that the coverage for the MSAC countries is 35%—which is exactly the overall average—and that of the LLDCs is 56%. This would suggest that the poorest of all have been making particularly good use of the GSP. However, with no more than 10 LLDCs, which do not belong to the list of ACP countries, and which account for only 1.4% of the GSP trade the observational basis for such an assertion is too narrow.

In order to examine the effect which a country's level of economic development—measured in per capita GNP—has on the utilization of preferences the developing countries were divided into four per capita income categories (see Table 23). The data obtained should again be interpreted with a good measure of caution since the ACP countries had to be lifted out of the various categories. But even if this results in certain shifts, it is still interesting to note that nearly one-half of all GSP imports come from the group of the most developed developing countries with a per capita income in excess of US $1,075 per annum. By contrast less than one-fifth of all imports comes from the poorer countries with a per capita income under US $520.

Table 23. *GSP Imports by Per Capita Income Categories of Supplying Countries, 1976*
(in Million UA and as a Percentage)

Per capita income	GSP imports	Percentage	Preference potential	Percentage
under $266	453	14.9	1,331	15.5
$266 to $520	140	4.6	478	5.5
$520 to $1,075	938	30.9	2,500	29.0
over $1,075	1,505	49.6	4,304	50.0
Total	3,036	100.0	8,613	100.0

Source: Own calculations based on SOEC and German Federal Ministry of Economic Affairs data. Grouping of developing countries by per capita income in accordance with *OECD: Development Co-operation, 1977 Review*, Paris 1977, pp. 155-157.

Yet conditions are very similar for the total trade in GSP products, the preference potential. This indicates that the structure of GSP trade does not occupy any special position. This is further confirmation of the finding that preferential trade represents a typical section of the total trade in GSP products.

c. Diversification and the utilization of preferences

This section differentiates between GSP products and preferentially-treated products. By the GSP products of a supplying country we understand all traded products included in the GSP if the country concerned was eligible for preference in respect of them. For these products, therefore, treatment on preferential terms could have been applied for. To be distinguished from these GSP products are the preferentially-treated products, i.e. GSP products for which GSP preference had in fact been applied for and granted. By definition the number of preferentially-treated products cannot be greater than that of GSP products. The ratio between preferentially-treated and GSP products reveals the degree to which an attempt was made actually to obtain for the products of a developing country the preferences to which it was entitled under the GSP.

Table 24 lists the supplying countries in accordance with the GSP products they imported into the EC in the reference year 1976. The number of imported GSP products fluctuates a great deal. Thus Yugoslavia imported about 682 different GSP goods. On the other hand, 12 countries, which have not been included or specified, dealt in fewer than 10 different GSP products. The connection between GSP products and preferentially-treated products is readily seen. To the extent that, from one group of 10 to the next, the average number of GSP products diminishes, so the average number of preferentially-treated products diminishes also. Because of this close correlation the group of specified top ten countries again includes nearly all strong supplying countries from Table 21. Only Venezuela and Pakistan, which in terms of value belong to the top ten, are not in the top ten countries with the most diversified range of products.

Let us return to the relation between preferentially-treated products and GSP products, the relation which reveals the extent of a country's efforts to make the fullest possible use of potential preferences. This ratio, as shown by Table 24, is not constant but likewise diminishes with decreasing degree of diversification (with diminishing magnitude). The top ten countries applied at least once for treatment on preferential terms for 69% of all GSP products. For the 11th to 20th country preferences were actually utilized only in respect of 59% of all GSP products. This degree of utilization declines steadily from one group of ten to the next.

Table 24. *Developing Countries by Number of GSP Products and Preferentially-Treated Products (Excluding Countries with Special Preferences), 1976* (Absolute and as a Percentage)

Country	Number of GSP products	Number of preferentially-treated products	Percentage
Yugoslavia	682	519	76
India	603	544	90
Hong Kong	483	310	64
Brazil	459	335	73
South Korea	418	327	78
Singapore	374	182	49
Romania	342	223	65
Mexico	338	240	71
Thailand	302	212	70
Malaysia	296	154	52
Average of top ten countries	430	305	69
Average of 11th to 20th country	203	121	59
Average of 21st to 30th country	105	35	34
Average of 31st to 40th country	64	20	32
Average of remaining 37 countries	26	7	16

Source: Own calculations based on SOEC and German Federal Ministry of Economic Affairs data.

The strongest supplier countries with a broad spectrum of products offered thus tried to make particularly good use of the preference facilities on offer to all developing countries. Yet in terms of value this does not result in any disproportionately large share of GSP imports for these strong countries. The fact that, in spite of the particularly high degree of utilization by the strong supplying countries, GSP trade nevertheless presents a fairly typical replica of the total trade in GSP products is no doubt due to the restrictive effect of maximum import amounts which, other things being equal, restrict a strong supplier to a greater extent than a weak one. Or put another way: Because the strong developing countries made better use of the opportunities granted them under the GSP than did the small ones they were able to neutralize the restrictive effects of maximum import amounts and maintain their share of GSP trade.

nd Actual GSP

own the scale, struc-
ng the period under
irst evaluation of the
o analyse the poten-
:ountries under any
e proportion repre-
)se EC imports from
itext of total imports
procedure [18] to the
way it is proposed,
e the GSP potential
t amounts charac-
)roduct-specific and
; GSP potential will
P imports. The sub-
he discrepancy be-
mance by analysing

18. For a detailed description of this procedure see Annex 3.

The developing countries, accounting as they do for more than one-quarter of total EC imports,[19] make a substantial contribution to the supplies of the nine EC countries. In 1976 the Community imported approximately 86 billion UA worth of products from that group of countries.[20]

Although the European integration process has, in relative terms, displaced imports from non-EC countries in favour of intra-Community trade, more than one-half of all imports still come from supplier countries not belonging to the Community; imports from developing countries, representing 51% (1976), are playing an exceedingly important part in EC supplies from non-EC countries.

The important position occupied by the developing countries in the pattern of EC imports quite obviously does *not* rest upon those products or those supplier countries which are the subject of the GSP. Indeed GSP products account for a mere 16% (1976) of total EC imports from developing countries. This means that 72.1 billion UA, or 84%, of total EC imports from developing countries are outside the GSP range of products. Not covered by the GSP are, above all, energy-producing and other raw materials, accounting for 70% alone. These are not as a rule dutiable and cannot in consequence be the subject of any preferential regulation. The dutiable products not included are predominantly agricultural products. Among dutiable industrial products the GSP does not cover, among others, a number of base metals, hides and skins and articles thereof, mineral products or textiles.

The entirely sensible exclusion of the predominantly non-dutiable raw materials and the striking disregard shown for a number of dutiable products not only in the agricultural but also in the industrial sector therefore reduces the potential volume of preferential imports to 16% (1976) of EC imports from developing countries.

This import potential, moreover, is reduced not only by the

19. Intra- and extra-trade of the EC.
20. See also Tables 25 and 26.

product effect but also by the limitations on the eligibility of certain supplier countries. Exclusion of countries during the period under review occurred mainly

— for textiles, which were importable on preferential terms only from such countries as had signed the Long-term Arrangement Regarding Trade in Cotton and Textiles,
— for jute and coir manufactures, in respect of which only India, Sri Lanka, Thailand and Bangladesh were eligible on the grounds of their special trade agreements with the EC, as well as
— in the case of Romania, which has only belonged to the circle of beneficiary countries since 1974 and has since become eligible for preference in respect of an increasing number of products.

This country effect reduces the GSP potential by 18% to 13% of total EC imports from developing countries.

The EC has concluded special association, co-operation and preferential agreements with a number of extra-European developing countries.[21] Compared with the GSP these agreements generally grant equivalent or more favourable—though in a few instances less favourable—trade preferences. For these countries, of course, the GSP performs a meaningful function only if their own special preference is inferior to the generalized preference. If, therefore, one excludes all those developing countries whose special preference was more favourable than or equivalent to GSP preference, then a further 22% of the remaining GSP potential is eliminated and this potential then diminishes to 10% of all imports from developing countries. If, moreover, one considers the surprising fact that the GSP "comprises" also a number of duty-free tariff headings and lines,[22] the result obtained so far is further reduced by 1.2 billion UA (= 14%) to 9% of all imports from developing countries.

The GSP potential, finally, is further reduced by one per-

21 See § 9.
22. Thus tariff headings 29.01, 33.01, 40.02, 44.05 and 47.01 include a large number of duty-free items.

Table 25. *Reduction of EC-6 and EC-9 Imports from Developing Countries to the GSP Potential by Agricultural and Industrial Products, 1973 and 1976*
(in 1,000 UA)

	1973 EC-6			1976 EC-6			1976 EC-9		
	CCT chapters 1-24	CCT chapters 25-99	CCT chapters 1-99	CCT chapters 1-24	CCT chapters 25-99	CCT chapters 1-99	CCT chapters 1-24	CCT chapters 25-99	CCT chapters 1-99
1. Total EC imports	24,822	111,796	136,618	35,484	195,031	230,515	50,738	270,372	321,110
2. *of these:* from non-EC countries	13,016	47,556	60,572	19,930	108,906	128,836	27,048	140,582	167,630
3. *of these:* from beneficiaries (incl. duty-free)	5,356 (1,124)	17,507 (14,881)	22,863 (16,005)	8,758 (1,839)	50,039 (41,616)	58,797 (43,455)	13,208 (2,774)	72,385 (59,304)	85,593 (62,078)
4. *of these:* GSP goods	135	2,574	2,709	903	7,172	8,075	1,668	11,800	13,468
5. *of these:* from eligible beneficiaries	135	2,048	2,183	900	5,799	6,699	1,664	9,437	11,101
6. *of these:* excluding developing countries with special preferences	110	1,682	1,792	665	5,092	5,757	1,232	7,381	8,613
7. *of these:* excluding duty-free goods	110	1,679	1,789	665	4,225	4,890	1,232	6,189	7,421
8. *of these:* excluding LDC's without notification	110	1,679	1,789	649	3,703	4,352	1,209	5,528	6,737
9. Actual GSP imports	29	582	612	308	1,677	1,985	731	2,304	3,036

Note: For the method see Annex 3.
Source: Own calculations based on SOEC and German Federal Ministry of Economic Affairs data.

Table 26. *Reduction of EC-6 and EC-9 Imports from Developing Countries to the GSP Potential by Agricultural and Industrial Products, 1973 and 1976 of Imports from Beneficiary Developing Countries*
(as a Percentage)

	1973 EC-6			1976 EC-6			1976 EC-9		
	CCT chapters 1-24	CCT chapters 25-99	CCT chapters 1-99	CCT chapters 1-24	CCT chapters 25-99	CCT chapters 1-99	CCT chapters 1-24	CCT chapters 25-99	CCT chapters 1-99
1. Total EC imports	—	—	—	—	—	—	—	—	—
2. *of these:* from non-EC countries	—	—	—	—	—	—	—	—	—
3. *of these:* from beneficiaries (incl. duty-free)	100 (21)	100 (85)	100 (70)	100 (21)	100 (83)	100 (74)	100 (21)	100 (82)	100 (73)
4. *of these:* GSP goods	3	15	12	10	14	14	13	16	16
5. *of these:* from eligible beneficiaries	3	12	10	10	12	11	13	13	13
6. *of these:* excluding developing countries without special preferences	2	10	8	8	10	10	9	10	10
7. *of these:* excluding duty-free goods	2	10	8	8	8	8	9	9	9
8. *of these:* excluding LDC's without notification	2	10	8	7	7	7	9	8	8
9. Actual GSP imports	1	3	3	4	3	3	6	3	4

Source: Own calculations based on SOEC and German Federal Ministry of Economic Affairs data.

79

centage point if one assumes strict application of the notification requirement. The GSP potential in that case—disregarding the maximum import amounts laid down in the GSP—would be a potential volume of preferential imports of 6.7 billion UA (1976) or 8% of all EC imports from developing countries. This exceedingly limited relative potential applies equally to agricultural products and to semi-finished or finished industrial products.

The continuous further development of the GSP ever since its introduction has had an only seemingly positive effect on the GSP potential through the inclusion of new products and through the extension of the circle of eligible developing countries. Although in 1976 a marked extension of agricultural products entitled to preference resulted in 4% more import products being covered by the GSP, this effect was offset by the duty-free products included in the GSP, products which evidently accounted for major portions of imports in 1976, so that the GSP potential, seen relatively, underwent no more than a slight change.

Even so there was quite a substantial *absolute* increase. Between 1973 and 1976 the GSP potential increased from 1.8 billion UA to 6.7 billion UA, i.e. by a factor of 3.7. Its growth, however, was in step with the equally dynamic increase in overall trade with the developing countries.

B. Comparison of Potential and Actual GSP Trade

The part played at present by the GSP in the Community's overall trade with developing countries emerges clearly if the GSP potential just discussed is compared with *actual GSP performance.* Whereas the GSP potential reflects the maximum scope of the GSP, actual GSP imports and their relation to that potential reflect the effectivity of the GSP, determined as this is by the limitation of GSP imports to certain maximum amounts on the one hand and the utilization of import opportunities on the other.

Against the background of total imports and of non-EC imports entering the Community of the Nine the actual GSP imports are of only marginal significance. In 1976 they amounted to less than 1% and 2% respectively. Only in respect of agricultural products of chapters 1 to 24 were slightly higher import figures recorded for the GSP, but even these remained below 3%. Similarly, in relation to EC-9 imports from developing countries enjoying GSP preferences in any form whatsoever the relative importance of GSP imports is slight; this again reflects the preponderance of mainly duty-free raw materials not covered by the GSP. However, the slight share of 3.6% represented by the GSP in total EC-9 imports from developing countries should not be seen as evidence of its only marginal importance but should, on the contrary, be interpreted as a starting point for its real function—the diversification of the one-sided export structure of the developing countries.

If, finally, actual GSP performance in 1976 is compared with the GSP potential, and if this is related to eligible countries, a significant discrepancy emerges: actual GSP imports in 1976 amounted to only 27.4% of potential imports. This strikingly low proportion, however, requires two-fold qualification.

Imports from developing countries with special preferential agreements were evidently in part regarded as GSP imports and statistically recorded as such, even though these special preferences were at least equivalent to, if not more advantageous than, those of the GSP. This unsatisfactory lumping together of general and special preferences, which will be discussed in greater detail later,[23] calls for a correction of the GSP results so far attained and for a different unit of reference for overall trade. Accordingly a general import ratio of 34.3% is found for the GSP.

Another distortion finally arises from the inclusion of a number of duty-free products in the GSP *and* demonstrably also in the GSP statistics. These are often tariff items which together with other dutiable lines make up a GSP product (e.g. 29.01, 33.01, 40.02, 84.06 and 89.01). Frequently, however, EC regulations list a whole tariff heading as a GSP product (e.g. 27.06, 37.06, 47.01, 49.01).[24] Since for this last-named category it has been possible to prove GSP imports in a number of instances, even though no

23. See § 9.
24. The German Customs Tariff is more accurate in this respect and only describes dutiable tariff items as GSP products.

reasonable explanation was found for this,[25] the registration of duty-free GSP products as GSP imports cannot be ruled out even for the former category. It should be pointed out, incidentally, that the EC regulations on the GSP in 1978 still contain duty-free GSP products.

Against that background the actual proportion of GSP imports can only be estimated. The upper limit is a proportion of 43.7%, the lower limit is the above-mentioned proportion of 34.3%; a proportion of 40% may thus be regarded as a realistic figure.[26]

In spite of a certain imprecision attaching to the estimates it is possible to state that the GSP has *not* so far succeeded in taking up the major portion of the GSP potential. The gap between GSP potential and actual GSP performance is particularly marked in respect of industrial products, where it amounts to approximately 35%; in the sphere of agricultural products, on the other hand, some 60% of the potential was in fact realized as GSP imports.[27] It is an interesting point that the corresponding figures for the Community of the Six come out even lower and that these underwent no appreciable change between 1973 and 1976.

§ 6. Impact of a-priori Limitations on GSP Performance

Analysis of the GSP potential has shown that actual GSP performance remained well below the theoretical possibilities. The principal explanation for this has to be seen in the a-priori limitations of the GSP which greatly reduce the potential volume of GSP imports. An attempt will be made in the following section to reveal the impact of these quantitative and formal limitations upon GSP performance.

25. Duty-free GSP imports cannot be explained by the adjustment of the external tariffs of the three new Member States either since such imports can be statistically proved also for the six original Member States.

26. Because of this uncertainty surrounding the data the statistical presentations of GSP imports disregard the problem of duty-free GSP imports.

27. Considering the numerous "ex-items" among agricultural products—which it is impossible to isolate from overall trade—the rate of realization for agricultural products might even in fact be a little higher.

A. Limitation of GSP Potential by Quotas and Ceilings

Community tariff quotas and ceilings, in their role of general upper limits on imports, are designed to keep reduced-duty and/or duty-free imports from developing countries as well as their associated competitive and structural effects within a scale tolerable for the EC. Considerations of the export interests of other countries enjoying special preferential agreements with the EC are likewise reflected in the delimitation of tariff quotas and ceilings. The maximum GSP imports for one preferential year (the so-called "preference offer") is arrived at, in accordance with the method of calculation usual hitherto, from the sum total of all maximum amounts plus the imports of agricultural products[28] which may be imported without limitations.

If these maximum admissible GSP imports are compared with the overall potential of GSP imports the limiting effect of ceilings and quotas imposed on EC imports from beneficiary developing countries is immediately seen. These import maximum amounts in conjunction with the limited eligibility of various supplier countries at present restrict the GSP potential by approximately 35% (1976) (see Table 27). It is also significant that this figure increased between 1973 and 1976, i.e. that potential GSP imports into the EC from developing countries increased during that period at a greater rate (68.9% p.a.) than did the GSP quotas and ceilings (64.9% p.a.). Because adjustments of maximum amounts are made in discrete quantities as the reference year for the basic amount is changed, the longest possible period of review should be used for the determination of the average annual growth. Between 1972 and 1978 the Community tariff quotas and ceilings were extended by an average of 34.1% p.a. (see Table 29), yet their growth was still only half as much as that of the GSP potential during the period under review.

---

28. Calculation of its "preference offer" is based by the EC Commission on the performance during the preceding year.

Table 27. *GSP Potential, Maximum and Actual GSP Imports 1973 and 1976*
(in Billion UA and as a Percentage)

Imports	In billion UA		in %			
	1973	1976	1973		1976	
Volume of potential GSP imports	1.79	8.61	100		100	
Maximum GSP imports (Preference offer)	1.25	5.60	70	100	65	100
Effective GSP imports	0.61	3.04	34	49	35	54

Sources: Own presentation and calculation based on *Commission of the European Communities: Scheme of generalized tariff preferences of the European Community for 1977* (COM) (76) 303 final, 30 June 1976, p. 2, and "Proposals from the Commission of the European Communities to the Council concerning regulations relating to the application for the year 1978 of the generalized tariff preferences of the European Community", in: *European Parliament: Working Documents 1977-1978*, Doc. 245/77 of 9 September 1977, p. 2, as well as on SOEC and German Federal Ministry for Economic Affairs data.

If therefore the scope of the granting of preferences (the preference offer) fails to keep pace with the growth of EC imports from beneficiary developing countries it is necessary to seek the reasons. The main explanation for this trend lies in the method of calculating ceilings and Community quotas with its typical lag of three to five years, as well as in the numerous deviations—chiefly on grounds of structure policy and cyclical policy—from the basic formula. Especially in the category of products graded as sensitive there have been repeated instances of the supplementary amount not being taken into account, or only to a fraction of its real extent (5% of EC imports from non-EC countries not enjoying GSP preferences), in the fixing of the Community tariff quotas.[29]

29. See also § 2 D.

B. Utilization of Quotas and Ceilings

1. Coefficient of utilization

The lag of Community quotas and ceilings behind the GSP potential—leaving aside other limitations—might be expected to lead to an increasing degree of utilization of these maximum amounts. In the category of sensitive products, in particular—a category in which the developing countries already command substantial shares of the market and exhibit high growth rates—one would expect the maximum amounts to be reached or indeed exceeded and the most-favoured-nation rate to be therefore reapplied. The trade-political value of the GSP would be particularly questionable in such cases since it would no longer be able to stimulate greater exports from the supplier countries and would at the most constitute a "customs duty present".

Murray uses a model calculation to demonstrate very clearly the magnitude of the probability of the limits of the Community quotas and ceilings being reached for alternative combinations of import market shares and growth rates of the supplier countries.[30] However, he overlooks the fact that the reference year for the basic amount is generally adjusted in a three-year rhythm. This means that the time at which the maximum limits are reached is transferred into the future. Murray moreover assumes an annual growth in non-EC imports of 10% though in fact this has been substantially higher for a number of years. Between 1973 and 1976 alone EC imports from developing countries in respect of GSP products increased—no doubt also due to inflation—by an average of approximately 40% per annum. This factor operates against the one mentioned above and ensures that ceilings and Community quotas are reached prematurely.

Even without an appropriate modification of Murray's model it can be observed that the calculation formula limits the GSP potential and—according to growth rate and market share of the imports—causes a more or less marked excess of imports no longer

---

30. See T. Murray, loc. cit., p. 68 ff.

Table 28. *Utilization of Community Tariff Quotas and Ceilings by Group Frequency and Sensitivity, 1973 and 1976*

	Utilization by groups and incidence							Total number of cases
	0%	>0 to <25%	25 to <50%	50 to <75%	75 to <100%	100%	>100%	
1973								
Sensitive goods	5	22	32	33	19	0	0	111
Hybrid goods	—	—	—	—	—	—	—	—
Semi-sensitive goods	18	18	21	14	10	0	28	109
Non-sensitive goods[a]	n.a.	n.a.	n.a.	n.a.	n.a.	n.a.	n.a.	n.a.
All goods[b]	23	40	53	47	29	0	28	220
1976								
Sensitive goods	2	7	18	21	26	1	—	75
Hybrid goods	0	11	6	6	5	—	1	29
Semi-sensitive goods	29	28	13	15	12	—	60	157
Non-sensitive goods[c]	196	227	80	41	41	—	185	770
All goods	227	273	117	83	84	1	246	1,031

[a] Not available (n.a.).

[b] Excluding non-sensitive and agricultural products.

[c] Excluding agricultural products for which no ceilings are fixed.

Source: Own calculations based on SOEC and German Federal Ministry of Economic Affairs data.

eligible for preferential treatment with the result that reintroduction of the most-favoured-nation rate is inevitable.

It is, however, significant that imports notified and admitted for GSP preference do *not* as a rule approach the general maximum amounts of ceilings or Community quotas.[31] This was found to be the case in 784 of 1,031 instances[32] in 1976 (see Table 28). They were reached or exceeded in 247 instances, though most-favoured-nation tariffs were reintroduced only 23 times. These instances of limits being surpassed predominantly concerned non-sensitive products in respect of which waiver of special surveillance of GSP imports had clearly resulted in a most liberal import practice. Yet the ceilings were exceeded also by an astonishingly large number of semi-sensitive products (40%). Any strict interpretation of the EC regulations would clearly have exerted a markedly unfavourable impact upon the entire GSP performance. This liberal importation practice, incidentally, has become much more pronounced for semi-sensitive goods compared with 1973. These liberalization effects will be examined in greater detail elsewhere.[33]

A striking feature, on the other hand, is the fact that in 227 instances, i.e. in 24% of all instances, the quotas and ceilings offered to the developing countries were not being made use of at all. These comprised two sensitive, 29 semi-sensitive[34] and 196 non-sensitive products; it was not that GSP preference was not applied for, through some omission, but that, in most cases, the developing countries were unable or only minimally able to deliver the goods. The latter, incidentally, was true also of 48 (20%) of the 241 non-sensitive agricultural products. Because of a lack of data concerning the ceilings of non-sensitive GSP products in 1973 it is unfortunately impossible to ascertain whether the problem of supply-conditioned non-utilization of the ceilings is gradually be-

31. The causes of non-utilization are analysed in § 6 B. 3.

32. Agricultural products of Regulation 40, which on principle are not subject to any quantitative or value limitations, are *not* included.

33. See § 6 C. 3.

34. Twenty-seven of these 29 instances were ceilings specially created for Yugoslavia and Romania.

87

coming less pressing as a result of an increased "growing into" such product areas by the developing countries. It must, however, be assumed that in many cases this will not be possible, or only partially possible, in the forseeable future as the real prerequisites of the production of these often high-quality industrial products are lacking chiefly in terms of technology and capital.

The general thesis that the far greater increase in GSP potential compared with the increase in the granting of preferences is bound to lead to a greater utilization of tariff quotas and ceilings does not appear to be borne out without differentiation. During the life so far of the GSP the highest utilization has only been 54% of that potential. Average utilization between 1971 and 1976 admittedly increased from 44% to the peak value of 54% (see Table 29), but its fluctuations during the past few years do not reveal any clear trend. The slight utilization of tariff quotas and ceilings during the first two preference years is probably due to the initially somewhat limited range of GSP participants. Ever since this became more or less stabilized the average coefficient of utilization has fluctuated about the 50% mark.

The different sensitivity categories admittedly reveal significant changes in the degree of utilization. The sensitivity structure of the utilization of Community quotas and ceilings reveals that the developing countries have shown great skill in taking increasing advantage of their marketing opportunities within the GSP framework in just those product areas in which they are particularly competitive.

It may have been a disappointment to them that these are the very groups of sensitive GSP products for which maximum import amounts frequently impede a free expansion of GSP exports into the EC and in which the relative lag of tariff quotas and ceilings behind the general growth of imports from those countries emerges as a restrictive factor.

It is not therefore surprising that in the group of *sensitive* GSP products the coefficient of utilization of Community tariff quotas is, *first of all*, higher than average (1976: 63.5%) and that, *secondly*, it increases vigorously over the years (1973: 38.4%; 1976: 63.5%) (see Table 30). This effect was also enhanced by

Table 29. *Volume of Granting of Preferences (Preference Offer) and Utilization, 1971 to 1978*
(in Million UA and as a Percentage)

Year	Volume of preference granted[a] (Preference offer) in million UA	Utilization in %
1971 (2nd half)	500	44.0[a]
1972	1,100	40.9[a]
1973	1,250	49.0
1974	3,250	53.9
1975	3,680	47.0
1976	5,600	54.2
1977	6,230	—
1978	6,400[b]	—

[a] Data of the EC Commission including the previous year's imports of agricultural GSP products not subject to any quantitative or value limitations.
[b] In EUA.

Note: The utilization coefficients published by the EC Commission had to be revised on the strength of available GSP performance for the years 1973 to 1976.
Sources: Own presentation and calculation based on *Commission of the European Communities: Scheme of Generalized Tariff Preferences*, loc. cit., p. 2, and "Proposals from the Commission of the European Communities", loc. cit., p. 2, as well as on SOEC and German Federal Ministry of Economic Affairs data.

the down-grading of the sensitivity of certain products and their inclusion in the group of hybrid or semi-sensitive products. It is also interesting that, on the other hand, it occurred only once in 1976 in this group of products that the Community quota was fully utilized (see Table 28).

A marked effect on the utilization of Member State shares is exerted by the breakdown proportion of Community quotas among the individual EC countries. Since this breakdown is determined not on products-specific grounds but is derived from general economic criteria and—allowing for modification for textiles—is uniformly applied to all sensitive products, there is bound to arise a divergence from the overall trade pattern, the more as there is no annual adjustment to structural changes.

Table 30. *Utilization of Community Tariff Quotas and Ceilings*[a]
by Sensitivity Groups, 1973 and 1976
(in Million UA and as a Percentage)

	Preference granted in million UA		Utilization in %	
	1973	1976	1973	1976
Sensitive goods	477	694	38.4	63.5
Hybrid goods	—	275	—	45.1
Semi-sensitive goods	142	799	61.3	123.5
Non-sensitive goods	631	3,832	54.2	38.7
All goods	1,250	5,600	49.0	54.2

[a] Including expected imports of non-sensitive agricultural GSP products not subject to any quantitative or value limitations.

Sources: Own calculation and presentation based on SOEC and German Federal Ministry of Economic Affairs data as well as on *Commission of the European Communities: Scheme of Generalized Tariff Preferences*, loc. cit., p. 2 and "Proposals from the Commission of the European Communities", loc. cit., p. 2.

Such changes arise not only from alterations over the course of time of the country-by-country distribution of real trade flows but also from the definition of Member State shares in a unit of account which no longer reflects actual parities between individual EC currencies. The distortion thereby produced is revealed by a correlation between EC country structures of Member State shares on the one hand and the structures of the EC's overall trade with eligible developing countries in respect of all sensitive GSP products. Correlation of the two matrixes produces a coefficient $r = 0.53$, a figure which shows that the breakdown key was not arbitrarily chosen but which nevertheless reveals a relatively slight connection between the two structures and therefore makes it appear probable that these distortions must have considerable negative effects in relation to the utilization of Community quotas.

The EC country structure of utilization of national quotas shows very clearly that the Federal Republic of Germany exhibits

90

by far the greatest coefficient of utilization (77.7%). Above-average performances are recorded also by Italy and the Benelux countries. Nearly all EC countries have been able, since the GSP came into force, to record marked increase in the utilization of import opportunities with respect to sensitive products (see Table 31).

Table 31. *Percentage Utilization of National Tariff Quotas by EC Member States 1971 to 1976*

EC Member State	1971	1972	1973	1974	1975	1976
Federal Republic of Germany	34	34.1	56.61	51.74	62.37	77.66
Benelux	24.2	32.9	47.08	54.41	58.37	61.29
France	14.6	20.1	28.86	39.42	42.18	55.65
Italy	29	37.8	47.19	53.65	44.14	64.86
United Kingdom	—	—	—	47.03	35.5	45.69
Ireland	—	—	—	14.02	13.14	28.08
Denmark	—	—	—	43.66	37.54	47.79
EC[a]	26	32.2	45.74	48.06	42.24	60.6

[a] Divergences from Table 30 are due to different methods of calculation. In the table above it was necessary to use the unweighted averages of national coefficients of utilization in order to obtain the longest possible time series.

Source: Own calculations based on SOEC and German Federal Ministry of Economic Affairs data.

Particularly striking is the increase in the coefficient of utilization in respect *of semi-sensitive* GSP products. Here actual GSP imports have already exceeded the ceiling limits. Average utilization in 1976 was 123.5%, representing double the 1973 figure. This over-utilization of the total ceiling amount is due—as already indicated—to the pronounced liberalization effects brought about by a generous administration of this trade.

Non-sensitive products were the only category to exhibit a decline in average utilization. This trend is quite obviously to be explained by a particularly marked extension of ceilings between 1973 and 1976 which, at a figure of +607% far exceeded the growth of GSP imports at +434%. Conditions are the reverse in the more sensitive areas. There GSP imports increased at twice the rate (+ 575%) of the maximum import amounts (+ 285%).

2. The rationale of the coefficient

This picture of the utilization of Community quotas and ceilings, however, requires closer study. The question arises as to whether this customary method of calculation of average utilization—a method time and again used also by the EC Commission—is not in need of amendment.

1. In order to ascertain the average coefficient of utilization the statistically ascertained actual GSP imports are compared with the volume of granting of preference (the preference offer) as it emerges from the sum total of all Community tariff quotas and ceilings plus the previous year's imports of agricultural products not subject to the above quotas or ceilings.
2. This method of calculation treats the non-sensitive agricultural products as quasi-ceiling-limited. In view of the fact that GSP imports of agricultural products have so far been steadily increasing this method as a rule results in an "artificial" improvement of the coefficient of utilization.
3. The total of "genuine" Community tariff quotas and ceilings also contains amounts for products in respect of which the developing countries are not at present competitive or capable of supply, or else are so only to a limited extent, and moreover will remain in that position in many areas for the forseeable future. These include high quality industrial products of the chemical industry, of the machine-tool and electrical engineering industries and automotive engineering, as well as numerous semi-finished products from base metals. No doubt the granting of preferential import facilities also for such products is sensible in principle, just as is their annual extension. But the developing countries cannot be expected from one day to the next, to move into such highly developed industrial areas or indeed not at all without foreign capital and know-how. The continuous raising of ceilings, accompanied as it inevitably is by a diminishing coeffi-

cient of utilization, reveals the evident industrialization lag and the low competitiveness of the developing countries. But it conceals the fact that these supplier countries are exceedingly skilful in achieving growing marketing successes also in non-sensitive areas. Beyond this point—if not before—the coefficient of utilization as hitherto used ceases to be useful.

At first glance it would seem sensible, in calculating the average coefficient of utilization, to exclude the non-sensitive agricultural products which are subject to neither ceilings nor quotas. The marketing performance of the developing countries in respect of these agricultural products might simply be shown by growth rates and, if necessary, by reference to the number of different products which the developing countries were or were not able to supply.[35]

As a result of this first correction the average coefficient of utilization for 1976 declines slightly from 54.2% to 54.0% (see Table 32). The decline for non-sensitive products is more marked —from 38.7% to 33.0%.

If the total of tariff quotas and ceilings is further reduced by the import limits laid down for GSP products not actually suppliable by the beneficiary developing countries a very much more positive picture of GSP utilization emerges: for all GSP products subject to quotas or ceilings which are actually suppliable by the beneficiary developing countries the average coefficient of utilization significantly amounts to 68.6% (see Table 32). A greatly increased figure of approximately 50% is found more particularly in the area of non-sensitive products.

A much more favourable result still is obtained if one calculates not the average coefficient of utilization but the average of coefficients of utilization ascertained for each separate GSP product. In this calculation each individual coefficient of utilization enters into the calculation of the average with simple weighting. While the coefficients of utilization exhibit a slight decline for sensitive, hybrid and semi-sensitive goods, they display a

---

35. See § 4.

marked upward leap for non-sensitive and subsequently also for all GSP products (see Table 32).

It would be wiser not to attempt an interpretation of these, after all, very divergent results, the more so as not only the individual methods but the criteria of the coefficient of utilization generally are open to criticism. In the past it seemed that the purpose of this yardstick was to represent the success of the supplier countries in utilizing the marketing opportunities granted to them, expressed by the total of all quotas and ceilings. Averaged over all products it has so far remained well below the 100% mark which seemed to reflect the ideal state: total utilization of all opportunities offered. What was overlooked was the fact that such an interpretation of the yardstick presupposes the strict application of ceiling and quota regulations. But since in the meantime a rather liberal administration has evolved not only for non-sensitive but also for semi-sensitive GSP products, one which even permits a manifold over-utilization of granted ceilings, the yardstick has totally lost its validity. Without additional information on the frequency of individual coefficients of utilization (see Table 28) the coefficient of utilization of 126.7% for semi-sensitive products, to quote just one example, can no longer be meaningfully interpreted. The coefficient of utilization hitherto in use is therefore now applicable, at best, to sensitive products only since for these products quotas are in fact under strict surveillance and over-utilization is ruled out as a matter of principle. For the remaining categories of products a totally different indicator suggests itself, one that might prove equally applicable to sensitive products.

3. Non-utilization as an alternative indicator

As an alternative indicator we might consider the absolute and relative extent of non-utilization as it emerges from the total of all positive differences between ceilings and GSP imports recorded. This means that all instances of ceilings and quotas being reached or exceeded are disregarded. An attempt will again be made to express the remaining import opportunities. In view of

94

Table 32. *The Effect of Different Methods of Calculation on the Coefficient of Utilization of Community Tariff Quotas and Ceilings for 1976*
(in Million UA and as a Percentage)

Goods	(1) Volume of preference granted in mill. UA (EC Commission data)	(2) Less "quotas" for non-sensitive agricultural products (1)	(3) Less quotas and ceilings for GSP goods not actually capable of being supplied (2)	(4) GSP imports	(5) Less GSP imports of non-sensitive agricultural products (4)	Utilization in % (6) (4):(4)	(7) (5):(2)	(8) (5):(3)	(9) Average utilization[a]
Sensitive goods	694	694	694	441	441	63.5	63.5	63.5	60.3
Hybrid goods	275	275	275	124	124	45.1	45.1	45.1	44.2
Semi-sensitive goods	799	799	779	987	987	123.5	123.5	126.7	113.3
Non-sensitive goods	3,832	2,832	1,880	1,484	936	38.7	33.0	49.8	223.1
All goods	5,600	4,600	3,628	3,036	2,488	54.2	54.0	68.6	184.4

[a] Excluding GSP products in respect of which the beneficiary developing countries were not in fact capable of delivery.

Sources: Own presentation and calculation based on *Commission of the European Communities: Scheme of Generalized Tariff Preferences*, loc. cit., p. 2, and "Proposals from the Commission of the European Communities", loc. cit., p. 2, and "Report drawn up on behalf of the Committee for Development and Co-operation on the proposals from the Commission of the European Communities", loc. cit., as well as on SOEC and German Federal Ministry of Economic Affairs data.

the liberal import administration in respect of semi-sensitive and non-sensitive products this represents a minimum. For products in respect of which no GSP and no most-favoured-nation imports have been established non-utilization might additionally be recorded separately as the sum of the ceilings concerned.

If such a calculation is performed for the preference year 1976 the following picture is obtained (see Table 33): non-utilization amounted to altogether 3.1 billion UA; this is 80% of the corresponding ceilings and Community quotas. It is at least to this not inconsiderable extent that the GSP offers to beneficiary supplier countries further preferential marketing facilities which are just as great as the present GSP trade. In the less sensitive product areas as well as in instances where maximum import amounts have already been exceeded an additional import potential may moreover be thought to exist in view of the more liberal administration that has come into being in this field over the past few years. Import opportunities, however, are qualified by the special supplier-country-specific maximum import amounts.

The remaining marketing opportunities are concentrated to 75% in the area of *non-sensitive* products. There a non-utilization of approximately 2.3 billion UA may be observed, of which 952 million UA, or 31%, are accounted for by ceilings which remained totally untouched. These are products in respect of which the developing countries possess no actual supply capability.

The question therefore arises as to what factors have led to the extensive non-utilization of Community quotas and ceilings. Possible factors are:

— lacking supply capability on the part of the developing countries;
— competitive disadvantages, e.g. in the form of higher production and transport costs, inadequate product quality, etc., which cannot be offset by the preferential margin;
— the restrictive effect of Member State shares and maximum amounts;

96

Table 33. *Non-utilization of Ceilings and Community Tariff Quotas and their Causes, 1976*
(in Million UA and as a Percentage)

| Goods | Non-utilized ceilings and Community tariff quotas in mill. UA | Non-utilization[a] | | | | | |
| | | Total | | Offer-conditioned | | Restriction-conditioned | |
		In mill. UA	In %	In mill. UA	In %	In mill. UA	In %
Sensitive goods	677	297	9.7	142	7.4	155	13.7
Hybrid goods	274	151	5.0	61	3.2	91	8.0
Semi-sensitive goods	396	311	10.2	228	11.9	83	7.3
Non-sensitive goods	2,525	2,293	75.1	1,487	77.5	806	71.0
All goods	3,872	3,052	100.0	1,918	100.0	1,135	100.0

[a] Sum total of all positive differences between Community tariff quotas and/or ceilings and GSP imports.

Source: Own calculations based on SOEC and German Federal Ministry of Economic Affairs data.

— non-compliance with formal requirements such as rules of origin and notification on requirement;
— insufficient incentives due to excessively narrow preferential margins;
— inadequate state of information on the part of those involved in the import trade, and
— non-tariff barriers.

As it is not possible to isolate or quantify the effect of all the above-named factors an attempt will be made first of all to separate the supply-determined non-utilization of Community quotas and ceilings—due to insufficient supply capability and competitiveness of the developing countries—from the remaining determinants which, in a wider sense, give rise to limitation-determined non-utilization, disregarding for the moment the effect of the preferential margin.

The predominant part (63%) of non-utilization is accounted for by insufficient supply capability and competitiveness of the beneficiary developing countries. These countries more particularly lack production and export capacities in respect of non-sensitive products. Such capacities are not only frequently too small but in most cases do not exist at all. Non-sensitive ceilings without any imports whatever account alone for 64% of ascertained non-utilization.

Similar problems exist also with regard to a considerable number of semi-sensitive GSP products. Although the developing countries have, generally speaking, proved their supply capability and competitiveness in respect of these, they are not sufficient to ensure full use of preferential import potentialities. It might be suspected that this is partly due to the restrictive effect of Member State shares and maximum amounts seeing that, given a large preferential margin, the developing countries might suddenly lose their competitiveness when the EC external tariffs are re-introduced. Since, however, only a very small part of supply-determined non-utilization is encountered in such cases either for semi-sensitive or for sensitive products, this thesis has to be rejected.

98

Limitation-determined non-utilization of ceilings and quotas accounts for 1.1 billion UA or 37% of total non-utilization. It is a very conspicuous fact that for this set of causes, too, the emphasis lies on non-sensitive products (806 million UA). As, however, quantitative or value a-priori limitations virtually do not occur in this category of products, other factors, such as

— the rules of origin;
— attractiveness of preferential margin, and
— state of information,

must be responsible for the fact that the major part of the import trade with developing countries takes place not via the GSP but on most-favoured-nation terms.

The remaining 329 million UA of limitation-determined non-utilization are finally accounted for by the more sensitive product categories which also represent the main field of application of quantitative and value limitations on imports. Particularly striking is the high level of non-utilization for the relatively few sensitive GSP products (155 million UA). Analysis of non-utilization clearly shows that insufficient supply capability and competitiveness on the part of the developing countries are the principal determinants. The quantitative and value limitations of the GSP —if one disregards the other factors—can, at most, explain 10% of total non-utilization. In consequence they do not possess anything like the importance that one might have expected them to have in view of the fierce criticism to which they have been subjected. At the same time their importance should not be underrated. In the more sensitive categories of products, which nowadays account for 50% of the GSP trade, 43% of non-utilization there observed is due to restrictions in the wider sense. Among them the quantitative and value limitations are probably the major factor since here the remaining determinants of non-utilization are largely eclipsed. If application of maximum amount and Member State share regulations were set aside, and if ceilings and Community quotas were maintained, the GSP trade in the more sensitive product areas might be increased by approximately 20%. Whether, in view of the protective effects of not only maximum amounts but also Member State shares, this would be desirable is another matter. The restrictive effects of maximum import amounts should not, however, be underestimated because quite often they become effective only after GSP imports have exceeded ceilings and Community quotas. It should finally be borne in mind that already more than half the GSP trade in the more sensitive products categories is being controlled by means of maximum import amounts. This point will be examined in greater detail later.[36]

The following section, therefore, will examine the scope and structure of all cases in which imports notified for GSP preference were affected—because of reaching the various upper limits—by the reintroduction of the EC's most-favoured-nation tariff.

C. Quantitative a-priori Limitations and their Impact on GSP Trade

1. Frequency and structure of application of limitations

During the period from 1971 to 1976 imports from developing countries were curtailed in 1,350 cases by the application of the different instruments of quantitative limitation (see Table 34). A striking feature is the almost steady increase in the frequency of these cases. Only in the recession year 1975 did their number decline, though in the following year it exceeded the frequency of 1974.

Of outstanding importance for the control of GSP imports are the Member State shares[37] and maximum amounts which were applied 617 and 615 times, respectively, between 1971 and 1976; this means that they were applied in 91%! of all cases. Community tariff quotas and ceilings, on the other hand, were far less frequent limitations on GSP imports (118 times). The increase in their frequency, too, clearly lags behind the very marked exten-

36. See § 6 C. 3.
37. For the determination of the frequency of utilized Member State shares see Annex 4.

100

sion of Member State shares and maximum amount instances.

Particular attention should be given to the Member State shares: with a declining number of sensitive GSP products the frequency of their utilization increased drastically. Member State shares—gauged by the frequency of their application—represent the most important control instrument of the GSP, one that is being applied on a greatly increasing scale (see Table 34).

Table 34. *Frequency of Utilization of Community Tariff Quotas and Member State Shares, Ceilings and Maximum Amounts by Sensitivity Groups from 1971 to 1976*

Goods	1971	1972	1973	1974	1975	1976	1971-1976
Sensitive goods	68	95	160	245	157	225	950
Community tariff quotas	—	—	—	1	—	—	1
Maximum amounts	46	61	70	67	42	46	332
Member State shares	22	34	90	177	115	179	617
Hybrid goods	—	—	—	—	23	28	51
Ceilings	—	—	—	—	1	—	1
Maximum amounts	—	—	—	—	22	28	50
Semi-sensitive goods	15	48	61	60	73	77	334
Ceilings	10	16	20	19	23	21	109
Maximum amounts	5	32	41	41	50	56	225
Non-sensitive goods	—	2	3	2	3	5	15
Ceilings	—	1	1	1	2	2	7
Maximum amounts	—	1	2	1	1	3	8
All goods	83	145	224	307	256	335	1,350
Community tariff quotas and ceilings	10	17	21	21	26	23	118
Maximum amounts	51	94	113	109	115	133	615
Member State shares	22	34	90	177	115	179	617

Source: Own presentation and calculation based on A. Pitrone: *EEC GSP Scheme*, Rome n.d., folded appendix p. 1-18, as well as on SOEC and German Federal Ministry of Economic Affairs data.

Table 35. *Number of GSP Products*[a] *Affected by Import Limitations according to Sensitivity, 1973 and 1976* (Absolute and as a Percentage)

Goods	Number of GSP goods[a]		Affected by limitations			
	Absolute		Absolute		in%	
	1973	1976	1973	1976	1973	1976
Sensitive goods	92	51	66	47	71.7	92.2
Hybrid goods	—	29	—	22	—	75.9
Semi-sensitive goods	105	100	45	55	42.9	55.0
Non-sensitive goods	829	947	3	4	0.4	0.4
All goods	1,026	1,127	114	128	11.1	11.4

[a] Including non-sensitive agricultural products not subject to any quantitative or value limitations.

Source: Own presentation and calculation based on A. Pitrone, loc. cit., folded appendix p. 1-18, as well as on SOEC and German Federal Ministry of Economic Affairs data.

Quantitative and value limitations on imports between 1971 and 1976 affected 152 of the approximately 1,100 GSP products. The range of regulated products is relatively well defined, even though fluctuations may be observed (see Table 35).

The emphasis in terms of products was clearly on textiles and textile manufactures. Nearly one-half of all cases were concentrated on this product area which, judged by the multiplicity of regulations issued in respect of it, exhibits the highest degree of sensitivity of all GSP product groups (see Table 36). Two further, though lesser areas of emphasis were represented by leather and leather goods in the wider sense—which likewise constitute a relatively sensitive product category—as well as by electrical engineering products.

It is not surprising that the control mechanisms of the GSP have most forcibly and most frequently operated in the group of *sensitive products.* In 950 (70%) of the altogether 1,350 cases in which the EC external tariff was reintroduced for individual or all countries, the products affected were sensitive products (see

Table 36. *Frequency of Utilization of National and Community Tariff Quotas, Ceilings and Maximum Amounts by CCT Sections, 1971 to 1976*

CCT section number	CCT section	Member State shares	Community tariff quotas and ceilings	Maximum amounts	Total
VIII	Raw hides and skins, leather, furskins and articles thereof; saddlery and harness; travel goods, hand-bags and similar articles	61	6	44	111
IX	Wood and articles of wood; wood charcoal; cork and articles of cork; manufactures of plaiting materials; basketware...	28	8	39	75
XI	Textiles and textile articles	364	62	193	619
XII	Footwear, headgear, umbrellas, sunshades, etc.	33	1	44	78
XIII	Articles of stone, of plaster, of cement, of asbestos, of mica and of similar materials; ceramic products; glass...	6	8	48	62
XVI	Machinery and mechanical appliances; electrical equipment	48	4	64	116
XVIII	Optical, photographic, cinematographic instruments and apparatus...	8	4	20	32
XX	Miscellaneous manufactured articles, incl. furniture, toys...	19	1	49	69
	Sub-total	567	94	501	1,161
I-XXI	All CCT sections	617	118	615	1,162

Source: Own presentation and calculation based on A. Pitrone, loc. cit., folded appendix p. 1-18, as well as on SOEC and German Federal Ministry of Economic Affairs data.

103

Table 37. *Cumulation of Import Limitations under the GSP, 1973 and 1976*

		Number of utilized maximum import quotas per GSP article								
		1	2	3	4	5	6	7	8	9
Number of instances	1973	54	36	18	6	4				
	1976	72	38	10	7	7	8	3	2	1

Source: Own presentation and calculation base on A. Pitrone, loc. cit., folded appendix p. 1-18, as well as on SOEC and German Federal Ministry of Economic Affairs data.

Table 38. *Frequency of Cumulation of Different Import Limitations under the GSP according to Types of Limitation, 1973 and 1976*

Type of limitation	1973	1976
Maximum amounts	113	133
Maximum amounts and Member State shares	45	32
Maximum amounts and Community tariff quotas and/or ceilings	8	11
Member State shares	90	179
Member State shares and Community tariff quotas	—	—
Community tariff quotas/ceilings	13	12

Source: Own presentation and calculation based on A. Pitrone, loc. cit., folded appendix p. 1-18, as well as on SOEC and German Federal Ministry of Economic Affairs data.

Table 34). In 617 cases they were affected by Member State shares and in 332 cases by maximum amounts. Only in one single case in 1974 did sensitive goods reach the Community tariff quota. It is therefore chiefly the Member State shares and maximum amounts which control the importation of sensitive goods from developing countries. This effect is intensified by the circumstance that both limitations as a rule occur together (1976: 32 times; see Table 38).

An increasing and cumulative number of individual limitations (see Table 37) account for GSP products affected by upper import limits. This is not, however, a case of cumulation of different upper limits (see Table 38). The reason, instead, is the rapidly growing number of Member State shares fully utilized in more and more EC countries. Here is, therefore, further evidence that the annual adjustment of quotas lags far behind the extension of overall trade. The increasing tightness of quotas is bound to lead to an increasing degree of utilization. It is moreover interesting to note that, given a diminishing number of sensitive products, the regulated remainder shows a marked increase. Whereas in 1973 some 72% of all remaining sensitive products were affected by Member State shares, the figure by 1976 had grown to 92% (see Table 35). As a number of products were being downgraded to the semi-sensitive categories a "hard core of sensitivity" began to crystallize. By 1976 only four of the altogether 51 sensitive products remained unregulated.

Hybrid GSP products—with one exception—were controlled exclusively by means of maximum amounts (see Tables 34 and 35). For 22 of the altogether 29 products of this sensitivity group imports exceeding the maximum country amounts in 1976 were curtailed. These 22 products alone accounted for 28 separate maximum amounts. Their striking cumulation is due to the numerous maximum amounts reduced below the normal 50% as well as to the maximum amounts once more reduced for particularly competitive countries; these maximum amounts might, if necessary, be administered by the individual EC States. In 1976 particularly competitive countries were subjected to this intensified maximum amount regulation in 22 out of altogether 28 cases (1975: 16 out of 22 cases). Since the introduction of hybrid GSP products in 1975 there have been altogether 50 maximum amount instances and one ceiling instance.

Semi-sensitive products have suffered a total of 334 limitations since 1971. Maximum amounts accounted for the major part of these restrictions (altogether 225 cases); in 109 cases the EC external tariff was reintroduced because of a crossing of ceiling limits (see Table 34). Ever since the Member State shares have greatly increased for sensitive products and the number of products has been reduced, the main emphasis of maximum amounts has shifted to hybrid and semi-sensitive products.

Control of semi-sensitive products is the main task also of the ceilings. Since 1971 some 92% of all oversteppings of ceilings occurred in this sensitivity group. In 20% of the instances of restrictions on semi-sensitive products in 1976 there was an overlap between maximum amounts and ceilings. At present more than one-half of all semi-sensitive products are regulated by means of limitations (see Table 35).

In line with their low degree of sensitivity *non-sensitive* GSP products relatively rarely experience the application of maximum import limits. Although, as will presently be shown, the calculated limits are often exceeded by a multiple, reintroduction of the most-favoured-nation tariff was practised only in exceptional cases. Since a special surveillance procedure is waived, appropriate action by the EC Commissions is normally taken only on the initiative of EC producers. This happened on no more than 15 occasions between 1971 and 1976. Imports of non-sensitive products (see Table 34) were regulated in roughly equal shares by ceilings (7) and maximum amounts (8). Of the altogether 947 non-sensitive GSP products only four were subjected to restrictive measures in 1976 (see Table 35).

2. Volume and structure of GSP trade controlled by limitations

The restrictive character of the GSP is illustrated not only by the frequency of the application of a-priori limitations but also in the volume of trade affected by them. It is significant that the 128 of altogether 950 GSP products regulated in 1976 by Member State shares or Community tariff quotas, ceilings and/or maximum amounts accounted for 40% of the total GSP trade[38] (see Table 39). This "restriction rate" was substantially higher still in the more sensitive product areas. There 124 of the 180 products which account for more than three-quarters of GSP imports in this category were affected. Nearly all hybrid imports were concentrated on 22 of altogether 29 hybrid products.

38. If those agricultural GSP products which are not in principle subject to any quantitative or value limitation are excluded, then as much as just under 50%! of remaining GSP imports are controlled by upper import limits.

These findings, however, require some modification since the interpretation of "restricted trade" also includes that part of GSP trade in a particular product which has remained duty-free in respect of certain supplier and/or recipient countries. Thus, if a maximum amount is reached in respect of a GSP product none but the GSP imports of the maximum account country should properly be viewed as "restricted trade". Much the same is true of cases affected by Member State shares.[39] If the calculations are appropriately corrected the "restricted trade", properly speaking, is found to amount to 878 million UA for 1976, or just under 30% of all GSP imports. Even when allowance has been made for this correction considerably higher proportions are found for the more sensitive product categories. There the figure averaged 55%. Regulation affected 55% of imports of sensitive products, 66% of imports of hybrid products and 54% of imports of semi-sensitive products.

It is clear that by far the strongest control function is exerted by maximum amounts. Although Member State shares are just as frequently applied for the purpose of limiting imports, in terms of the "restricted trade" accounted for by them (54%) *the maximum amounts are certainly the most important instruments of control by the GSP.* It is interesting also that Member State shares (19.5%) account for an even smaller proportion of the "restricted trade" than do ceilings (26.8%). This is a further illustration of the fact that sensitive products require a particularly high specific regulation effort.

It is not only the marked increase in the frequency of import-restricting measures that suggests that Member State shares and Community tariff quotas, ceilings and maximum amounts are affecting ever larger portions of the entire GSP trade and thereby continually extending the "restricted trade". Another indication is the development of this "restricted trade" in the broadest sense, showing as it does a rapid increase from 28% to 40% of all GSP trade between 1973 and 1976 (see Table 39).

Thus the scope for unregulated GSP trade is being steadily

39. See the notes on method in Annex 5.

Table 39. *GSP Imports Affected by Import Limitations according to Type of Restriction and Degree of Sensitivity, 1973 and 1976*
(in Million UA and as a Percentage)

	1973					1976				
	SEN	HYBR	SSEN	NSEN	Total	SEN	HYBR	SSEN	NSEN	Total
1. GSP imports (in mill. UA)	183	—	87	342	621	441	124	987	1,484	3,036
2. GSP imports affected by limitations in the wider sense[a] (in mill. UA)	113	—	56	6	169	322	119	746	32	1,218
3. GSP imports affected by limitations in the strict sense[b] (in mill. UA)						244	82	532	20	878
3.1. by maximum amounts						73	82	299	18	472
3.2. by Member State shares						171	—	—	—	171
3.3. by Community tariff quotas and ceilings						—	—	233	2	235

Table 39 (continued)

	1973					1976				
	SEN	HYBR	SSEN	NSEN	Total	SEN	HYBR	SSEN	NSEN	Total
4. GSP imports (in %)	100	—	100	100	100	100	100	100	100	100
5. GSP imports affected by limitations in the wider sense [a] (in %)	61.5	—	63.9	1.7	27.6	72.9	95.6	75.6	2.1	40.1
6. GSP imports affected by limitations in the strict sense [b] (in %)						55.3	65.9	53.9	1.3	28.9
						100	100	100	100	100
6.1. by maximum amounts						29.8	100	56.2	91.7	53.7
6.2. by Member State shares						70.2	—	—	—	19.5
6.3. by Community tariff quotas and ceilings						—	—	43.8	8.3	26.8

[a] Total imports of *products* entirely or partially affected by limitations.
[b] Total imports of *product flows* affected by limitations.

Note: For the determination of GSP imports controlled by upper import limits see Annex 5.
Source: Own calculations based on SOEC and German Federal Ministry of Economic Affairs data.

narrowed down for the supplier countries. On the grounds of sensitivity alone a potential 50% of their imports into the EC run the risk of being affected by import limitations. At least 30% of the present GSP trade is already being effectively excluded from any further granting of preferences, because of maximum limits having been reached, which means that the supplier countries are, at the most, able to market additional products on preferential terms to the extent that quotas, ceilings and maximum amounts are being increased.

3. Liberalized application of limitations

No doubt this scope would be very much narrower still if, over the course of the years, the EC had not adopted a liberal practice in the application of a-priori limitations. This liberalization manifests itself in different forms:

1. Although the most-favoured-nation tariff was reintroduced this was done only when the upper limits laid down in the EC regulations on the GSP has already been exceeded.
2. Reintroduction of the most-favoured-nation tariff was waived altogether, even though GSP trade had exceeded the upper import limits.
3. Although numerous applicants had not yet effected the required notification they were not denied GSP preference. Inadequate certificates of origin were also temporarily handled in a generous manner.

A liberal application of quantitative and value limitations on imports may be observed in all product categories, even in respect of sensitive products. Admittedly in that category, because of strict surveillance and the more or less automatic reintroduction of external tariffs, it represents an exception. The Community tariff quotas—using 1976 conditions as a basis—are never exceeded. Individual national quotas, and more often maximum amounts, are being applied only reluctantly. In seven instances application of the maximum amount rule was waived altogether (see Table 40).

110

Table 40. *Frequency of Upper Import Limits Being Exceeded[a] according to Sensitivity and Type of Liberalization,[b] 1976*

Import limit	Type of liberalization	Sensitive goods	Hybrid goods	Semi-sensitive goods	Non-sensitive goods	All goods
Community tariff						
quotas/	A + B	1	1	60	185	247
ceilings	A	0	0	39	183	222
Member State shares[c]	A + B	14	—	—	—	14
	A	0	—	—	—	0
Maximum amounts	A + B	40	27	112	379	558
	A	7	0	66	376	449
All limitations	A + B	55	27	172	564	819
	A	7	0	105	559	671

[a] The criterion chosen was an exceeding of limits by 5% or more.

[b] Liberalization Type A: Limit exceeded without reintroduction of external tariff;
Liberalization Type B: Limit exceeded with delayed reintroduction of external tariff.

[c] As national quota instances had to be derived from GSP import data, differentiation between liberalization types A and B was impossible. Strict application on the part of individual Member States was assumed.

Source: Own calculation based on SOEC and German Federal Ministry of Economic Affairs data.

Liberal handling of imports is more conspicuous in the remaining product categories, especially in respect of non-sensitive products. There the absence of special surveillance of GSP imports inevitably results only rarely in the reintroduction of the most-favoured-nation rate. In consequence, limits are frequently exceeded, especially in the case of maximum amounts which are often exceeded by a multiple.

Remarkable, finally, has been the liberalization in the group of semi-sensitive products, where, in spite of surveillance, maximum amounts and sometimes also ceilings were exceeded by substantial amounts without GSP imports being curtailed (1976: 105 times; see Table 40).

Generally speaking the most frequent practice is total waiver of the application of quantitative or value limitations; this is due mainly to non-sensitive imports not being subject to surveillance. In the more sensitive product categories the predominant method is delayed reintroduction of the EC external tariff. But even here liberalization has come a long way: in over 40% of all cases of limits being exceeded no measures were taken by the customs authorities in spite of surveillance.

This liberal handling of maximum import amounts contributes in an astonishing degree to the overall GSP performance. If the exceeding of limits in 1976 is quantified a "liberalization effect" of approximately 700 million UA is found. This value represents more than 20% of all GSP imports during that year. A considerable share in this remarkable result was provided by the liberalized imports in the more sensitive product categories which account for approximately one-half of the total effect. A more detailed, product-specific, analysis shows that the major part of this effect is due to generously handled imports of petroleum processing products of tariff heading number 27.10. They alone accounted for maximum amounts being exceeded to the extent of 200 million UA.

The EC proceeded liberally also in the application of formal a-priori limitations. Thus, especially in the early years of the GSP, many developing countries were permitted preferential imports into the EC in spite of inadequate certificates of origin.

112

A similar attitude was shown by the customs authorities in the absence of notification. By the middle of 1972 a mere 32, and by the beginning of 1974 only 60, countries and territories had met this requirement. In spite of the fact that as late as 1976 numerous beneficiaries had not yet named their customs authorities or deposited samples of their stamps, 17 developing countries nevertheless entered into enjoyment of GSP preferences that year. This resulted in liberalized imports of approximately 320 million UA, i.e. approximately 10% of all GSP imports. Romanian imports alone contributed 233 million UA to this effect. Worth mentioning also were imports from Libya, Saudi Arabia and the Yemen Arab Republic.

4. Protective and restrictive effects of maximum amounts

The discovery that by far the strongest control of GSP trade is exerted by maximum amounts seems a reason for subjecting this a-priori limitation to somewhat closer analysis. Member State shares and Community tariff quotas as well as ceilings are designed exclusively to keep GSP imports from developing countries to a tolerable scale in order thereby to meet the protective needs of affected sectors of the economy as well as the export interests of other countries associated with the EC by special association, co-operation or preferential agreements. The institution of maximum amounts, on the other hand, serves ambivalent purposes: on the one hand it has a restrictive effect, just as the other upper import limits, in that it curtails GSP imports whenever they reach the predetermined levels or, if practised liberally, somewhat later. They therefore protect the same circle of interested parties. On the other hand, however, the maximum amount arrangement serves as a corrective for competitive conditions in the separate GSP markets which are frequently characterized by the predominance of a small number of often more highly developed countries. To ensure that the benefits of preference were shared out more evenly among GSP beneficiaries maximum country amounts were created, generally at the level of 50% of ceilings or Community tariff quotas, but sometimes at a more restrictive level for particularly competitive developing countries.

The institution of maximum amounts has repeatedly been the object of fierce criticism, mainly on the grounds that the competitive developing countries were being needlessly restricted in utilizing the advantage of preference without any benefit being derived from this restriction by the remaining beneficiaries. The result, it was claimed, was merely an additional protective effect for certain sectors of the economy within the EC rather than protection for the less developed supplier countries.

It should be pointed out straight away that the import limitations so far imposed accurately concentrate on the supplier countries which hold a leading position in GSP trade and in overall trade. Between 1971 and 1976 some 90% of all maximum amount cases were accounted for by the countries listed in Table 41. The same countries held a 65% share of GSP trade in 1976. It is also revealing that the "normal maximum amount" of 50% already represents the exception rather than the rule. Just under 80% of all maximum amount cases are accounted for by reduced maximum country amounts with emphasis on the 20% and 30% rates (see Table 41).

The question of whether maximum amounts are predominantly protectionist of predominantly competition-corrective is answered by an examination of the supplier country structure of the 104 GSP products,[40] whose imports in 1976 were regulated by maximum amounts (see Table 42). To start with, it was found that the institution of maximum amounts provides protection both for competitive and for less competitive countries.

Admittedly the protection enjoyed by competitive developing countries is confined to a mere 21 out of the 104 GSP products concerned. Only in one single case was Yugoslavia the sole supplier country, and only in that case did the maximum amount fail in its function of providing protection for other GSP participants. In all other cases—and they were approximately 80%—protection was provided for at least one lesser supplier country which did not belong to the 10 most competitive GSP import countries.

40. Affected CPG items.

Table 41. *Developing Countries Affected by Maximum Amounts according to Frequency of Limits Reached and Maximum Amount Rates, 1971 to 1976*

Developing countries concerned	Special maximum amounts	10%	15%	20%	25%	30%	35%	40%	45%	50%	All maximum amounts
1. Yugoslavia	22	3	2	52		45		1		32	157
2. Hong Kong	15		3	65		27				9	119
3. South Korea	2		4	29		54				22	111
4. India				3		37		1		20	61
5. Brazil			2	2		5		1		17	27
6. Pakistan			2	2		18				3	25
7. Singapore				9		6				3	18
8. Romania				5						12	17
9. Iran				6		5				1	12
10. Mexico				3		7				2	12
Sub-total	39	3	13	176		204		3		121	559
Remaining 17 countries		3		17		29				7	56
All 27 countries concerned	39	6	13	193		233		3		128	615

Source: Own calculation and presentation based on A. Pitrone, loc. cit., folded appendix p. 1-18 as well as on SOEC and German Federal Ministry of Economic Affairs data.

In the case of one-third of all GSP products regulated by maximum amounts six or more minor supplier countries enjoyed protection as a result of these maximum amounts.

It may be concluded that the institution of maximum amounts, like all other import limits, has a restrictive effect and indeed is bound to have such an effect. The advantage of this restriction, on the other hand, is already demonstrably benefiting *also* those less competitive developing countries from whose point of view the maximum amounts represent a welcome protection, especially if maximum amount rates are reduced and an increased number of countries is thereby enabled to participate in the GSP.

It might be objected that it is not the number of GSP participants that decides on the restrictive or even protectionist character of maximum amounts but the unused GSP potential, expressed by non-utilization of Community tariff quotas and ceilings. It is true that GSP products affected by Member State shares and maximum amounts do exhibit a considerable restriction-conditioned non-utilization (approximately 200 million UA) in which the maximum amounts certainly have a share.

It should, however, be borne in mind that such a non-utilization, to the extent that it is due to maximum amounts, can be entirely desirable. Certainly an immediate utilization of remaining ceilings and quotas would be more advantageous; but these gaps can just as well be interpreted as a useful encouragement to new supplier countries to export to the EC on preferential terms. Non-utilization due to maximum amounts should not therefore be assessed only from a short-term point of view. Since minor supplier countries have already gained a foothold in markets governed by maximum amounts, that non-utilization represents their future marketing potential on preferential terms, a potential into which they can grow. Of course, the protection provided by maximum amounts, thus understood, is meaningful only in the case of GSP products enjoying a generous scale of quotas or ceilings; otherwise there would be a pointless share-out of small and minute shares in imports. This danger exists mainly for the more sensitive products.

Some doubt also attaches to the practice of the EC Commis-

Table 42. *Representation of the Less Competitive Developing Countries in Imports of Maximum-Amount-Controlled GSP Products, 1976 by Frequency Categories*

Frequency of less strong suppliers among the developing countries[c]	Number of GSP goods affected by maximum amounts[a]
0	22[b]
1 to 5	47
6 to 10	13
11 to 15	13
over 15	9

[a] CPG items concerned.

[b] Only in one instance was no other competitive country represented apart from the maximum-amount country (Yugoslavia).

[c] Countries not among the 10 biggest supplier countries.

Source: Own calculation and presentation based on A. Pitrone, loc. cit., folded appendix p. 1-18, as well as on SOEC and German Federal Ministry of Economic Affairs data.

sion in using per capita income and import and export data for sharing out the markets as fairly as possible among the supplier countries. Even though the measures taken in respect of certain semi-sensitive textile products[41] are based on entirely sound criteria, there must be considerable doubt about as to whether the totality of GSP markets can be subdivided with such scientific precision in favour of the minor supplier countries, and as to whether such highly complex arrangements are in fact still comprehensible to those countries. Yet transparency and clarity of preferential terms is a vital factor in the stimulant effect of the GSP, especially with regard to investment incentives.

D. The Effects of the Rules of Origin

The rules of origin were laid down in order to prevent abuse of preferences by non-beneficiary countries. Under these rules a GSP product is entitled to preference only if it meets the following three conditions:

41. See § 2 D. 2. d.

— It must have been produced wholly in the beneficiary developing country or, if materials of parts were imported, these must have undergone sufficient working and processing in the developing country.

— It must be consigned directly, i.e. without further processing, from the beneficiary country to the EC.

— Fulfilment of these requirements must be supported by documentary evidence.

The rules of origin are designed to prevent abuse of the GSP; they should cease to apply at the point where they merely serve to prevent imports which, in the spirit of the GSP, should properly enjoy preference. It will be necessary to examine to what extent the rules of origin are fulfilling their purpose.

At present about three-quarters of all GSP imports consist of products considered as wholly obtained in countries benefiting from the GSP.[42] Few problems as a rule arise in connection with the issue of a certificate of origin.

As the developing countries are increasingly integrated in international trade, however, the proportion of products the materials for which have in part been imported from other countries and which have merely undergone working or processing in the preference-claiming country is increasing. In each such case the criterion for eligibility is whether such processing was sufficient. As a general rule the EC applies the criterion of the so-called "tariff leap" into a different four-digit heading number of the Brussels Tariff Nomenclature (BTN). There are, however, numerous exceptions to this rule. An extensive list, "List A", enumerates those manufacturing processes which, while resulting in a change in the tariff heading, are not regarded as sufficient. "List B" contains the reverse cases.

Apart from the fact that certain beneficiary countries are not yet using the BTN the long lists of exceptions result in considerable information problems especially for the lesser developing

---

42. See T. Murray: *Trade Preferences for Developing Countries*, loc. cit., p. 87 footnote.

countries. Added to this is the fact that virtually any system of preferences of the industrialized countries that proceeds in accordance with a "processing criterion"[43] in turn possesses its own lists of exceptions.

In answering the question—decisive in connection with the granting of preferences—as to whether sufficient working or processing has taken place the EC considers solely the preference-claiming country directly consigning to the EC. Any previous transformations performed in other countries, even if these were likewise beneficiary developing countries, are regarded as irrelevant. Cumulative origin, which preserves this status for products even after they have crossed a frontier, is recognized by the GSP only in respect of three regional groupings—the ASEAN, the MCCA and the Andean countries.

It is obvious that such a set of rules which obstructs international division of labour and the specialization of individual countries, does not make sense either on fundamental considerations of market economy or from the development policy point of view. It might be argued in justification that the simple rule of origin makes documentation very much easier. Since, however, other industrialized countries have for some time been practising the rule of cumulative origin, and since the EC itself grants this more advantageous rule to the above-named three regional groupings and, under the Lomé Convention, to all ACP states, such an argument does not carry much weight.

Another justification for preserving simple origin might be the argument that the benefit of preferential terms should be enjoyed only by the developing country which actually performed the decisive processing operations and that any purely "merchant countries", which merely market the products manufactured in other developing countries, should be deprived of the opportunity of gleaning additional profits. This argument does not carry much conviction either. Quite apart from the fact that, on market economy considerations, there is no harm in a developing country specializing in services, such as the marketing of prod-

43. Some of them also apply the "value added criterion". See also § 10.

ucts, it would not be very consistent if the question of incidence and of passing on the preferential margin among the developing countries were to be judged by yardsticks other than those between importer and producer within a developing country—since for preferential treatment it is irrelevant who benefits from the preferential margin.

The requirement of the GSP that GSP products must be consigned direct from the beneficiary developing country to the EC affects more particularly the landlocked countries without sea ports. The GSP in such cases only permits transport through third countries when it is established that the products do not enter into commerce or consumption and have only undergone operations intended to keep them in good condition. Certain problems arise if the products are to be stored for any length of time, handled, repacked or divided for distribution to different recipients while in the third country. If such operations, designed to maintain their competitiveness, are not tolerated by the GSP the landlocked countries are bound to be seriously handicapped. Unless these third countries are likewise eligible developing countries the introduction of the cumulative origin rule would automatically solve this problem.

Even though the entire complex of certification of origin was handled rather generously by the EC, at least during the initial period of the GSP, it is surely obvious that a large number of strict regulations, even if they are not applied, must exert a certain deterrent and unnerving effect. For one thing, countries which consign only small quantities to the EC may well have been deterred from applying for preferential treatment because the whole administrative effort required for GSP acceptance seemed excessive to them. For another, a producer, when making investment decisions, will naturally not wish to rely on the fact that a generous interpretation once practised will necessarily be practised also in the future. Now that the EC's rules of origin are being strictly interpreted it seems likely that, alongside their proper task of preventing abuse of the GSP, they also tend to exclude from the GSP a not inconsiderable portion of potential preferential trade.

120

§ 7. Size, Structure and Effects of Preferential Tariff Reductions

A. Methodological Remarks

The following analysis of the effects of the GSP on the customs revenues of the EC countries on the one hand, and of the effects of the tariff concessions upon the volume and structure of GSP trade on the other, is based on a comparision of most-favoured-nation tariff rates and GSP rates of duty for each individual product comprised in the GSP. Collection of the data gave rise to a number of problems, some of which were solved only by approximation.

— To ensure that a preferential customs duty defined at the CPG level could be related to a uniform most-favoured-nation rate of duty it was necessary in such cases—since distribution of preferential imports among NIMEXE items contained in the GSP is not known—to work out an unweighted average.
— Tariff suspensions in favour of non-eligible third countries— in so far as these were compatible with GSP products in terms of time and subject—were taken into consideration. It was not possible to include in the analysis differential most-favoured-nation rates of the EC countries—in particular those of the new Member States. In such cases the customs rate of the Community of the Six was used as a general principle.
— For a number of agricultural products the preferential customs duties of the new Member States differ from those of the Community of the Six. As the purpose of this measure was to ensure a uniform preferential margin regardless of different external tariffs the margin of the Community of the Six was used as the basis of calculation also in respect of the new Member States.
— Additional duties, variable components and levies, e.g. for sugar, were not taken into consideration either in the most-favoured-nation rates or in the preferential rates. This did not, however, lead to a distortion of the results since preferential treatment under the GSP does not, as a matter of principle, extend to such additional levies.

121

— Because of the huge effort involved in the collection and processing of the data the analysis had to be confined to two years of review—1973 and 1976.

B. Tariff Revenues Foregone

Loss of revenue by the EC customs authorities due to partial or total customs reductions within the framework of the GSP amounted to 63.030 million UA in 1973. By 1976 the loss of customs revenue had increased by 423% to 266.806 million UA; the rate of increase therefore was slightly below the growth rate of GSP imports (which totalled 496%) and that of total imports of GSP products from beneficiary developing countries (amounting to 480%). The percentage loss of customs revenue from GSP trade diminished from 10.3% in 1973 to 8.8% in 1976;[44] the percentage share of the loss of customs revenue in the total trade in GSP products by the developing countries similarly somewhat declined from 3.5% in 1973 to 3.09% in 1976. This suggests a diminution in the preferential margin or else a redistribution of GSP imports which will have to be examined in greater detail.

The absolute magnitude of the loss of customs revenue does not, of course, mean very much; what matters for the assessment of the importance and tolerability of these customs revenue losses in their relation to the EC's total customs revenue. Assuming the average customs charge on EC imports from non-EC countries to be 7% the figure obtained for the drop in EC customs revenue owing to the GSP amounts to 1.5% in 1973 and 2.3% in 1976. Although these figures reveal a rising trend, due to the disproportionately large increase in imports of GSP products from developing countries compared with total imports from non-EC countries, the *budgetary significance* of the loss in revenue resulting from the GSP is likely to remain relatively *slight* also in the immediate future.

44. This result, in terms of order of magnitude, is entirely compatible with a very cautious estimate of the Commission which put the loss of customs revenue in 1977 at approximately 300 million EUA. See "Proposals from the Commission of the European Communities", loc. cit.

122

C. Preferential Margin

One of the essential factors in the effectiveness of any preferential system is the preferential margin. The greater this preferential margin the greater the benefit to the competitiveness over competing third countries and domestic producers. The developing countries, in consequence, are anxious on the one hand to obtain the greatest possible tariff concessions within the framework of the GSP—although a further lowering of preferential rates is possible only in respect of agricultural products—while on the other hand preventing their own preferential margin from being trimmed down as a result of reductions in the most-favoured-nation rate for *all* non-EC countries.[45]

The preferential margin weighted with GSP trade flows amounted to 10.3% in 1973. By 1976 this average customs advantage for every preferential trade item had dropped by 1.5 percentage points to 8.8%. This decline in the preferential margin may be due to various reasons:

— The most-favoured-nation rate charged on GSP products may have declined between 1973 and 1976.
— The eligible products newly included in the GSP during that period may have carried a lower preferential margin.
— The structure of GSP trade may have shifted in favour of products with a lower preferential margin.

A glance at the unweighted preferential margin, which has remained virtually constant from 1973 to 1976 at approximately 10%, shows that the decline of the preferential margin cannot be explained either by changes in the most-favoured-nation rates or by an increased inclusion of low-tariff products in the product lists of the GSP. This means that structural shifts must have taken place which call for a closer examination of the amount of the preferential margin in certain areas of the GSP.

---

45. For the problems stemming from this pattern of interests of the developing countries for the general tariff reduction talks (the Tokyo Round) see T. Murray: *Trade Preferences for Developing Countries*, loc. cit., p. 136, as well as § 11 A.

Table 43. *Average Preferential Margin as a Function of the Degree of Sensitivity, 1973 and 1976*
(as a Percentage)

Degree of sensitivity/ economic sector	Average preferential margin in %	
	1973	1976
Sensitive products	11.8	12.1
Semi-sensitive and hybrid products	11.6	8.9
Non-sensitive products	8.9	7.8
Agricultural products	3.63	6.75
Semi-finished and finished industrial products	9.8	9.55
of these: ECSC products	6.3	6.3
textiles	13.4	13.3
of these: sensitive textiles	13.9	14.6

Source: Own calculations based on SOEC and German Federal Ministry of Economic Affairs data.

Table 43 lists the preferential margins, weighted by the trade volumes concerned, according to degree of sensitivity and to economic sectors. As expected, the preferential margin—and hence also the EC external tariff[46]—is highest for sensitive products, followed by semi-sensitive and non-sensitive products. Differentiation by economic sectors makes it clear that the tariff concessions in the agricultural sector in 1976 resulted in a situation in which the lowest preferential margin attached no longer to agricultural products but, for the first time, to ECSC products. The preferential margin for textiles remained uniformly high; indeed for sensitive textile products it continued to rise between 1973 and 1976.

A striking feature is the decline of the preferential margin for semi-sensitive products by more than 2.5 percentage points—in spite of the fact that the extension of GSP items in the areas of

46. Only in the case of agricultural products does the preferential margin rule out conclusions about the EC external tariff.

Table 44. *Distribution of GSP Trade and Total Trade in GSP Products as a Function of the Size of the Preferential Margin 1973 and 1976* (as a Percentage)

Preferential margin in %	GSP Trade 1973 in %	Total trade in GSP goods 1973 in %	GSP Trade 1976 in %	Total trade in GSP goods 1976 in %
0.0- 0.9	0.1	0.1	1.5	13.3
1.0- 1.9	0.4	0.2	1.3	0.9
2.0- 2.9	2.2	1.3	8.8	4.6
3.0- 3.9	3.7	3.2	6.1	6.5
4.0- 4.9	4.0	3.8	3.4	3.1
5.0- 5.9	9.0	6.0	7.0	2.8
6.0- 6.9	9.4	7.2	6.7	3.9
7.0- 7.9	14.3	12.2	17.1	13.2
8.0- 8.9	10.0	10.4	6.7	4.9
9.0- 9.9	6.6	3.6	10.5	6.5
10.0-10.9	4.6	3.4	3.0	5.9
11.0-11.9	3.3	2.6	5.6	4.3
12.0-12.9	6.6	2.8	3.6	0.6
13.0-13.9	3.8	5.0	3.9	5.4
14.0-14.9	2.8	7.0	2.1	7.1
15.0-15.9	0.9	0.7	1.2	1.3
16.0-16.9	2.0	2.8	1.8	1.0
17.0-17.9	5.2	13.6	2.2	6.9
18.0-18.9	0.8	2.0	0.9	1.0
19.0-19.9	0.3	0.3	0.3	1.3
20.0-20.9	1.2	1.0	1.3	1.9
21.0-21.9	—	—	—	—
22.0-22.9	0.2	0.0	0.1	0.2
23.0-23.9	0.0	0.0	0.2	0.2
over 24.0	8.6	10.8	4.6	3.1
Total	100.0	100.0	100.0	100.0

Source: Own calculations based on SOEC and German Federal Ministry of Economic Affairs data.

semi-sensitive and hybrid products was predominantly at the expense of the sensitive products carrying a higher preferential margin. The explanation lies in the dynamic development of item 27.10 (light oils, medium oils, heavy oils) which, with a below-average external tariff of 6% in 1976, accounted for more than one-sixth (18.3%) of the total GSP trade compared with a relatively insignificant proportion of 1.9% in 1973. This exceptional effect, due to developments in the petroleum market, goes a long way to explain the decline of the preferential margin generally. A further explanation is the fact that preferential imports of agricultural products—enjoying an increasing but nevertheless below-average preferential margin—have expanded at a particularly striking rate since 1973, by a factor of 23, and have in consequence depressed the overall average.

Table 44 attempts to answer the question as to the extent to which the size of the preferential margin affects the structure of GSP trade. Comparison of the distribution of GSP trade and of total trade among preferential margins reveals no systematic correlation. Nor can any empirical confirmation be found for the thesis that GSP imports from developing countries have in the course of time concentrated on those products which enjoy especially high customs concessions: correlation between coincidence—the relation between total imports and GSP imports—and the size of the preferential margin in fact declined from 1973 to 1976.

D. Incidence and Stimulant of GSP Preferences

An important criterion of the effectiveness of the preferential margin is its incidence: if the customs benefit in the form of higher selling prices is passed on to the producers in the developing countries then their improved profit situation provides favourable conditions for an increase in investments. If, on the other hand, the importer is able to retain the preferential margin as an additional profit then he will endeavour to exploit his import demand in favour of the developing countries and to the detriment of the relatively dearer products from third countries; this would result for the sellers in the developing countries in an investment-stimulating quantity effect. The same result would arise if the importer passed on the customs benefit to domestic buyers in the form of lower market prices.

126

Customs theoreticians differ on the actual response to be expected from importers. The extreme case, though entirely feasible, would be that of the importers, having obtained their products predominantly from developing countries benefiting from preferences, exploiting the weak bargaining position of the supplier countries in order to keep back the entire preferential margin without increasing their imports and without lowering the market price. Such action would be rational given completely price-inelastic demand or market saturation. Under realistic conditions, however, it may be assumed that for most of the products there exists a normal demand function and that, even given market saturation, competition of importers amongst each other and their rivalry for market shares will favour a passing-on of the preferential margin to the consumer.

Any of these three types of incidence—back-shifting to the producer, on-shifting to the ultimate purchaser, and retention by the importer—can only have beneficial effects on the developing countries if the preferential margin is wide enough to offset possible cost disadvantages of the developing countries. It is impossible to generalize on which of the three types of incidence is typical of the GSP. The incidence option must depend on the bargaining strength of the sellers in the developing countries— which probably means that the more competitive developing countries will again enjoy an advantage—on the degree of sensitivity of the product, determining as it does the probability of preferential treatment, and on the market situation for each separate GSP product, which may vary a good deal from one EC country to another. Individual data cannot therefore be generalized and any package statement on the incidence of the preferential margin under the GSP must be purely speculative. What is essential for the effectiveness of the GSP is that, regardless of the findings of primary incidence, the sellers in the developing countries are at least assured of a quantity effect.

The stimulant effects of the preferential margin arise—according to the type of incidence—from the price and/or quantity effects of tariff cuts. The question therefore arises as to whether the acceleration of the growth rate due to preference is merely a short-term process occurring at the introduction of a preferential system. Customs theory would suggest that the dynamic effects of tariff cuts are spent as soon as a new point of equilibrium is reached between supply and demand and that any further growth of trade can be effected only by the "normal" determinants of the interplay of supply and demand. Hence the growth rate, following a short-term rise, would after a brief period of adjustment—admittedly at a higher level—merge into the path of long-run growth.

However, in the field of international trade and more particularly in that of trade relations with developing countries a considerable number of reasons suggest that the theoretical premise of instant adaptation to changed data patterns is in need of considerable qualification. Thus without any doubt knowledge of the market is incomplete: both on the side of the exporters and on that of the importers information on the GSP—if only because of its complexity and continually changing structure—spreads but slowly. The consumer similarly is unable to recognize immediately a GSP-determined change in price relations or make allowance for it in his consumer decisions—especially since consumer preferences only change slowly. A further retarding element is the fact that importers are reluctant to abandon traditional trade relations predating the introduction of the GSP. The incidence process, too, can be of a longer-term nature: it is conceivable, for instance, that importers will carefully examine the supply situation before deciding to pass on the preferential margin.

Yet another obstacle lies on the side of the developing countries which are unable, because of their (in the short term, low) elasticity of supply, to respond instantly to an extension of demand by the installation or preparation of new production capacities. If developing countries, by means of enlarging production, succeed in realizing economies of scale then such a saving of costs will intensify the effect of the preferential margin and impart new dynamism to the development of trade. The same effect is achieved by increasing tariff concessions within the framework of the GSP; what comes to mind here is an increase of the average margin of preference for agricultural products. Finally continuous liberalization and enlargement of the GSP will ensure that the preferential margin develops its growth-accelerating effect for more products from more countries. The duration and intensity of the effectiveness of the above-listed factors differs a good deal. Nevertheless, it would seem that their combined effect has been that the "pure" dynamic effects upon GSP trade, i.e. those resulting from the benefit of the preferential margin, have not yet been exhausted during the existence of the GSP so far and that in all probability they will continue to operate in the foreseeable future.

§ 8. Growth of GSP Trade

A. Determinants of Growth in GSP Trade

GSP trade underwent a tempestuous upsurge between 1973 and 1976. Total GSP imports increased from 612 million UA to 3,036 million UA, representing an average annual growth rate of 70%. This growth is now to be reduced to its separate components. It is not intended to perform an exact breakdown; the values given should merely be taken as estimates of the order of magnitude of the individual effects.

Generally speaking five major factors have contributed to the development of GSP trade:

1. The *EC enlargement effect:* as a result of the enlargement of the EC, the number of preference-giving countries after 1974 increased from six to nine.
2. The *pure growth* of GSP trade.
3. The *country list effect:* in the GSP the countries eligible for preference in respect of a certain product group are grouped together in country lists. These lists have been subject to modification with the result that, as the circle of eligible developing countries widened, the volume of GSP trade also underwent changes.
4. The *product effect:* the number of products included in the GSP has been steadily rising, with positive results for GSP trade.
5. *Other* influencing factors.

We shall begin by dealing with those factors whose effects cannot be accurately quantified.

As surveillance of import limits is being liberalized the volume of trade increases. Since, on the other hand, upper import limits in the sensitive areas increase more slowly than the volume of trade,[47] these limits are increasingly often reached, which triggers off a counter-effect.

The volume of GSP imports rises or falls according to whether imports from developing countries enjoying special preferences either superior or equivalent to the GSP are acknowledged and recorded as preferential imports within the GSP framework.

Thanks to an improved recording procedure, reasonably accurate import data—which still had to be estimated for non-sensitive trade in 1973—are now available. This is a factor which likewise has an effect on the statistically recorded volume of trade.

What all these factors have in common is that while statements can be made on the direction in which they change the trade volume, hardly anything can be said about their magnitude. In view of this indeterminacy it seemed justified to proceed from the hypothesis that these often opposite effects will cancel each other out and that they may therefore be disregarded in their overall effect.

Among the remaining four factors the EC enlargement effect can be isolated with relative ease. The necessary data on this are listed in Table 45.

In 1976 some 35% of GSP imports went to the three new EC Member States. This percentage share, however, looks different if expressed in EUA instead of in UA. Since among the new Member States the economic preponderance was with weak-currency countries the enlargement effect if expressed in UA results in an over-estimate. In real terms, as the calculation in EUA shows, they only accounted for 25% of total imports. Even so the new Member States' share in the GSP trade is far above

47. See § 6 A.

Table 45. *Base Data for the Calculation of the EC Enlargement Effect:*
GSP Imports
(in Million UA and/or Million EUA)

	1973		1976	
	Mill. UA	Mill. EUA	Mill. UA	Mill. EUA
EC-6	612	639	1,985	2,183
EC-9	—	—	3,036	2,921
Difference			1,051	738
Proportion of difference of EC-9 imports			35%	25%

Source: Own calculations based on Statistical Office of the European Communities, loc. cit., p. 112, and SOEC and German Federal Ministry of Economic Affairs data.

their share in the total trade (13%) and also in excess of their share of the EC's GNP of approximately 19%. The GSP imports of the six original Members therefore amount to 1,985 UA (1976) or 2,183 EUA (1976).

Considering that in the fixing of EUA parties the economic weight of each country is reflected also in its GSP trade, one may normally assume approximate parity between EUA and UA for preferential imports as a whole. For GSP trade the divergence in 1976 amounted to less than 4%. However, the exclusion of several weak-currency countries which were taken into consideration in the fixing of the EUA parities results in a situation when this approximate parity between EUA and UA is no longer ensured. The divergence between EUA and UA figures for 1976 amounts to 10%. This is too big a difference to be tolerable. For that reason the figures available in UA from the GSP statistics for 1976 will henceforward be converted into EUA by means of a "parity surcharge" of 10% in order to adjust them to the real purchasing power ratios.

If the EC enlargement effect is disregarded GSP trade increased from 639 million UA in 1973 to 2,183 million EUA in

1976. This represents an annual increase of 51%. How this growth is to be allocated to the other effects will be seen from the following considerations.

For methodological reasons we shall first estimate pure GSP growth so that product and country list effects may then be determined as the balance. Pure GSP growth may be thought of as being made up of two components:

— the growth in GSP imports which would have occurred even without the introduction of the GSP, and
— a "GSP supplement" reflecting the stimulant effects of the GSP.

These two growth components will now be examined in greater detail.

Since the determination of pure growth requires the elimination of the product and country list effects this calculation can only be performed for products in respect of which the content definition has undergone no change between 1973 and 1976. To eliminate the country list effect it is, moreover, necessary to deduct from the 1976 data all trade flows with those developing countries which in 1973 were not yet eligible for preference in respect of that particular product. For the sake of simplification it was assumed that the range of countries eligible under the GSP for a particular group of products has continually grown and that it was not therefore necessary to exclude any flows from the 1973 GSP trade data in order to eliminate the country list effect.

Following the exclusion of those products which exhibited changes of code during the period under review, and which it would therefore have been exceedingly difficult to trace throughout that period, imports worth 477 million UA still remained of the 1973 GSP trade worth 639 million EUA; this means that 75% in value of imports were taken into account in the sample. In respect of these products GSP imports to a total of 1,182 million UA were established from countries which were eligible for preference with regard to them also in 1973. Including the "parity surcharge" of 10% this makes 1,300 million UA or an annual growth rate of 40%. On the plausible assumption that the

132

changes in product code which led to the product's exclusion from the survey were independent of the growth trend of the product concerned it is possible now to transfer the growth figure thus determined by a random sample to the totality of GSP imports. Proceeding from GSP imports in 1973 to a value of 639 million EUA we arrive, given an annual growth rate of 40%, at a preference figure in 1976 of 1,753 million EUA.[48]

This then leaves a balance as against the total trade of the Community of the Six of 430 million EUA which by definition must be attributed to the product and country list effects. The breakdown of the balance between these two effects will not be discussed.

The number of items included in the GSP increased during the period under review by approximately 10% and the number of items in respect of which the developing countries were capable of delivery increased by 22%.[49] It should, however, be remembered that some of the new items were created by splitting old ones and that these do not therefore represent a real extension. It may also be assumed that the newly included items initially recorded below-average trade volumes. An increase of 20% due to the product effect may therefore be accepted as an upper limit.

As for the country effect, it is possible to make unambiguous statements for one country: Romania, not entitled to benefits in 1973, recorded the fourth highest GSP imports into the EC in 1976. Romanian imports into the Community of the Six should therefore be attributed to the country effect[50] and are readily available for a rough calculation.

48. The "parity surcharge" was taken into account also in calculating the growth rate.
49. See Tables 5 and 6.
50. There may be some argument about whether Romanian GSP imports of products which in 1973 had not yet been included in the system of preferences should be assigned to the product effect or to the country list effect. An analogous situation exists for other overlap points between different effects—with some exaggeration, for instance, British imports from Romania of products not yet enjoying preference in 1973. The problem of four mixed sub-effects arising from three independent mutually overlapping effects will here be disregarded. It should, however, be borne in mind that, according to the "sequence of reduction" chosen, the weight of the individual effects will fluctuate.

Considering that imports from Romania in 1976 amounted to 233 million UA we arrive, in line with our assumptions and including the "parity surcharge", at imports of 167 million EUA into the original Member States of the EC as the minimum value for the country list effect. In reality this is likely to be considerably greater as for a whole number of countries there has been a considerable extension of preference possibilities.[51]

As for the breakdown of the as yet unassigned 431 million EUA, the following may be stated: No less than 167 million EUA are due to the country list effect and no more than 350 million EUA[52] may be attributed to the product effect. In the graphical presentation (Diagram 1) the two effects, in the absence of other criteria, have been equally shared out in a ratio of 1:1.

B. Preferences and their Impact on the EC's Trade with Developing Countries

1. Theoretical approaches

Any lowering of existing customs barriers renders possible additional trade between the countries concerned. If, as in the case of the GSP, that tariff cut is preferential, then the effect will be not only trade creation but also trade diversion since products from countries not benefiting from the tariff cut will now be relatively more expensive and will be displaced by products from beneficiary countries.[53]

In its original form the concept of trade creation and trade diversion is based on a general welfare-economic approach: it is a development of the argument, which dates back to Ricardo, that the initiation of trade leads in each participating country to a better utilization of production factors and thereby promotes the general welfare as well as the welfare of each individual country.

51. Thus the large group of dependent countries and territories (including Hong Kong and Macao) were not eligible for preferential imports of footwear until 1975 included.
52. This is 20% of 1,752 million EUA.
53. On preference theory generally see Annex 7.

Diagram 1. *The Various Growth Determinants of GSP Trade in 1976*
(Quantities in Million EUA)

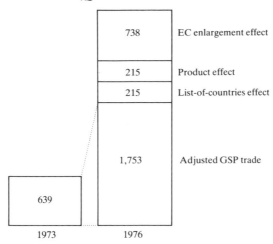

738	EC enlargement effect
215	Product effect
215	List-of-countries effect
1,753	Adjusted GSP trade
639	

1973   1976

Source: Own presentation based on SOEC and German Federal Ministry of Economic Affairs data.

Any diminution of trade, on the other hand, or any diversion due to preferential tariff cuts, leads to a less efficient allocation of inputs and this is reflected on the debit side of the welfare scale. The excess of trade creation over trade diversion may be viewed as an indicator of the overall welfare gains resulting from the tariff cut.[54]

This marginal-analysis approach is based on premises which cannot be met in the specific case of trade with the developing countries. For that reason a number of authors have meanwhile produced different arguments, some of which contradict the classical approach.[55] In particular it is now being suggested that, in contrast to the classical model, one cannot proceed from pre-

54. See also J. Viner: *The Customs Union Issue*, New York and London, 1950.

55. The first approach towards a single-country viewpoint was made by Gehrels. The argument from the point of view of the developing countries was subsequently put forward by Linder, who postulated a concept of "efficient trade diversion". Most recently Murray has once more come up with a theoretical analysis of non-reciprocal preferential systems. See F. Gehrels: "Customs Unions from a Single-Country Viewpoint", in: *The Review of Economic Studies*, Vol. 24 (1956-57), No. 63, p. 63 ff., St. B. Linder: "Customs, Unions and Economic Development", in: M. S. Wionczek (Ed.): *Latin American Economic Integration, Experiences and Prospects*, New York etc. 1966, p. 40, as well as T. Murray: *Trade Preferences for Developing Countries*, loc. cit., p. 104 f.

sumption of full employment of input in the developing countries. That is why a sub-optimal allocation due to trade diversion is still regarded as preferable from the point of view of a developing country benefiting from trade diversion and from the development-policy point of view it is not the net result between trade creation and trade diversion that should be taken as a measure of benefit but the sum of the two effects. This means that the distinction between trade creation and trade diversion loses much of its relevance.

Apart from questions of method there are other points to be borne in mind in an analysis of trade creation and trade diversion. Especially in the case of a reduction of customs duty on the products of a developing country it can hardly be assumed that the country's elasticity of supply is sufficiently great to be able to satisfy the increased demand immediately. This is especially true in the area of semi-finished and finished industrial products which, after all, represent the bulk of GSP products.

In that case it is possible that importers may in the short run react not with quantitative but with price changes and that, as a result of improved export conditions, investments may be induced in the developing countries even though these will bear fruit only in the long term. Since these long-term effects can greatly exceed the short-term ones, the relatively short time that has elapsed since the coming into force of the GSP makes it impossible to observe more than a fraction of the entirety of trade-creating effects.

While these long-term effects—which cannot be taken into consideration in a short-term analysis—result in the overall effect of the GSP being underestimated, there is, on the other hand, an effect which tends to lead to an overestimation of the results. Just because the developing countries are scarcely able to react in the short term with an expansion of production it is entirely conceivable that the countries themselves may divert their trade flows from supplier countries with tariff barriers to supplier countries without tariff barriers. Such a "trade diversion"— which, viewed from the EC, appears as a trade creation—does not produce a net positive effect, in terms of development policy,

136

for the trade-diverting developing country since its volume of production and exports has remained constant. Since, however, GSP products have meanwhile come to be granted preferences by most other industrialized countries this effect may be disregarded.

2. The role of preferences

The question of trade-creating and trade-diverting effects is now to be answered by a comparison of differential growth rates. If the GSP actually produces the effects it is presumed to produce then the rate of growth of GSP trade must be greater than comparable growth rates. This means that, over the course of time, the proportion of GSP products imported from eligible developing countries must have increased compared with the total of imports from non-EC countries.[56]

Table 46 shows the growth rates of EC imports from non-EC countries and from developing countries for different periods of time. In order to achieve the best possible matching of products with GSP products the dates listed refer only to semi-finished and finished industrial products of Sections 5 to 8 of the Standard International Trade Classification (SITC).[57]

Although the definition of developing countries used here does not fully agree with that of the GSP—the GSP moreover practices selection by defining only certain developing countries as eligible with regard to certain products—and although SITC Sections 5 to 8 also comprise products which are not all included in the GSP, and vice versa, the table nevertheless reflects several trends: The rate of growth of imports of semi-finished and fin-

56. This line of argument more or less follows Balassa who assumes a constant ratio between imports and gross national product (GNP) and who attributes such changes in the growth rate of imports as exceed the growth of the GNP to integration effects. See B. Balassa: "European Integration: Problems and Issues", in: *The American Economic Review, Papers and Proceedings*, Vol. 53 (1963), No. 2, p. 175-184.

57. See Statistisches Bundesamt, Wiesbaden: *German translation of the Standard International Trade Classification*, rev. 2, of the United Nations, 1975, Stuttgart, Mainz 1976.

Table 46. *Average Annual Growth Rates of EC-9 Imports of Products of SITC Sections 5 to 8, 1965 to 1973 and 1973 to 1976 and Share of Developing Countries in the Trade of Non-EC Countries* (as a Percentage)

Imports	Annual growth rates in %		Proportion of non-EC imports in %		
	1965-1973	1973-1976	1965	1973	1976
Total non-EC imports	13.9	19.3	100.0	100.0	100.0
Imports from					
Class 2 countries	13.3	20.9	16.5	15.7	16.3

Because of the availability of sources, the calculation, unlike that in Annex 1, is based on the SOEC definition of developing countries (Class 2).

Source: Own calculations based on SOEC, Statistical Office of the European Communities: *Monthly External Trade Bulletin, Special Issue 1958 to 1976*, Luxembourg 1978, p. 40 ff.

ished industrial products from developing countries between 1973 and 1976 was approximately 20% per annum. It was therefore roughly in step with the growth rate for all non-EC imports. For that reason the share which imports from developing countries held in non-EC imports remained more or less constant.

Table 47 narrows down the analysis to the various growth rates for trade in GSP products. The rates listed represent "pure" growth; the country list, product and EC enlargement effects have been deducted in the calculation. Processed petroleum products, many of which are included in the preferential system but are not included in SITC Section 3, as well as agricultural products of SITC Sections 1 and 2 (in which GSP products only have a slight share) have likewise been eliminated.

The rate of growth of imports of GSP products from non-EC countries, amounting as it does to 21.2%, is approximately of the same order of magnitude as the corresponding rate for SITC Sections 5 to 8, which amounts to 19.3%. The growth rate for imports of GSP products from developing countries eligible in accordance with country lists is conspicuously greater, at 30.7%, and also clearly in excess of the growth rate for imports of semi-finished and finished industrial products from developing countries which, over the same period of time, amounted to 20.9% (see Table 46). The corresponding rate for actual GSP trade is a little higher still (33.2%).

Table 47. *Average Annual Growth Rate of EC Imports of GSP Products from Selected Groups of Countries and their Share of Non-EC Trade, 1973 to 1976*
(as a Percentage)

Imports of GSP products	Annual growth rate 1973-1976	Proportion of non-EC imports in % 1973	1976
From non-EC countries overall	21.2	100.0	100.0
From developing countries enjoying preferences, according to list of countries	30.7	7.1	9.2
GSP trade	33.2	2.4	3.7

Source: Own calculations based on SOEC and German Federal Ministry of Economic Affairs data.

In view of the fact that these rates were considerably in excess of the growth of non-EC trade there was also a substantial increase, over the three-year period from 1973 to 1976, of their share of non-EC trade. The developing countries eligible on the basis of lists now hold a share of 9.2% of the EC's total non-EC trade in preferential products, as against a 7.1% share in 1973;[58] during that period the share of GSP trade rose from 2.4% to 3.7%.

To sum up: The rate of growth of the trade in GSP products of the countries eligible in accordance with country lists is clearly in excess of the comparable growth rates. The eligible developing

58. It is not surprising that this share is still small by comparison with the non-EC trade shown in Table 6, considering that the table covers the trade of *all* developing countries whereas here we are considering only the trade of countries eligible in accordance with country lists.

countries have, in respect of GSP products, increased their share of imports. Hence an indispensable condition for the presence of trade-creating and/or trade-diverting effects produced by the GSP is met. With a view to pinpointing the particularly dynamic areas Table 48 lists the growth rates according to CCT Sections. Data available on the agricultural sector, which was still fairly insignificant in 1973, were too few and this sector was therefore excluded.

Any particular group of products can only be said to exhibit a trade development favourable to the developing countries if the growth rate of imports from eligible developing countries exceeds that of non-EC imports generally. The increase in non-EC imports into the EC is therefore regarded a trend indicator. However, an above-average increase in imports from eligible developing countries can only be attributed to the effects of the GSP provided that preferential imports exhibit a similarly high or even higher upturn. If, on the other hand, GSP imports increase at average rates then such a development, favourable though it is to the eligible developing countries, cannot be assigned to the GSP. In that case there must be other causes.

If both criteria are simultaneously applied to the data of Table 48 the following major sectors stand out as having presumably undergone certain trade-diverting effects through the GSP:

— hides, furskins and articles thereof (VIII);
— paper and articles thereof (X);
— textiles and textile articles (XI);
— footwear, umbrellas (XII);
— stones, glass, ceramic articles (XIII);
— pearls, coins, precious stones (XIV);
— precision instruments and apparatus (XVIII);
— miscellaneous manufactured articles (XX).

Table 48. *"Pure" Growth Rates of EC Imports of GSP Products from Selected Groups of Countries by CCT Sections (Excluding Agricultural Products), Annual Averages for 1973 to 1976*
(as a Percentage)

CCT section		Average annual growth of imports of GSP products in %		
		From non-EC countries	From eligible developing countries	GSP trade
V.	Mineral products	47.7	181.2	201.2
VI.	Chemicals	25.2	17.4	20.9
VII.	Artificial resins and plastic materials	24.6	39.4	33.8
VIII.	Hides and skins and articles thereof	31.6	43.4	51.2
IX.	Wood, cork and articles thereof	23.8	15.8	22.6
X.	Paper and paperboard and articles thereof	18.2	36.4	36.6
XI.	Textiles and textile articles	8.2	25.8	34.7
XII.	Footwear, umbrellas, etc.	26.2	35.7	40.9
XIII.	Articles of stone, ceramic products, glass and glassware	23.2	28.2	33.3
XIV.	Pearls, coins, precious stones	4.0	32.5	62.8
XV.	Base metals	25.4	21.0	25.3
XVI.	Machinery, electrical equipment	23.0	40.4	33.3
XVII.	Vehicles, etc.	13.1	10.9	10.7
XVIII.	Instruments and apparatus, clocks, recorders and reproducers, etc.	24.2	56.0	59.6
XIX.	Arms and ammunition	31.3	16.8	2.3
XX.	Miscellaneous manu-factures	26.2	31.1	40.4
XXI.	Works of art, etc. [a]	—	—	—
All GSP products[b]		22.3	36.1	41.4

[a] In 1973 not yet included in the GSP, hence no growth rates calculable.

[b] These growth rates have been arrived at by including CCT section V and are not therefore comparable with those in Table 47.

Source: Own calculations based on SOEC and German Federal Ministry of Economic Affairs data.

Chapter 3

THE EC'S GSP IN THE FRAMEWORK OF PREFERENTIAL TRADE RELATIONS BETWEEN INDUSTRIALIZED AND DEVELOPING COUNTRIES

Any analysis of the EC's GSP would be incomplete unless the trade preferences granted under this system were viewed in the context of comparable arrangements between industrialized and developing countries. The EC's GSP is merely one element in a worldwide network of preferential trade relations between these two groups of countries and therefore calls for a comparative study that would include both the differences in effectiveness and the reciprocal impact of the different agreements. Interestingly enough, these are by no means confined to preferences granted to developing countries by the rest of the industrialized countries. Of considerable importance also are the numerous special free trade area and association agreements, preferential agreements and co-operation agreements concluded by the EC itself with selected countries. The questions to be examined in the following sections will therefore concern, firstly, the relative rank which the GSP occupies by comparison with the other preferential trade arrangements of the European Communities and, secondly, a comparison of the GSP with the preferential systems of other industrialized countries.

§ 9. General and Special Trade Preferences of the EC

A. Preferential Trade Policy of the EC

The GSP should be viewed as part of a tight network of agreements by means of which the EC is shaping its relations with non-EC countries. Only if this fact is borne in mind can the position at present occupied by the GSP be properly assessed.

The EC's foreign trade policy has given rise to a differentiated hierarchy of preferences. If examination is confined to tariff concessions then access to the Community markets is graduated as follows:[1]

1. The highest degree of preferences is enjoyed by the Member States themselves; these are not subject to any intra-Community limitations.
2. Next follow those non-EC countries whose exports into the EC are subject to reduced customs duty or are totally exempt from such customs duty on the basis of free trade area, association, co-operation and/or preferential trade agreements.
3. A third group embraces all GATT countries. Their exports into the EC are subject to the normal most-favoured-nation terms.
4. The bottom rung in the hierarchy of preferences is finally held by countries without GATT status.

Analysis of the preferential status occupied by the GSP requires a detailed examination of the second group which includes not only the GSP but also all other preferential arrangements with non-EC countries.

Many of these are of greater scope and also very much older than the GSP. Thus, for example, the Yaoundé Convention and the agreements with Greece and Turkey had long been in force before, in 1964, at the first international trade conference in Geneva, UNCTAD I, discussions began about the worldwide introduction of a General System of Preferences in favour of the developing countries. These agreements, however, differ not only in their age and content; more importantly, they stem from different reasons.

Whereas the EC's GSP springs from a general demand by the developing countries for special treatment in international trade, the special preferential agreements are based—apart from development-policy involvement—also on the EC countries' special links and their own interests. The specific historical, economic and political relations which certain Member States during their

1. See T. Murray; *Trade Preferences for Developing Countries*, loc. cit., p. 119.

colonial period maintained with overseas, principally African, countries and territories called for special economic arrangements if those spheres of influence were to be maintained (Yaoundé Convention and Arusha Agreement). Such considerations played a part also at the time of Britain's accession to the EC. Added to this was the aim of establishing closer relations with the whole of Black Africa as Europe's natural complement in terms of economic geography (Lomé Convention).

Special relations were also the reason which induced the EC to conclude association agreements with a number of less well developed European countries in the hope that this would bring these countries closer to the Community and possibly fully integrate them at a later date (e.g. Greece). The EC's preferential policy finally reflected its endeavour—even without the explicit option of accession—to maintain generally close trade and economic relations with the countries of the Mediterranean and Middle East in view of the numerous historical, economic, political and cultural links between those areas and the Community (e.g. Mashriq and Maghrib Co-operation Agreements).

The diverse reasons underlying these preferential agreements have resulted in a situation in which the group of non-EC preferences exhibits its own hierarchy. The numerous agreements have become a close web of relations which is in no way based on uniform structural principles. In spite of the harmonization of numerous agreements, for instance within the framework of the Lomé Convention, and in spite of a global policy towards the Mediterranean littoral states considerable differences continue to exist in the preferential status of beneficiary countries.

Preferential treatment ranges from preferential trade agreements through co-operation arrangements to free trade area and association agreements with the option of accession to the EC (see Table 49). Preferences are granted by way of non-reciprocal tariff cuts or exemptions, by industrial, technological, socio-political and financial agreements, by purchasing guarantees in respect of specific products such as sugar, by stabilization schemes for export earnings, by the creation of free trade areas and by the progressive introduction of customs unions.

That motives other than those of development policy played a part in the formulation of the agreements between the EC and non-EC countries is reflected also in the fact that even industrialized countries and countries with disputable developing-country status are granted preferences. Thus the EFTA countries enjoy preferences, just as do Greece, Spain, Israel and Turkey, although these are not internationally or universally regarded as developing countries.

If one considers the great variety of types of preference then one finds that the GSP has a relatively limited preferential status. All it offers—as will be shown presently—to such developing countries as do not enjoy more favourable agreements with the EC is customs duty concessions and/or customs duty exemption within the framework of certain upper limits; financial transfers or measures for industrial or technological co-operation are not provided for in the GSP. The quality of tariff preferences under the GSP compared with those of the other agreements will be examined in the following passages.

B. Differential Features of General and Special Preferences

The EC's foreign trade policy towards non-EC countries has given rise to a *differentiated structure of preference*. The objectives and structure of the numerous agreements differ so much from one another that a preference gradient has inevitably come into being. As indicated in the introduction to this section, the GSP in consequence is seen to occupy a *subordinate preferential status* because, in contrast to most agreements, it is confined to pure tariff preferences and does not contain arrangements concerning, for instance, other trade preferences such as purchasing guarantees or stabilization schemes for export earnings, or industrial and technological co-operation, or indeed financial transfers. The quantitative and qualitative importance accruing to the GSP from its tariff preferences is determined, on the one hand, by the value of the customs advantages of the other agreements and, on the other, by the extent of overlap.

In the subsequent comparison of general and special tariff

Table 49. *Trade Agreements between the EC and Non-EC Countries (as at Beginning of 1978)*

Type of agreement	Countries and groups of countries enjoying preferences
1. Free trade area	(i) *EFTA countries:* Iceland, Norway, Austria, Portugal[a], Sweden, Switzerland, Liechtenstein, Finland (ii) Faroë Islands, Israel[l]
2. Association agreements	(i) Cyprus, Greece[j], Malta, Turkey
3. Agreements on commercial, industrial, socio-political and financial co-operation	(i) *Maghrib countries:* Algeria, Morocco, Tunisia (ii) *Mashriq countries:* Egypt, Lebanon, Syria, Jordan (iii) *ACP countries:* preferences at present enjoyed by 53 countries of Africa, the Caribbean and the Pacific (iv) Overseas countries and territories[c]
4. Preferential agreements	(i) *Generalized system of tariff preferences for developing countries:*[b] enjoyed at present by 115 independent countries and 27 dependent countries and territories (ii) Spain[k] (iii) *Agreements on handloom products:*[d] Bangladesh, India, Pakistan, Sri Lanka, Laos, Thailand, El Salvador, Honduras, Indonesia (iv) *Agreements on handicraft products:*[e] Bangladesh, India, Pakistan, Philippines, Sri Lanka, Iran, Indonesia, Thailand, Bolivia, Peru, Malaysia, Panama, Paraguay, El Salvador, Honduras, Uruguay, Ecuador, Laos, Chile (v) *Agreements on jute manufactures:*[g] India, Thailand, Bangladesh (vi) *Agreements on coir manufactures:*[g] India, Sri Lanka (vii) *Agreement on sugar:* India[f]

146

Table 49 (continued)

5. Non-preferential trade and economic agreements	(i)	*Agreements on textiles:*[h] Romania, Yugoslavia, Egypt, Hong Kong, Japan, Macao, India, Pakistan, Iran, South Korea, Malaysia, Singapore, Brazil, Colombia, Sri Lanka, Indonesia, Philippines, Thailand, Argentina, Guatemala, Mexico, Peru, Uruguay
	(ii)	*Agreements on transit traffic:* Austria, Switzerland
	(iii)	*Other agreements:* Yugoslavia, Bangladesh, India, Pakistan, Sri Lanka, Argentine, Brazil, Mexico, Uruguay, Canada, Iran[i], China

a   Additional industrial, technical, social and financial co-operation. Portugal applied for accession to the EC on 28 March 1977.

b   Strictly speaking not an agreement but an autonomous tariff-policy measure by the EC.

c   Provisional regulation since 1 August 1975, effective until the coming into force of the decision to associate with the EC.

d   Agreement on trade in silk and cotton fabrics manufactured on handlooms.

e   Agreement on trade in certain handicraft products.

f   Preferential treatment consists of a sugar purchase guarantee which matches the sugar protocol of the Lomé offer concerning the granting of general customs preferences.

g   The preferential tariffs are granted within the framework of the EC's offer concerning the granting of generalized tariff preferences.

h   Textile agreements of the EC within the framework of the Multi-Fibre Agreement.

i   Expired; renegotiations in progress since 20 December 1976.

j   Greece applied for accession to the EC on 12 June 1975.

k   Spain applied for accession to the EC on 28 June 1977.

l   Additional industrial, technical and financial co-operation.

Source: Own presentation based on Commission of the European Communities: *List of Main EEC Agreements with Other Countries*, Europe-Information, External Relations (1978), No. 6.

147

preferences allowance it is chiefly the present situation that will be borne in mind. It should not, however, be forgotten that the preferential status of the various agreements has fluctuated considerably over the period of application of the GSP and that these fluctuations have a considerable bearing on the effectiveness of the GSP. Thus the enlargement of the EC and the subsequent progressive reduction of tariffs between the EC and EFTA,[2] as well as the Lomé Convention, as a result of which a number of new developing countries of the ACP zone for the first time acquired preferential status, all greatly modified the scope, structure and quality of preferences in the past.

Moreover, the GSP itself underwent countless changes in the course of its development. Both the product spectrum and the range of beneficiary countries have been continually extended, the preferential margins for agricultural products have increased, and upper import limits have been adjusted.[3]

1. Preferences for agricultural products

A common characteristic of all preferential arrangements between the EC and non-EC countries are the limited customs benefits in the area of agricultural products of chapters 1 to 24 and of such processed agricultural products of chapters 25 to 99 as are subject to the Common Agricultural Policy. Although the EC was anxious to liberalize the importation of typical export products of the beneficiary countries as much as possible, it found itself invariably obliged, in doing so, to grant priority to the preferential advantages of the Community countries and to ensure a graduation of preferences for non-EC countries. That is why the EC's preferential agreements as a rule comprise a *selection* of agricultural products in respect of which in most cases preferential customs duty reductions—much more rarely customs duty exemption—are granted. Agricultural products subject to regulations are largely excluded or, in a few

2. See UNCTAD: *The Generalized System of Preferences: Effects of the Enlargement of the European Community*, Geneva 1973, TD/B/C. 5/8.
3. See § 2.

instances (e.g. for overseas countries and territories and for the ACP countries), granted tariff cuts. In spite of these restrictions a relatively high liberalization quota is often reached. Thus the co-operation agreements with the Maghrib countries result in over 90% of their agricultural exports to the EC enjoying preference. Preferential tariff cuts for Spain cover approximately two-thirds of all Spanish exports to the EC. By contrast the liberalization measures in the field of agricultural products are relatively slight under the EFTA agreement and also under the agreement with Cyprus.

Another striking feature is the fact that the preferential margin and the product spectrum of the agreements tend to divide the markets or "reserve" them for certain partner countries. Thus the benefit arising to the Maghrib countries from the tariff cuts lies mainly in their preferential treatment as against other non-EC countries which are granted no, or only slight, preferences in respect of the same products.[4] Thus in the much-contested market for citrus fruit tariff cut in favour of the Maghrib countries amounts to 80%, while Israel was granted only 60% and Spain a mere 40%.[5]

We find therefore that a considerable preference gradient exists between the different agreements in respect of chapters 1 to 24, both with regard to the product spectrum and with regard to the preferential margin.

In the area of agricultural products, which are nearly all subject to customs duties and/or levies, the GSP occupies a relatively *weak preferential position*. Even though as a general rule there are no quantitative limitations on imports[6] and even though the number of eligible products has steadily increased,[7] the GSP clearly comprises fewer tariff items than the bulk of the other

4. See W. Vogel: "Abkommen der Europäischen Wirtschaftsgemeinschaft mit Algerien, Marokko und Tunisien", in: *Mitteilungen der Bundesstelle für Aussenhandelsinformation, Beilage zu den NfA*, Vol. 26 (1976), No. 163, p. 3f.

5. See ibid.

6. Exceptions for coffee, tobacco and pineapples.

7. Including jute and coir products the number of agricultural GSP products rose from 147 in 1971 to 307 in 1978.

agreements.[8] Although it still ranks above, say, the EFTA preferences, it holds the lower end of the preferential scale alongside these.

A similar picture is found when one ascertains the extent to which the GSP is able to provide actual preferences for exports from the beneficiary countries. It turns out that the GSP is *not* able to provide preferences for the agricultural exports from beneficiary developing countries into the EC.[9] This is true in particular of those countries which have no special preferential agreements with the EC and are therefore dependent on the GSP. By contrast the preferential agreement with Spain—as mentioned above—covers two-thirds of its agricultural exports to the EC. The co-operation agreements with the Maghrib countries confer benefits on approximately 94% of all dutiable exports from those countries to the EC.[10] The ACP agreement is even more comprehensive, conferring as it does preferences on 99% of dutiable EC imports from those countries.[11]

The inferior preferential status of the GSP is further confirmed if its *preferential margin* is compared with that of other agreements. Of the 307 processed agricultural products included in the GSP 225 enjoyed customs duty reductions and only 82 customs duty exemption in 1978. The ACP Agreement, on the other hand, totally liberalized the importation of 385 of the total of 1,244 tariff items and created preferential advantages over third countries for all (sic) other products of chapters 1 to 24, both in the form of tariff cuts and by the lowering or abolition of fixed or

8. Thus the ACP Agreement in 1975 granted preferences to all 1,244 tariff items of chapters 1 to 24. See UNCTAD: *Effects of the Generalized System of Preferences of Developing Countries Sharing their Special Tariff Advantages as a Result of the Implementation of the System. The GSP and the Lomé Convention*, Geneva 1977, p. 6, TD/B/C. 5/49/Add. 1 (hereinafter quoted as UNCTAD: TD/B/C. 5/49/Add. 1).

9. See § 5. The scope of the GSP in 1976 extended to only 2% of agricultural imports from developing countries.

10. See UNCTAD: *Effects of the Generalized System of Preferences on Developing Countries Sharing their Special Tariff Advantages as a Result of the Implementation of the System: The GSP and the EEC/Mahgrib Co-operation Agreements*, Geneva 1977, p. 9, TD/B/C. 5/49/Add. 2 (hereinafter quoted as: UNCTAD: TD/B/C. 5/49/Add. 2).

11. See UNCTAD: TD/B/C. 5/49/Add. 1, p. 7.

variable import levies[12] not affected by the GSP. While therefore preferential agricultural imports to the EC from GSP beneficiary countries consisted of 86.2% duty-reduced and 13.8% duty-free preferential items,[13] EC imports from the ACP countries consisted of 2% duty-reduced and 98% duty-free or levy-exempt products.[14]

Comparison with the Maghrib Agreement similarly shows the GSP to be less favourable. Although the degree of liberalization under this agreement is less than that under the ACP Agreement, nevertheless approximately 52% of preferential and dutiable products from Morocco, Tunisia and Algeria are exempt from duty and 48% enjoy reductions.[15]

As for quantitative limitations on imports of agricultural products no substantial differences can be established between the different preferential agreements. The GSP and the other agreements all contain quantitative upper limits on imports in respect of a small number of products but these are of no great importance in the general picture.

The limited advantage which developing countries with special preferential agreements would be deriving from the GSP if they were solely dependent on the GSP is shown by two UNCTAD studies which reveal the situation for the ACP and Maghrib countries on the basis of import data for 1974. The basis of the calculation was the 1976 version of the GSP.[16] The comparison was between the import potential under alternative preferential systems, the restrictive effects of the GSP's upper limits on imports being disregarded. It was found that the ACP agreement covers 99% of all dutiable agricultural imports into the EC from those countries while the GSP would confer preference on only 22%.

Conditions are similar with regard to the Maghrib Agreement.

12. Data for 1975, see UNCTAD: TD/B/C. 5/49/Add. 1, p. 6.
13. Own calculations for 1976.
14. See UNCTAD: TD/B/C. 5/49/Add. 1, p. 8.
15. Own calculations based on imports in 1974 according to UNCTAD: TD/B/C. 5/49/Add. 2, p. 8 ff.
16. See UNCTAD: TD/B/C. 5/49/Add. 1 and Add. 2.

As a result of this agreement 94% of dutiable agricultural imports are covered by Maghrib preferences. The GSP, on the other hand, especially in the area of agricultural products, in no way allows for the typical export structure of Algeria, Tunisia and Morocco. It covers merely 8% of dutiable imports from those countries.

2. Preferences for industrial products

Significant differences in the structure of the generalized and the special preferential agreements exist also in respect of the industrial products of chapters 25 to 99.

Although numerous special agreements cover a very wide *product spectrum* and in consequence frequently liberalize virtually the entire trade in semi-finished and finished industrial goods, the GSP—as it does with agricultural products—excludes certain products and product groups. This applies, among others, to processed agricultural products subject to the EC's Common Agricultural Policy. A particularly striking fact is that the GSP excludes raw materials from preferential treatment and that, in consequence, a preference gradient emerges for dutiable products of this category, especially with regard to the ACP Agreement and to the co-operation agreements with the Maghrib and Mashriq countries. But there are also a number of other import products in respect of which the product spectrum of the GSP falls short of the scope of comparable preferential agreements. Excluded, among others, are certain

— products of the chemical and allied industries,
— artificial resins and plastic materials,
— leather and articles thereof,
— wood, cork and articles thereof,
— textiles and textile articles,
— metals and articles thereof, as well as
— manufactures of the electronic industry.

In respect of the above-named products other non-EC countries with special preferential agreements enjoy preferential treatment

152

in the form of customs duty reduction or customs duty exemption. A clear preference gradient, due to a narrower product spectrum, exists in particular between the GSP on the one hand and the ACP Agreement on the other.

If the ACP countries were solely dependent on the GSP it would be obvious how little the GSP preferences in fact match the export structure of those countries. In respect of products of CCT chapters 25 to 99 the ACP Agreement comprises *all* dutiable EC imports while the GSP would provide duty-free access to the market for only just over one-half (55%) of them. From the point of view of the Maghrib countries, on the other hand, the GSP would seem to be substantially better adapted to their export structure. Its scope, at any rate, extends to 87% of dutiable EC imports.[17]

With regard to the *preferential margin*, on the other hand, the preferential status provided by the GSP appears considerably more favourable. As in most agreements, the EC grants customs duty exemption in respect of GSP products. Only in a few individual agreements, e.g. with Spain, are customs rates reduced. This means that the preferential items included in the GSP generally receive uniform customs treatment without the differentiation between beneficiary countries that applies with regard to agricultural products.

Admittedly the benefit of customs duty exemption is considerably diminished for the beneficiaries of the GSP by its numerous quantitative limitations. The application of tariff quotas and national quotas, of ceilings and maximum amounts frequently results, especially in the case of sensitive, hybrid and semi-sensitive products, in the reintroduction of the most-favoured-nation tariff and hence to exclusion from the circle of beneficiaries from tariff preferences.[18] The other preferential agreements, by contrast, only exceptionally envisage quantitative limitations on imports. Thus the ACP Agreement contains quotas for certain alcohols, and the co-operation agreements with the Maghrib and Mashriq

17. See UNCTAD: TD/B/C. 5/49/Add. 1 and Add. 2.
18. See § 6.

countries impose limits on the importation only of certain selected petroleum products, phosphate fertilizers, and cork and cotton articles.[19] It is interesting, however, that the upper limits
frequently match the total exports from these countries into the
EC and hence do not exhibit any of the restrictive effects of the
quantitative limitations of the GSP.[20]

3. Other differential features

The value of tariff preferences depends not only on product
spectrum, preferential margin and quantitative limitations but
also on such factors as reciprocity and safeguard clauses. As for
reciprocity, i.e. the obligation to grant reverse preferences, there
used to be considerable differences between various agreements
prior to 1975. It was only the ACP Agreement that rescinded the
obligation of the original Yaoundé and Arusha countries to grant
the EC preferential access to their markets as a collateral. The
reciprocity clauses of the earlier agreements were often criti-
cized, especially by the USA, on the grounds that they discriminated against non-EC countries and infringed the most-favoured-nation regulations of GATT. Most of the ACP countries
abolished their reverse preferences shortly after the coming into
force of the Lomé Convention. At present, admittedly, the following states are still granting imports from the EC more advantageous treatment than under most-favoured-nation terms
(as of April 1977): Benin, Upper Volta, Mauritius, Mauritania,
Niger, Senegal and Tonga.[21] The new co-operation agreements
with the Maghrib and Mashriq countries likewise no longer con-

19. Quota restrictions on duty-free imports from countries enjoying special preferences may moreover result from the fact that the importation of certain textile articles
originating in a number of non-EC countries is at present, under the agreements on
international trade in textiles as well as under bilateral agreements with the non-EC
countries concerned, subject to Community approval as well as to an upper limit regulation. One such textile-exporting non-EC country enjoying special preferential agreements is Egypt.
    20. See also UNCTAD: TD/B/C. 5/49/Add. 2, p. 11.
    21. See "Written Question No. 52/77", *Official Journal of the European Communities*,
Vol. 20, No. C 162 of 11 July 1977, p. 32.

tain reciprocity clauses. The GSP similarly does not oblige the beneficiary countries to grant it any reverse preferences.

Yet there are other agreements, such as the association agreements with Greece and Turkey, and also the EFTA free trade agreement, which cover liberalization of their imports from the EC countries. Unless they have to be put into effect as soon as the agreement comes into force, these reserve preferences have to be implemented by means of a graduated reduction of customs tariffs.

The various agreements further differ on their *rules of origin*. This may well result in quite substantial discrimination against EC imports otherwise "eligible" for preference. In this connection the ACP countries enjoy particular preference benefits. The requirements concerning the extent of working and processing of a product in its country of origin are lower under the ACP Agreement than in other agreements, including the GSP. The ACP Agreement, moreover, grants all beneficiary countries the right of cumulative origin: such a regulation is in part in the free trade area agreement with the residual EFTA as well as in the Maghrib Agreement, though not at present in the Mashriq Agreement. The GSP grants the right of cumulation to three regional groupings—the Andean group, the MCCA (the Central American Common Market) and the ASEAN countries. The GSP, on the other hand, does not provide for the bilateral cumulation permitted under the ACP, the Maghrib and the Mashriq Agreements.

Safeguard clauses are designed to avert major import-induced disruptions in individual economic sectors or regions. They are nowadays a regular feature of all preferential trade agreements between the EC and third countries. Yet the GSP is downgraded in this respect, too, by comparison with the other agreements. This is due, on the one hand, to the arrangement under which the GSP preferences that have to be fixed afresh every year are harmonized beforehand both with associated countries and with the ACP countries by way of a consultation procedure. On the other hand the EC Regulations on the GSP expressly emphasize the general as well as the special safeguard clause in favour of the ACP countries:

> "Moreover, it is evident from the conclusions worked out
> in UNCTAD that this offer, while being of a temporary
> nature, does not constitute a binding commitment and, in
> particular, may be withdrawn wholly or in part at a later
> date; whereas this possibility may be adopted *inter alia* with
> a view to remedying any unfavourable situations which
> might arise in the ACP states following the implementation
> of the generalized preference scheme."[22]

Although these conditions are bound to be seen as disadvantageous by the developing countries not enjoying special agreements with the EC, and consequently dependent on the GSP, many developing countries evidently regard the EC's more comprehensive preference concessions in favour of selected countries as more important than the inevitably associated discrimination against the others. This is confirmed by the resolution again adopted at the international trade conference in Nairobi in 1976 (UNCTAD IV), in which it is stated:

> "The generalized system of non-reciprocal, non-discriminatory preferences should be improved in favour of the
> developing countries, taking into account the relevant interest of those developing countries enjoying special advantages as well as the need to find ways and means of
> protecting their interests."[23]

The adoption of such resolutions is not, of course, surprising if one remembers that of the 115 independent developing countries existing at present 62 (sic) enjoy special preferential agreements with the EC.

The safeguard clauses of the GSP also reflect another inter-

---

22. "Council Regulation (EEC) No. 3019/76 of 13 December 1976 opening, allocating and providing for the administration of Community tariff quotas for certain products originating in developing countries", in: *Official Journal of the European Communities,* Vol. 19 (1976) No. L 349, p. 1.

23. *Resolution 96 (IV) of the United Nations Conference on Trade and Development,* Section I, A, paragraph (a), quoted from UNCTAD: TD/B/C. 5/49, p. 3.

esting difference between generalized and special preferential agreements. When it is pointed out that "this offer, while being of a temporary nature, does not constitute a binding commitment and, in particular, may be withdrawn wholly or in part at a later date", then this emphasizes the autonomous character of the GSP which, unlike the other preferential agreements, is not an agreement arrived at by negotiation but a *unilateral measure* of the EC. The EC thus—as on other occasions—interprets decisions taken within the framework of the United Nations as not being binding under international law.

4. Preferential status of the GSP

Analysis of the structural differences between the GSP and the other preferential trade agreements with non-EC countries has shown that the GSP occupies an inferior preferential status. It represents a unilateral measure by the EC without obligation under contract law or international law; it is confined purely to tariff preferences, it has a comparatively narrow product spectrum, it offers smaller preferential margins in respect of agricultural products and it provides for restrictive quantitative limitations on large sections of the trade with beneficiary countries. Finally, the rules of origin are by no means as liberal as those of other major preferential agreements, and the safeguard clauses convey greater advantages to the special preferential agreements.

C. Overlapping of General and Special Preferences

1. Modes of overlapping

The range of countries enjoying benefits under general and special preferences is by no means sharply defined. There is a good deal of overlapping since of the (at present) 147 beneficiary countries and territories of the GSP 70 (sic) are enjoying special tariff preferences (see Annex 1). Most of these belong to the ACP group or to the other overseas countries and territories

(OCT). As the GSP confers benefits on developing countries only and—apart from Yugoslavia, Romania and Gibraltar—on no European ones, a number of non-EC countries enjoying EC preferences are left with no more than their special tariff concessions without any option (EFTA, Greece, Turkey, Spain, Malta, Israel, Faroë Islands). This does not necessarily mean that the remaining countries enjoy double concessions since the product spectra of the agreements differ from one another and since the lists of countries enjoying GSP benefits exhibit product-specific differences.

Utilization of optionally available preferences is not subject to any regulation, i.e. the declarant is free to choose whichever preference he prefers. Customs formalities depend solely on the application and the evidence of preference submitted.

The overlapping of general and special preferences produces a number of interesting effects.

a. Favourable GSP preferences

In spite of the generally inferior preferential status of the GSP the system in some ways offered and still offers more favourable customs treatment than other agreements. Thus Egypt and Lebanon, prior to the conclusion of their co-operation agreements with the EC, found it generally more advantageous to make use of generalized preferences—at least until the reintroduction of the most-favoured-nation rate because of upper import limits having been reached. Only then did it make sense to claim special customs preference. Given rational behaviour and complete information there was therefore a possibility of *cumulation of preferences.* As a result of a general harmonization of preferences this effect has now become a marginal phenomenon. More favourable GSP preferences are still being found mainly in the field of certain agricultural products (e.g. fruit of tariff heading No. 08.10).

b. Equal GSP preferences

More important are those cases where general and special preferences are equally advantageous. This is nowadays true of large portions of EC imports from eligible developing countries provided one looks solely at the customs burden. In the sphere of semi-finished and finished industrial products, especially (products of chapters 25 to 99), the GSP, the ACP Agreement and the co-operation agreements with the Maghrib and Mashriq countries all offer the same customs benefits.

It appears therefore that an *option* between general and special preferences exists in respect of imports from developing countries enjoying benefits under both heads. In deciding in favour of the one or the other preference the other preferential features of course play an important part. At first glance it might seem an excessive risk, especially in respect of sensitive and semi-sensitive products of chapters 25 to 99, to declare imports for the GSP because, as soon as the various upper import limits are reached, the most-favoured-nation rate of duty may be applied. There is, moreover, the danger that the products may not come up to the criteria of the—compared with other agreements—stricter application of the rule of origin and that, in consequence, they may not qualify for benefit under GSP preference. Since, finally, GSP preference confers no kind of specific advantage over special preference, the GSP at first does not seem to be a genuine alternative and the preferential status of these countries is thus purely nominal.

The fact that these developing countries are nevertheless being listed among the countries and territories enjoying GSP preferences is probably due to the fact that by its very nature the GSP is designed to be non-discriminatory and that the preferences therefore must be offered to all developing countries without distinction.

Cumulation of general and special preferences may therefore arise also when these tariff preferences are equal. Unregulated access of special-preference developing countries to the GSP moreover holds the danger that they may impair the effectiveness of the GSP (*displacement effect*).[24]

24. In the light of these conditions it is conceivable that suppliers and/or importers who are in a position to cumulate preferences may deliberately use this displacement effect as a market-policy instrument. There is not, however, any solid evidence of any such market strategy.

c. Unfavourable GSP preferences

Less favourable customs preferences are offered by the GSP in respect of the bulk of agricultural products. Even in cases where it lays down the same tariff rate the GSP is frequently inferior since agreements such as that with the ACP countries additionally provide for a lowering or abolition of fixed or variable import levies. Preferential status under the GSP will probably therefore as a rule be of a *nominal* nature only for the ACP, Maghrib and Mashriq countries. Displacement or cumulation effects might, at the most, arise for a small number of quantitatively regulated agricultural products. All other cases of overlapping will again be instances of inadequate information on the part of those involved in the import or of an unsatisfactory mixing of general and special preferences.

2. Size of overlapping

Analysis of the GSP potential has already shown that the inclusion in the GSP of developing countries with special preferences lends the GSP a breadth of scale it does not really possess.[25] If one allows for imports from developing countries which, on the strength of special agreements with the EC, enjoy either equal or more favourable preferences, then the preferential *potential* of the GSP[26] for 1976 is reduced by 22.4%. This calculation disregards the fact that the EC's preference policy has meanwhile embraced a number of further developing countries. Thus the co-operation agreement with the Mashriq countries has placed Egypt and Lebanon on an equal or better footing in customs treatment and has also embraced Syria and Jordan, both of which had in the past been dependent on the GSP alone. The same effect was produced by the enlargement of the group of ACP countries by the Cape Verde Islands, the Comoros, Sao

25. See § 5.
26. Imports of GSP products from eligible developing countries.

160

Tomé and Principe, the Seychelles, Surinam, Djibouti[27] and Papua New Guinea.

If the preferential *potential* of the GSP as determined for 1976 is appropriately adjusted and the analysis thus based on presently valid preference relations the GSP import potential is reduced by altogether 24.2%.

Statistics of GSP imports do not show anything like such a pronounced overlapping between general and special preferences. As a general rule the ACP and Maghrib countries, as well as the overseas countries and territories, opt for their special preferences. Nevertheless application for GSP preference is made from time to time, even though this does not at first sight offer any obvious advantages. As a result, the actual GSP performance for 1976 is distorted by 86 million UA or 2.8%. If a notional allowance is made also for the Mashriq and the new ACP countries then recorded GSP imports are reduced by altogether 113 million UA of 3.8% (see Table 50).

The fact that the GSP statistics continue to record imports from developing countries enjoying special customs preferences clearly testifies to the still inadequate state of information on the part of the supplier countries, and perhaps also on that of the import trade and of direct importers. It furthermore confirms that the customs administration of the different preferential systems has not yet begun to distinguish accurately between general and special preferences.

The fact that in itself special preferential imports are recorded as GSP imports is probably no more than a blemish. Nor would it matter very much if it were not for the fact that it might curtail the marketing opportunities of other developing countries which do not enjoy special preferences. In the *calculation* of Community tariff quotas and ceilings for semi-finished and finished industrial products the countries enjoying special preferential agreements are excluded, in the GSP, with regard to the basic amount and accounted for in respect of the supplementary amount, like

27. The former French Afars and Issas Territories had enjoyed special preferences as OCT territories even before their independence.

Table 50. *GSP Imports from Developing Countries with Special Preferences, by Groups of Countries, 1976* (in 1,000 UA)

Group of countries	Chapters 1-24			Chapters 25-99					Chapters 1-99				
	SEN	NSEN	Total	SEN	HYBR	SSEN	NSEN	Total	SEN	HYBR	SSEN	NSEN	Total
1. ACP	9	2,655	2,664	2,278	28	39,520	4,910	46,736	2,287	28	39,520	7,565	49,400
2. OCT	—	18	18	—	—	18,268	86	18,354	—	—	18,266	106	18,372
3. Maghrib	—	953	953	2,293	86	10,542	3,949	16,870	2,293	86	10,542	4,902	17,823
Total 1-3	9	3,626	3,635	4,571	114	68,330	8,945	81,960	4,580	114	68,328	12,573	85,595
4. Mashriq[a]	—	714	714	9,310	44	13,274	2,986	25,615	9,310	44	13,274	3,700	26,328
5. New ACP[b]	—	549	549	—	—	—	1	1	—	—	—	550	550
Total 4-5	—	1,263	1,263	9,310	44	13,274	2,987	25,616	9,310	44	13,274	4,250	26,878
Total 1-5	9	4,889	4,898	13,881	158	81,604	11,932	107,576	13,890	158	81,760	16,823	112,473

[a] Egypt, Syria, Jordan and Lebanon.
[b] Cape Verde Islands, Comoros, Sao Tomé and Principe, Seychelles, Surinam, Djibouti and Papua New Guinea.

Note: Discrepancies in columns and lines due to rounding errors.
Source: Own calculations based on SOEC and German Federal Ministry of Economic Affairs data.

the rest of the non-EC countries, with a mere 5%. For the purpose of *charging* the EC Regulation should ensure that imports which are duty-*free* on the grounds of another preferential tariff arrangement granted by the Community should *not* be charged against tariff quotas or ceilings.

Views on the interpretation of this regulation evidently differed among the individual EC countries. The Federal Republic of Germany until the end of 1977 believed that this Regulation aimed at drawing a clear line between general and special preferences. In consequence, while GSP preference was granted to products from the ACP, Maghrib and Mashriq countries, provided a certificate of origin was submitted on Form A, the imports were *not* in fact charged against the tariff quotas or ceilings of the GSP, nor were they statistically recorded as GSP imports. Because other EC countries followed a different procedure the German Federal Ministry of Finance issued a decree in 1978 in accordance with which the Federal Republic of Germany now also accepts imports from special-preference developing countries wholly and entirely as GSP imports, charging them against upper import limits provided that GSP preference is applied for with the appropriate Form A certificate of origin. It is therefore to be expected, possibly even on an increasing scale, that imports from developing countries with special preferences will continue to contribute to the utilization of quotas and ceilings and to the premature reintroduction of the most-favoured-nation rate. This could be the more serious as they enter into the calculation of the upper limits with only 5% of their imports during the reference year in question and might in consequence displace the other supplier countries which are dependent on the GSP alone. The above-mentioned risk of maximum amounts being reached is already being met in the way that a second certificate of origin for the alternative preference is kept in readiness or is demanded from the exporting country and submitted to the customs authorities subsequently.

In 1976 it was mainly the United Kingdom and Italy, but also the Benelux countries and Denmark, that charged goods notified for GSP preference from special-preference developing countries against national quotas and ceilings, more especially with regard to products which they imported from the ACP countries (see Table 51). These developing countries did not reach the maximum amounts. Admittedly their GSP imports in 1976 were taken into account in 43 of the altogether 179 cases in which national quotas were exhausted. As for GSP products whose ceilings were reached, developing countries with special preferential agreements were involved in *all* (23) cases. Of the total GSP imports from those countries,[28] amounting to 86 million UA, 32 million UA, or 37%, were accounted for in 1976 by GSP products affected by the import limits referred to above (see Table 51).

There are clear indications that special-preference developing countries were comparatively more strongly represented in trade in sensitive, hybrid and semi-sensitive goods, whose importation in 1976 was limited by ceilings and Member State shares, than they were in the total GSP trade. This suggests that, alongside a cumulation of general and special preferences, displacement effects were also present.

Overlapping between general and special preferences is likely to continue also in future. This view is supported by the circumstance that the Federal Republic of Germany, and possibly some other EC states, have been changing over since 1978 to the charging of such imports. Besides, the further development of EC preferential policy towards individual countries or groups of countries is likely to operate in the same direction. This can already be seen clearly with regard to the 21 Member States of the Arab League who, within the framework of what has become known as the "European-Arab Dialogue", have for some time been negotiating a co-operation agreement with the EC. Such an agreement, in the view of the Arab side, is to include, among other things, a preferential trade arrangement modelled largely on the ACP Agreement. So far, however, the EC has given no indication of any intention to extend the trade policy concessions

---

28. Account is taken here only of the ACP and Maghrib countries and of the OCT territories.

Table 51. *GSP Imports from Developing Countries Enjoying Special Preferences of Products Affected by Member State Shares and Ceilings, by EC Countries, 1976*
(in UA)

	France	Benelux	Federal Republic of Germany	Italy	United Kingdom	Ireland	Denmark	Total
ACP	—	228,804	—	8,430,891	14,319,032	—	418,007	23,396,734
OCT	—	293,831	—	—	1,350,285	—	—	1,644,116
Maghrib	—	906,203	—	5,982,070	126,110	—	6,429	7,020,812
Total	—	1,428,838	—	14,412,961	15,795,427	—	424,436	32,061,662

Source: Own calculations based on SOEC and German Federal Ministry of Economic Affairs data.

165

of the ACP, Maghrib or Mashriq agreements to all Arab states.[29]

The current negotiations between the EC and Iran about an association agreement are likewise concerned with customs preferences, to be modelled, in the Iranian view, on the ACP Agreement. For the moment, however, the EC has declared this demand to be unacceptable.[30]

§ 10. Appraisal of Preferences Granted by the EC Compared to Those of Other Industrialized Countries

A. Beneficiaries

As mentioned at the beginning of this study the original hope of arriving at a uniform system of preferences granted by all OECD countries soon proved to be an illusion—with the result that today eleven different preferential agreements exist alongside each other. To examine all these preferential systems in detail would exceed the scope of this study; in consequence, attention will be drawn only to their essential divergencies.

Even in their selection of beneficiary countries the industrialized states proceeded in different ways. Although all country lists are based on the developing countries belonging to the Group of 77, Finland and Japan, for instance, refused to extend benefits to dependent countries and territories. Another controversial point is the granting of preferences to Communist countries: Bulgaria and Romania are recognized as beneficiaries by Norway, Sweden and Switzerland; the Mongolian People's Republic enjoys GSP customs benefits on the part of Japan and Switzerland; and Korea and Vietnam are included in the circle of beneficiaries by neutral Finland and Sweden.

Hong Kong and Macao, because of their great export capaci-

---

29. See D. Lerche: *Grundlagen und Perspektiven des Euro-Arabischen Dialogs, Schriften des Deutschen Instituts für Entwicklungspolitik* (DIE), Vol. 46, Berlin 1977, p. 43.

30. See Anonymous: "Kluft zwischen Teheran und EG", in: *Handelsblatt* of 13 July 1978.

ties, occupy a kind of special position among the developing countries; to the extent that they enjoy benefits at all—as does Hong Kong under the GSP of the EC and of Japan—they are as a rule subject to particularly severe restrictions. Much the same applies to Israel which, with the exception of the EC, is granted preferences in all western industrialized countries (see Annex 6).

The USA is the only preference-giving country that has explicitly compiled a list of negative criteria which—regardless of a country's state of development—prevent inclusion in the GSP. The following accordingly are not eligible for preferences:

1. Communist countries unless they are IMF or GATT members;
2. countries participating in producer cartels and thereby contributing to an artificially curtailed supply or to increased prices of products of vital importance to the American market;
3. countries granting reciprocal preferences to other industrialized countries, in particular the EC.

Added to these there are three further criteria which debar from GSP participation all countries participating in the illegal drug trade and countries which have expropriated US property without adequate compensation.

Although these clauses leave relatively ample scope for decision by the President and Congress, they have nevertheless resulted in the non-inclusion of all Communist countries with the exception of Romania, of all OPEC countries, of the Mediterranean countries Spain, Portugal and Greece, and of Somalia, Uganda and the Yemen People's Republic. In its selection of countries enjoying GSP benefits the USA is trying to use a development-policy instrument for the accomplishment of economic and political aims of a different kind. Whether such a tie-up is compatible with the original objectives of the GSP is, of course, questionable.

B. Product Coverage

The main emphasis in the granting of preferences by all western industrialized countries lies—as laid down in the original offer of the OECD countries in 1969—on the industrial products of tariff chapters 25 to 99. It is interesting to note that the exclusion of raw materials, as practised by the EC, is not provided for in the preferential systems of most other industrialized countries, even though the practical significance of preferential tariffs for raw materials is obviously slight.

In the overall view the EC is rather generous as far as the number of products covered by the GSP is concerned: nearly all other major industrialized countries refuse, at least in part, the granting of preferences in areas so important to the developing countries as textiles, leather articles and footwear, or petroleum products. Apart from the EC only Switzerland and—with slight exceptions—Japan grant virtually across-the-board preferences for textiles.

It is again the GSP of the USA that contains a particularly long list of exceptions: no preferences are granted in respect of any textiles included in the Multi-Fibre Agreement or to footwear, petroleum and petroleum products, clocks and watches, or a selected list of steel and glass manufactures regarded as sensitive, or certain electronic products.

Table 52 shows the quantitative relations between total imports, imports dutiable under most-favoured-nation terms and products flows covered by the GSP. If one disregards the preferential systems of the socialist countries column 7 shows that lesser industrialized countries such as Austria, New Zealand and Norway offer the most comprehensive preference opportunities. Yet compared to the great trading nations Japan and the USA, the EC's GSP comprises a much bigger portion of dutiable imports. Whether this also results in a correspondingly greater benefit to the developing countries depends on the customs advantages and the restrictive elements of the various systems of preferences.

C. Depth of Tariff Cuts

Scope and type of tariff cuts are handled differently by the different systems of preferences. The Scandinavian countries (Norway, Sweden, Finland) and the USA in an exemplary manner grant complete exemption from customs duty to the developing countries in respect of all products covered by the GSP. In other systems a very common practice is merely the reduction of most-favoured-nation rates, also in respect of industrial products: thus Australia's GSP as a rule provides for tariff cuts by 10%, Austria and Canada reduce the customs burden for beneficiary developing countries in respect of industrial products by one-half or one-third. A number of industrialized countries such as Austria, Switzerland and Japan practise differential tariff cuts as an instrument for protecting their domestic producers in areas particularly threatened by competition, especially in the textiles sector. Austria and Switzerland additionally lower the preferential margin with regard to particularly competitive developing countries; thus Austria's GSP grants the Mediterranean countries Greece, Portugal, Spain and Turkey a preferential margin of only 30%; Switzerland, alongside an appropriate general discrimination against Greece and Spain in respect of a few products, also grants Hong Kong, Macao, Yugoslavia and Turkey a preferential margin reduced by comparison with other developing countries.

It should therefore be remembered that it is not only quantitative limitations but the preferential margin itself that are used to regulate the scale and structure of preferential trade.

D. Quantitative Limitations

Except for the universal "escape clause", which applies to all western systems of preferences and which offers the possibility, in the event of serious market upheavals, of revoking the granting of preferences either partially or wholly, only three other industrialized countries—apart from the EC itself—practise quantitative a-priori limitations.

Australia lays down an annual import maximum in respect of

Table 52. *Imports into Preference-giving Countries from Beneficiary Developing Countries, 1974*
(in Million US Dollars[a] and as a Percentage)

Preference-giving countries and CCT tariff chapters	All goods	Dutiable goods	Goods covered by GSP	Prefer-ential trade	Goods covered by GSP in % of		Preferential trade in % of		
					(4)/(2)	(4)/(3)	(5)/(2)	(5)/(3)	(5)/(4)
(1)	(2)	(3)	(4)	(5)	(6)	(7)	(8)	(9)	(10)
1. Austria									
1-24	240.0	169.9	94.1	—	39.2	55.4	—	—	—
25-99	932.1	717.2	668.3	—	71.7	93.2	—	—	—
1-99	1,172.1	887.1	762.4	—	65.0	85.9	—	—	—
2. Australia*									
1-24	180.9	76.6	35.6	—	19.7	46.5	—	—	—
25-99	1,404.4	437.4	226.1	—	16.1	51.7	—	—	—
1-99	1,585.3	514.0	261.7	—	16.5	50.9	—	—	—
3. Canada*									
1-24	582.0	326.0	52.0	—	8.9	16.0	—	—	—
25-99	3,838.0	640.0	470.0	—	12.2	73.4	—	—	—
1-99	4,420.0	966.0	522.0	—	11.8	54.0	—	—	—

Table 52 (*continued*)

4. EC*									
1-24	6,773.6	4,834.0	1,270.6	315.8	18.8	26.3	4.7	6.5	24.9
25-99	48,098.7	5.836.2	3,536.7	2,292.8	7.4	60.6	4.8	39.3	64.8
1-99	54,872.3	10,670.2	4,807.4	2,608.6	8.8	45.1	4.8	24.4	54.3
5. Finland*									
1-24	211.1	102.0	8.7	3.4	4.1	- 8.5	1.6	3.3	39.1
25-99	364.7	39.8	24.9	20.3	6.8	62.6	4.8	39.3	64.8
1-99	575.8	141.8	33.6	23.7	5.8	23.7	4.1	16.7	70.5
6. Japan*									
1-24	3,232.6	2,475.9	271.2	250.5	8.4	11.0	7.7	10.1	92.4
25-99	29,566.0	23.962.9	2,448.9	1,215.7	8.3	10.2	4.1	5.0	49.6
1-99	32,798.6	26,438.8	2,720.1	1,466.2	8.3	10.3	4.5	5.5	53.9
7. New Zealand*									
1-24	87.3	82.0	76.0	—	87.7	92.7	—	—	—
25-99	585.3	250.0	246.0	—	42.0	98.4	—	—	—
1-99	672.6	332.0	322.0	—	47.9	97.0	—	—	—
8. Norway									
1-24	131.8	21.0	17.5	1.3	13.3	83.3	1.0	6.2	7.4
25-99	621.4	33.2	20.7	9.4	3.3	62.3	1.5	28.3	45.4
1-99	753.2	54.2	38.2	10.7	5.1	70.5	1.4	19.7	28.0

Table 52 (continued)

(1)		(2)	(3)	(4)	(5)	(6)	(7)	(8)	(9)	(10)
9. Sweden										
	1-24	353.1	198.2	26.2	23.3	7.4	13.2	6.6	11.8	88.9
	25-99	1,455.8	223.2	89.3	62.3	6.1	40.0	4.3	27.9	69.8
	1-99	1,808.9	421.4	115.5	85.6	6.4	27.4	4.7	20.3	74.1
10. Switzerland[b]										
	1-24	443.0	360.0	43.0	25.4	9.7	11.9	5.7	7.1	59.1
	25-99	1,108.1	1,074.5	465.7	183.9	42.0	43.3	16.6	17.1	39.5
	1-99	1,551.1	1,434,5	508.7	209.3	32.8	35.5	13.5	14.6	41.1
11. USA*										
	1-24	7,055.7	3,908.7	918.3	—	13.0	23.5	—	—	—
	25-99	17,080.4	14,436.5	2,412.8	—	14.1	16.7	—	—	—
	1-99	24,136.1	18,345.2	3,331.1	—	13.8	18.2	—	—	—
Total (1-11)	1-24	19,291.1	12,554.3	2,813.2	N/A	14.6	22.4	—	—	—
	25-99	105,054.9	47,650.9	10,609.4	N/A	10.1	22.3	—	—	—
	1-99	124,346.0	60,205.2	13,422.6	N/A	10.8	22.3	—	—	—
Total (4, 5, 6, 8, 9, 10)	1-24	11,145.2	7,991.1	1,637.2	619.7	14.7	20.5	5.6	7.8	37.9
	25-99	81,214.7	31,169.8	6,586.2	3,784.4	8.1	21.1	4.7	12.1	57.5
	1-99	92,359.9	39,160.9	8,223.4	4,404.1	8.9	21.0	4.8	11.2	53.6

Table 52 (continued)

12. Hungary	1-24		651.4	384.6	346.2	53.1	90.0	53.1	90.0	100.0
	25-99		470.7	250.3	215.9	45.9	86.3	45.9	86.3	100.0
	1-99		1,122.1	634.9	562.1	50.1	88.5	50.0	88.5	100.0
13. USSR	1-99		4,059.8	1,224.0	1,224.0	30.1	100.0	30.1	100.0	100.0
Overall total (1-13)	1-99	129,527.9	62,064.1	15,208.7	6,190.2	11.7	24.5	4.8	10.0	40.7

a Information on the preferential agreements of Bulgaria, Poland and Czechoslovakia is inadequate.

b The dutiable imports of Switzerland in column (3) do not contain any items in respect of which the most-favoured-nation rate was only partially reduced.

Note: Information from the listed preference-giving countries and estimates of the UNCTAD Secretariat (marked by *).

Source: UNCTAD: *Fourth General Report on the Implementation of the Generalized System of Preferences*, Geneva 1977, TD/B/C. 5/53, p. 10 and 11.

43 preferential products; the major part of preferential imports, however, is not subject to any controls. Japan's GSP provides for a system of quantitative limitations that greatly resembles the EC's regulations. There, too, agricultural products may be imported on preferential terms to an unlimited amount; only in the industrial area are quotas laid down. Calculation of the total quota is also based on a fixed basic amount equalling the 1968 volume of imports, in terms of value, from beneficiary countries and on a supplementary amount which—unlike the EC formula —comprises 10% of the imports from all other countries during the year before the preceding year.

Imports from individual developing countries are limited by maximum amounts which are uniformly fixed at 50% of the quota. The Japanese preferential system also contains parallels with the grouping of products into sensitivity categories as under the EC's GSP: Japan's GSP has established three product groups in accordance with the frequency of current controls of preferential imports (daily, monthly, never) and the delay period after which the normal tariff rate is reintroduced (after two days, after one month, only as required).

The American GSP contains no ceilings applying to all developing countries. Instead the so-called "competitive need provisions" were introduced as an incentive to diversification of exports and as a protection for less competitive supplier countries. Under these provisions a developing country is excluded from preferential imports in respect of a product if its imports during one year exceed

— 25 million US $ or
— 50% of total US imports of the product concerned.

The value of the absolute import limit is adjusted annually in proportion to the USA's gross national product. The maximum import share of 50% refers both to preferential and to most-favoured-nation imports.

The "competitive need provisions" are not applied if the preferential product in question is not supplied by any domestic manufacturer; it is clear, therefore, that the introduction of this a-priori limitation was due not only to developmental objectives but also to consideration of the interests of domestic producers.

E. Rules of Origin

The function and purpose of the rules of origin is to prevent abuse of the GSP. Nearly all systems of preferences therefore contain appropriately strict factual and formal requirements as to evidence of origin.

There are virtually no problems in the treatment of goods which are manufactured in one developing country only. If, however, manufacture of the imports requires additional products then the fundamental rule is that, to qualify for preference, sufficient working or processing of such preliminary products must take place in the developing country. Preferential systems here apply two different criteria:

1. The process criterion—also described as the criterion of the tariff leap—presupposes that, as a result of the production process in the developing country, the product moves to another four-digit heading number of the BTN. In addition to the EC the following countries regard this tariff leap as sufficient evidence of working or processing in the preference-claiming developing country: Austria, Finland, Japan, Norway, Sweden and Switzerland. In order to meet the diverse character of the products the preferential systems in each case contain lists of exceptions, i.e. products which, in spite of the tariff leap are not accepted for the granting of preferences (List A) and, conversely, products for the manufacture of which no complete tariff leap is necessary (List B).

2. The value added criterion—applied by Australia, Canada, New Zealand and the USA—proceeds from the condition that the value of imported materials and components must not exceed a given percentage of the value of the exported final product. Australia and New Zealand require a value added by the developing country of not less than 50%, while Canada regards an added value of 40% and the USA an added value of 35% as sufficient justification of origin.

All western systems of preferences stipulate direct consignment to the preference-giving country. Interruption of transportation is permissible only for technical reasons; during such time preferential goods must remain under the continuous surveillance of the customs authorities.

All systems make it a condition for the origination of the goods to be attested by a certificate of origin. Most industrialized states apply the Form A certificate on which not only the exporter but also a governmental or correspondingly authorized organization in the developing country confirms origination in accordance with the rules. New Zealand is alone in contenting itself with the signature of the exporter.

A particular problem is what is known as bilateral origin. Australia, Canada and, up to a certain point, Japan regard materials and components from their own countries, if used in the manufacture of products by the beneficiary countries, as being on an equal footing with products from the beneficiary country—eligibility for preference is not therefore affected by the use of such inputs. This practice, on the one hand, tends to enlarge the range of beneficiary developing countries but, on the other hand, this ruling on bilateral origin might result in economic dependence on the preference-giving country, a dependence not necessarily desirable on development-policy considerations.

A major aspiration of the developing countries in connection with GSP reforms concerns liberalization of the rules of origin by the recognition of cumulative origin. In that case products would not forfeit their eligibility for preference if several beneficiary countries participated in their manufacture. Legitimation of origin would thus depend on the exported product having been manufactured in the beneficiary developing countries generally rather than in one particular country. So far Australia is the only western industrialized country to accept such multilateral cumulation unrestrictedly. The EC and the USA apply cumulative origin to certain regional economic associations and free trade areas, while the other western systems of preferences have not carried out any such liberalization of the rules of origin. It is worth mentioning that the USA's GSP as applying to preferential products from free trade areas permits the use of materials and products imported from countries not belonging to the free trade area in question up to a limit of 35% of the value of the final product, while the system of preferences of the EC in an analogous case requires a value added of no less than 95%.

F. Results

The qualitative comparison of the different systems of preference reveals no clear superiority of any one preference scheme over the rest.

In respect of range of products included, the EC's GSP may be said to occupy a favourable position; few other systems include textiles, footwear or petroleum products. The depth of the tariff cut may also be regarded as relatively generous, especially if the continuous growth of the preferential margin in the agricultural sphere is taken into consideration.

With regard to formal a-priori limitations the EC's GSP scarcely differs from other preferential systems; the partial recognition of cumulative origin may be regarded as particularly positive from the point of view of the developing countries. At the same time, no other GSP contains a comparable scale of quantitative a-priori limitations. This is due, on the one hand, to the extension of the preference offer also to sensitive product categories, and, on the other, to the fact that the EC regards it as necessary to take special measures for the purpose of "burden sharing" by the Member States. An important part is played also by considerations for other preferential and association agreements, a point that does not arise to the same extent for other industrialized countries.

It is not possible on the basis of the above criteria to quantify the advantages and disadvantages of the EC's GSP by comparison with other systems of preferences. What ultimately decides the efficacy of a system is the volume of preferential trade it generates. Unfortunately—as Table 52 shows—data on the volume of preferential imports by the western industrialized countries are available only to a limited extent.

The ratio between the EC's GSP imports and imports from beneficiary countries dutiable at the most-favoured-nation rate was 24.4% in 1974—the most favourable ratio of all the listed western industrialized countries. Admittedly, the conversion rate —i.e. the relation between GSP imports and GSP potential—is substantially higher in Sweden and Finland. This result seems entirely plausible since the realization rates reflect the formal and quantitative limitations. The quantitative limitations of Japan's GSP, which are very similar to the EC's limitations, accordingly result in an almost identical ratio between preferential trade and preference potential.

UNCTAD has calculated the volume of preferential imports which would have entered the USA in 1974 if the US preferential system, introduced only in 1976, had then been in force.[31] The—imaginary—realization rate of only 18.16% thus computed would seem to suggest that the "competitive need provisions" exercise a strongly restrictive effect, surpassing even the effects of quantitative limitations in the EC's system. However, the period under review is still too short for any final assessment.

31. See UNCTAD: *Review of the Schemes of Generalized Preferences of Developed Market-Economy Countries. Trade Implications of the United States Scheme of Generalized Preferences*, Geneva 1977, TD/B/C. 5/47, Annex IV, p. 9.

178

Chapter 4

ECONOMIC AND DEVELOPMENTAL ASSESSMENT OF THE EC'S GSP AND POSSIBILITIES OF ITS IMPROVEMENT

§ 11. Economic and Developmental Assessment of the GSP

A. Economic Development in LDC's and the GSP

The developmental objective of the EC's non-reciprocal system of preferences in favour of the developing countries is an effective increase in their exports and export earnings and, as a result, the promotion of their industrialization and the acceleration of their economic growth generally. In line with the idea of "aid by trade" the EC countries are to open up their markets to the export products of the less developed countries by abolishing protection for their domestic industries. Such protection distorts actual competitive conditions and prevents the developing countries from gaining a foothold in areas in which they are in fact competitive and cost-advantageous.

By introducing the GSP in 1971 the EC, following many years of discussions on generalized systems of preferences, met the demand of the developing countries and either abolished or lowered the customs barriers for semi-finished and finished industrial products as well as for certain agricultural products. From a developmental point of view this measure should be seen in the light of the fact that the EC absorbs approximately 30% of all the export products of the developing countries and therefore represents these countries' most important market; access to this market has now been made easier for them.

However, the EC's GSP covers only a small proportion of the developing countries' exports; more than 70% of them consist of energy-producing and other raw materials which will continue to constitute their traditional export products. These are largely duty-free. The GSP also disregards a number of dutiable goods

179

which predominantly include agricultural products. In addition to this limitation of the product spectrum the scope of the GSP is reduced also by restrictions on the eligibility of certain supplier countries. Likewise the dual preference position of the numerous countries which are associated with the EC or have special preferential agreements with it also has a negative effect on the effective scope of the GSP which, allowing for these factors, shrinks to a potential of approximately 8% of all EC imports from all developing countries. Thus the GSP provides no facilities at present for over 90% of their exports.

This is undoubtedly a very restricted scope for a generalized system of tariff preferences. It should, however, be remembered that it is virtually one of the purposes of the GSP to extend its own scope of validity by encouraging the diversification of the raw-materials-dominated production and export structure of the developing countries in order thus to enable them, on an increasing scale, to supply semi-finished and finished industrial products instead of their traditional export goods. Considerable growth-stimulating effects are expected of such a restructuring process.

It is certainly a positive feature that the EC's GSP offers, in the area of industrial products, a very broad product palette which covers virtually all dutiable goods. The preferential systems of the other trade partners of the developing countries, i.e. the USA and Japan, are far more restrictive in this respect. It may be objected that the developing countries are not capable of supplying a number of these products; this is in fact true of 25% of all GSP items.

Yet what matters in terms of development policy is the offer—and this is obviously being taken up by these countries. The number of GSP products delivered by them is perceptibly increasing, and this is an indication of just that diversification which is an avowed goal of the GSP and in the attainment of which the GSP is clearly playing a part.

Generally speaking there are clear signs that the GSP has a trade-stimulating effect. The EC's preferential trade with beneficiary developing countries and in preferential products has increased dramatically. The annual growth rate between 1973 and 1976 was approximately 70%. This vigorous increase was of course due also to a number of improvements in the GSP, improvements which consist mainly in a substantial broadening of the range of preferential agricultural products and in an enlargement of the circle of eligible supplier countries. A special stimulus was provided also by the enlargement of the EC and this has been reflected in GSP performance since 1974. But even after adjustment for all these factors it can still be observed that the growth of GSP imports is clearly greater than that of any comparable parameter. GSP trade increases disproportionately both by comparison with total third country imports and by comparison with general imports from developing countries. The beneficiary countries, in consequence, are gaining increasing shares of third country markets, and this suggests positive trends towards a successful trade diversion in their favour.

Tariff preferences represent a stimulus which—given appropriate market conditions—is by no means reflected in a once-only or sudden surge of growth. Inadequate information of the market participants, the often highly complicated structure and continuous amendment of the GSP, as well as the fact that traditional trade relations and consumer preferences change only gradually—all these mean that preference-conditioned growth stimuli become effective only after a lapse of time. The relatively low elasticity of supply of the developing countries frequently in fact rules out any comprehensive short-term success of the GSP. The establishment of new production capacities and the solution of associated problems of capital and technology is more often accomplished in the medium term and frequently only in the long term. This means that any economies-of-scale effects, which can be a great deal more important for the conquest of new markets and the enlargement of market shares than tariff preferences themselves, take a very long time to bear fruit.

In view of all this any system of generalized tariff preferences can only be expected to achieve the desired growth, diversification and export targets very gradually. The clear indications of the success of the GSP system, which began to be seen within a relatively short period of its effective life, were by no means to be expected automatically, especially as there was the danger that the a-priori quantitative and value limitations would have a negative effect on preference-induced growth impulses.

There can be no doubt that the import limits as well as the other a-priori limitations—including, more especially, the rules of origin—have acted as a brake on the expansion of GSP imports from developing countries especially in the more sensitive product areas. This effect has been largely due to the disproportionately small extension of quotas and ceilings for more or less strongly competing imported products. At present approximately 30% of all GSP imports represent what is known as "restricted trade", i.e. imports in respect of which further growth was no longer possible because upper limits had been reached or exceeded. This controlled GSP trade moreover exhibits an upward trend. At present, on the grounds of sensitivity alone, over 50% of the GSP products exported by the developing countries to the EC potentially carry the risk of being affected by restrictive measures. Any kind of quota-governed or ceiling-governed granting of preferences should, of course, be rejected on development policy grounds; but even if it is accepted as an economic necessity the question might still be asked as to what scale of "restricted trade" can just about be justified.

Yet the problem of quantitative and value limitations, whose total abolition must be the long-term developmental objective, should not divert attention from the as yet unused opportunities offered by the GSP. The substantial degree of non-utilization of community tariff quotas and ceilings, amounting to approximately 3 billion UA in 1976, is only partly (to about 10%) due to the (in any case fairly liberal) application of limitations. The remaining 90% of unused market potential must be explained by other factors. These include the restrictive effect of the rules of origin as well as a large number of other, non-tariff trade barriers which are not as a rule reduced by generalized systems of preferences. However, the major reason behind non-utilization is probably the lack of delivery capability and competitiveness on the part of the developing countries. It is significant that in respect of one-quarter of all GSP products no imports—either on preferential or on most-favoured-nation terms—can be ascertained. These products include a large number of high-quality industrial products which, it may safely be assumed, will not form part of the typical export range of the developing countries in future either. As for the rest—and also for such GSP products as the developing countries have shown themselves to be capable, in principle, of delivering—the reason is the lack of, or the inadequate scale of, production capacities and/or the lack of, or still inadequate level of, competitiveness. This means that better utilization of the marketing opportunities provided by the GSP depends largely on general progress in the economic development of those countries. There is a need to overcome the lack of capital and technology, to develop domestic markets, to establish and extend the infrastructure, to improve educational and training facilities, to create an efficient credit and banking system—to list but a few of the most important prerequisites. Beyond that, there is a need to fulfil, in the export sector, the qualitative requirements made on products, to ensure suitable packaging and range of choice, and generally to obtain accurate knowledge of conditions in the markets. In addition to market research and marketing there is also a need for efficient sales organizations and export financing systems. Transport and insurance are likewise in need of appropriate development.

Against this background it will be seen that the GSP can only to a very limited extent achieve its objectives in the short term. But it offers to those developing countries for which an export-oriented industrialization and growth strategy is at all a realistic possibility, a promising *long-term* promotion framework in spite of all its patent inadequacies. It should moreover always be remembered that tariffs represent only one of a great many competition determinants in foreign trade and that those other determinants can very easily neutralize or offset any preferences. As for the other trade barriers, it is not so much generalized systems of preferences as international negotiations, such as those within the framework of GATT, that provide a suitable forum for discussion on the lowering or abolition of those barriers.

It has often been asked whether the developing countries would not have been far better advised to dispense altogether with the benefits of generalized systems of preferences and instead achieve general and fundamental tariff cuts within the framework of the GATT negotiations.[1] This problem is indeed of some importance in that any general, GATT-agreed, tariff cut, while eroding the preferential advantage of the developing countries, possesses the virtue of letting all developing countries come into enjoyment of tariff cuts in respect of all products, whereas preferential systems stipulate exceptions both with regard to the eligibility of individual countries and with regard to the product spectrum. Exports to the preference-giving industrialized countries are moreover subject to quantitative limitations, with the result that a large proportion of the trade is then transacted on most-favoured-nation terms.

In order to answer the question as to whether the advantages of a general tariff cut exceed those of generalized preferences a number of basic assumptions have to be made with regard to the tariff cut formula, the elasticities of supply and demand, the elasticity of substitution and finally the expected improvements in generalized systems of preferences. Since such basic assumptions are controversial it is hardly surprising that no uniform opinion has so far emerged. What is important in this connection is that the assessment of appropriate calculations must appear different from the point of view of competitive and more advanced developing countries and from that of poorer countries which, after all, are far less affected by the quantitative limitations of the preferential systems than are the competitive ones, and which—as in the EC's GSP—are often totally exempted from limitative measures if they belong to the group of "least developed countries".

At the present moment it seems that the majority of devel-

---

1. See inter alia R. E. Baldwin, T. Murray: "MFN Tariff Reductions and Developing Country Trade Benefits under the GSP", in: *The Economic Journal*, Vol. 87 (1977), No. 345, p. 30-46, as well as UNCTAD: *Other Questions Related to the Operation of the Generalized System of Preferences and the Multilateral Trade Negotiations*, Geneva 1977, TD/B/C. 5/52.

oping countries wish to keep to their preferential treatment within the framework of generalized systems of tariff preferences while at the same time endeavouring to offset the undeniable erosion of preferences by obtaining substantial concessions from the industrialized countries through improvements in their preferential systems.

B. Repercussions on EC Countries

The GSP aims at integrating the developing countries into the international economy to a greater extent. Its objective is an increase in their exports and/or export earnings. This should represent a contribution to the further advancement of their national economies, an advancement that is greatly dependent on the financing of their considerable import requirements. This developmental objective is reflected in the economic policy of the industrialized countries by their introduction of a generalized system of tariff preferences. From its very inception an effort had been made to allow the greatest possible circle of beneficiary countries to enjoy the benefits of such a liberalization of trade.

From the economic-policy point of view, however, the GSP is more than just an instrument of development policy, considering that it affects external economic relations generally. It not only touches on the volume and structure of imports from the developing countries but indirectly encourages the intensification of *reciprocal* trade, the inducing of factor movements, and hence the improvement of the international division of labour generally.

The structure of the EC's GSP, just as that of other industrialized countries, at the same time clearly reflects an endeavour to control the structural implications of intensified economic relations by limited liberalization. For the EC there is the additional point that it has entered into special obligations towards a number of countries and that these obligations demand consideration of their interests and hence a policy of graduated preferences.

The economic-political problem of the GSP for the EC countries therefore lies in the fact that a compromise has to be struck in its shaping, application and further development between several different objectives. These are the objectives to be reconciled:

— trade with the developing countries should be liberalized and the benefits of access to the market should be made available to the largest possible circle of beneficiaries;
— this should contribute to an improved international division of labour;
— it should provide a check on growing competitive pressure on EC industries;
— it should take account of the EC's common agricultural policy as well as its common policy in the ECSC field;
— it should safeguard the interests of associated countries and of countries enjoying special preferences;
— and it should finally keep within tolerable limits the financial burdens stemming from customs duty forfeited due to the GSP.

Even at first glance doubts are bound to arise as to whether the efficacy of the GSP must not inevitably suffer from the conflicting nature of the aims it pursues and from the additional considerations it must bear in mind. Certainly, after a thorough analysis of the GSP, it should be stated that these conflicts cannot fail to affect GSP performance. In particular, the EC's measures to preserve the interests of the domestic economy have been clearly effective. Because of its fundamental economic-policy importance this aspect will now be examined in greater detail.

Prior to introduction of the GSP the EC, and with it the other industrialized countries, clung to the maintenance of numerous tariff and non-tariff barriers because it was feared that growing competitive pressure resulting from liberalized imports not only from developing countries might well, in many sectors, lead to intolerable structural crises which might jeopardize the very existence of a number of industries, to serious redundancies and to considerable social and political tension. These anxieties were given greater weight than the advantages which might have resulted from their own growth from an intensified—even

186

though less complementary than substitutive—division of labour between themselves and the developing countries.

The introduction of the GSP undoubtedly inaugurated a new phase in trade relations between the EC and the developing countries. It was a first step by the EC countries towards freeing themselves from the open conflict between a more or less protectionist foreign trade policy and the prescription of an export-oriented industrialization and growth strategy, a prescription that had been recommended to the developing countries for decades. Nevertheless the above-mentioned misgivings concerning total liberalization of trade with the developing countries were not easily brushed aside. The structure, application and further development of the GSP revealed very clearly that account continued to be taken in a great number of ways of the need to protect the domestic economy. This was done by

— grouping GSP products in sensitivity categories,
— limiting the import volume by quotas and ceilings and
— thereby often limiting its growth,
— by restricting the eligibility of certain supplier countries,
— by exempting certain products, and
— by often only reducing instead of totally abolishing the customs duty burden.

Quite obviously any excessive liberalization of agricultural products is considered questionable. There are misgivings about possible incompatibility with the EC's Common Agricultural Policy and also about the preferential benefits of associated and special-preference third countries. In the industrial sphere the preferential benefits are greatly narrowed down, for instance in respect of raw materials of the first stages of processing, in respect of iron and steel products (ECSC) as well as in respect of the more sensitive products of the GSP generally, including among other things:

— textiles,
— clothing,
— footwear,

187

— leather goods,
— wood processing products,
— certain electrical engineering products.

These are product areas which in fact were subject to considerable tariff protection prior to the introduction of the GSP[2] and which now selectively enjoy more or less restrictive treatment under the GSP in view of the fact that they are also products in respect of which the developing countries—mainly on the grounds of raw material and/or labour-intensive manufacture—might be exceedingly competitive. This restrictive treatment is expressed in tightly fixed tariff quotas which are under fairly close surveillance and are only slowly adjusted over the course of time, with the result that the granting of preferences often lags a good deal behind the increase in overall trade.

To assess the economic-policy importance of limited liberalization under the GSP it is necessary first of all to point to the foreign-trade importance held by imports from developing countries generally and on preferential terms in particular. At present EC imports from developing countries in the field of semi-finished and finished industrial products amount to approximately 8% (1976) of total EC imports;[3] this is roughly also the upper limit of fully liberalized GSP imports, though at present these amount to only a little over 1% of total EC imports. No doubt this global approach conceals the position of developing countries in individual markets; but in overall economic terms imports from other industrialized countries are of far greater relevance. Competition with them raises much greater structural problems than imports from developing countries.[4] General technical progress and the increased productivity resulting from it are also likely to have far greater effects in terms of structural policy and employment policy. One should not therefore over-

2. See J. B. Donges, G. Fels, A. D. Neu et al.: *Protektion und Branchenstruktur der westdeutschen Wirtschaft, Kieler Studien* No. 123, Tübingen 1973, p. 25.

3. Intra- and extra-Community imports.

4. See also J. M. Finger: "The Generalized Scheme of Preferences—Impact on the Donor Countries", in: *Bulletin of Economic Research*, Vol. 25 (1973), No. 1, p. 44 and 54.

rate the effect of imports from developing countries, especially since GSP-induced imports have not only trade-creating but also considerable trade-diverting effects which have no consequences for the EC producers.

Nevertheless, economic policy cannot be denied the right to take measures in favour of structurally weak sectors of the economy; indeed this is a positive part of its economic, social and political duties. The question is merely what period of validity such measures should have. This calls for a fundamental decision on whether threatened sectors should be given protection in permanence or only for a certain period of adjustment. On this point there ought to be consensus that measures such as the maintenance of a protective tariff should only be of a temporary nature and should be exceedingly limited since, from an overall economic point of view, greater advantages may be expected from integration into the world economy. Some important advantages of an open trade policy lie in the productivity gains from reallocation of input, in the supply to consumers of a broader palette of products, and in the price-dampening effect of well-functioning competition. In relation to the developing countries a point of particular importance is that a liberal trade policy results not only in increased imports from those countries but substantially contributes to the strengthening of their purchasing power, which is reflected in a growing export demand. In this way import-conditioned employment losses are almost completely offset by the creation of new jobs in export industries.[5]

If on principle one decides in favour of an economic policy which aims at welfare gains from specialization and division of labour, then a long-term concept is needed for a gradual opening up of markets, and such a concept should include the GSP. In a transitional period towards globally liberalized foreign trade the GSP represents, both in terms of development policy and of economic policy, a rational and acceptable instrument.

5. See D. Schumacher: *"Beschäftigungswirkungen von Importen aus Entwicklungsländern nicht dramatisieren"*, in: *DIW-Wochenbericht*, Vol. 45 (1978), No. 1, p. 6-11, as well as D. Schumacher: *800 Erwerbstätige für den Exports in Entwicklungsländern beschäftigt*, in: *DIW-Wochenbericht*, Vol. 45 (1978) No. 5, p. 58-61.

§ 12. Quantitative and Qualitative Improvement of the EC's GSP

A. Guiding Principles

The economic-political analysis of the GSP has shown that a balance has continually to be struck in its shaping, application and further development between a multiplicity of aims and considerations. Because the GSP lies at the intersection of numerous individual economic-policy areas, which include developmental, trade, agricultural, structural and foreign policy, it found itself encumbered with a variety of aims, sub-aims and also instruments. Economic-policy theory teaches that the conflict affinity between ends and means is the greater the more the employment of means is restricted by limiting conditions and the less the instruments can be shielded from other aims in their effects.[6] In consequence, the GSP is not free from tensions or conflicts. Over the years it has become increasingly complex, with the result that its efficacy has suffered considerably. This situation makes it desirable to examine the GSP in the light of a few principles which should provide guidelines just as much for a sound preferential policy as for other areas of economic policy. The principles discussed below make no claim to exclusiveness—but they probably are among the most important. The order in which they are presented does not imply any priority ranking.

If the GSP is examined with a view to *completeness* it is immediately seen that not all dutiable products are objects of the granting of preferences and that, moreover, the concession is not granted uniformly to the totality of developing countries. The GSP is incomplete also with regard to the preferences granted for "handlooms" and "handicrafts", which might very well be included in the GSP. These are ceiling-governed tariff concessions for the trade in certain hand-made products and in silk and cotton fabrics woven on handlooms. Only a limited number of developing countries[7] benefit from these preferences.

6. See A. Borrmann, D. W. Vogelsang et al.: *Zum Verhältnis von Aussenwirtschafts- und Entwicklungspolitik*, Hamburg 1975, p. 39.
7. See § 9.

190

Differentiation of eligibility between one country and another on the basis of different lists would generally seem to be a questionable practice. It involves application of a variable definition of the concept of "developing country" and this leads to questionable results. One might ask why Romania should be denied developing country status for one part of GSP products, or why only a small circle of countries is granted preferences in respect of jute and coir products or for "handlooms" and "handicrafts". If this arrangement is intended to be an attempt at regulating the competitive strength of individual supplier countries then surely the maximum amounts would provide a more suitable instrument. If the intention is to stipulate certain requirements as to origin and to working or processing, then this could be controlled by the rules of origin. If genuine doubt exists as to developing country status, as for instance in the case of the so-called newly industrializing countries, then this should be covered by a general and not a product-specific decision. Against this background it is possible, therefore, to formulate the principle of *non-discrimination combined with preservation of equal opportunity*. This principle, moreover, should govern the GSP's rules of origin, which differ according to degree of integration, resulting in a patent disadvantage for non-integrated developing countries, and which, moreover, do not cover all integration movements. Another violation of the principle of non-discrimination is represented, in principle, by the preferential gradient between the GSP and the other preferential agreements of the EC (such as the ACP, Maghrib and Mashriq Agreements); indeed the gradient is increasing all the time. Although these measures are politically motivated, they result in the creation of different classes of developing countries.

The problem of the developing countries enjoying special preferences also raises the question of the delimitation of the different agreements. On the basis of the principle of the *right of objection* it is difficult to see why these countries are excluded, for instance, from the calculation of the basic amount of quotas and ceilings but are admitted for charging provided they apply for GSP preferences on Form A. This is not just a statistical blemish but a case of factual handicap in the granting of preferences under the GSP.

The GSP is open to criticism also on the grounds of *clarity* and *unambiguity*. Its complexity has now reached such a degree that in the last analysis the existing system can only be understood and interpreted by experts.[8] As this phenomenon is observed also in other preference-giving industrialized countries the question has repeatedly been asked as to whether the generalized system of preferences can really be regarded as either "general" or a "system".[9] By its increasing complexity the GSP erects its own non-tariff barriers. Instances of this are the multiplicity of individual EC Regulations which are difficult of access even in terms of language, the numerous often interlocking quantitative limitations, the rules of origin and, above all, the regulations in the textile field which will soon yield nothing to the regulations governing the EC's agricultural policy.

Another principle, closely related to those of clarity and unambiguity is that of *uniformity*; this is being infringed by the diverse administration of the GSP in the different Member States. Thus, for instance, there is a difference of opinion on charging the imports of developing countries enjoying special preferences against tariff quotas and ceilings. Nor is there any uniformity in the administration of tariff quotas and ceilings, some countries practising the first-come-first-served and others the prior-allocation system. Uniformity would, moreover, require a renunciation of national quota arrangements as there is justified doubt as to whether national quotas do not run counter to the principles of a uniform customs area. A particular problem in this context is also the application of import limitations which is handled in different Member States with very different degrees of liberality. Liberal interpretation also suggests that it might be better to raise ceilings, customs quotas and maximum amounts, inasmuch as they are subject to surveillance, rather than grant

8. "Report drawn up on behalf of the Committee on Development and Co-operation on the Proposals from the Commission of the European Communities", loc. cit., p. 19.
9. See ibid., p. 7.

permission for them to be exceeded and thereby confuse the participants about the actual level of permitted preferential imports. This would be desirable also under the heading of clarity and unambiguity.

Finally much greater importance should be attached in the shaping and application of the GSP to the aspect of *continuity*. This should be reflected, above all, in annual extension of the framework of preferences in such a way that divergencies from the general method of calculating ceilings and quotas are kept within very narrow limits. This would be just as important with a view to making long-term planning of marketing opportunities possible for the exporting countries as would be the preservation of the degree of sensitivity of the individual GSP products, though a lowering of that degree might be desirable.

B. Selected Measures

The principles here postulated should serve as guidelines for the further quantitative and qualitative development of the GSP in its various areas. In conclusion a few reflections will be voiced concerning an improved formulation of the quantitative and formal a-priori limitations as well as of the product and country range of the GSP.

1. Restriction of quantitative a-priori limitations

In terms of development policy the *Community tariff quotas and ceilings* must be seen as a restrictive feature of the GSP. Even in terms of economic policy their abolition can be accepted as a long-term objective. Other industrialized countries have set an example in this field. The aim and purpose of the Community tariff quotas and ceilings are the controlled opening-up of the market for preferential imports from the beneficiary countries which—while bearing in mind the need to protect the interests of certain sectors of the economy—require a long-term liberalization concept. Realization of such a concept demands that the formula chosen for the extension of the scope of preferences is applied consistently and is deviated from only within narrowly circumscribed areas, provided the basic concept requires this. Short-term special interests should not be allowed to influence the process of a gradual opening-up of the market. The question should also be asked to whether it might not be possible to define a product area in respect of which quantitative a-priori limitations do *not* apply *on principle*. Any assignment of products to that category should be *final*. The developmental advantages of such an arrangement are obvious:

Granting of preferences achieves its maximum effectiveness through customs duty exemption and gives investment decisions by producers in the beneficiary developing countries the security and long-term orientation they need. Given high demands on its applicability and a similarly sparing application as in the past, such a measure might be supplemented by an "escape clause".

For the remainder of GSP products under surveillance and under quantitative limitations it would be desirable to re-examine the troublesome problem of *Member State shares*. In economic terms the EC represents a uniform economic area within which specialization is supposed to find its own level freely in accordance with prevailing competitive conditions. A Member-State-specific regulation of imports from third countries probably infringes that principle, especially if this is done mechanically and in an undifferentiated manner on the basis of a rigid timetable and quota system which might possibly have some justification in overall foreign trade but not for each individual market. Any transfer of a macro-relation to a partial market is bound to reduce the efficacy of the system and should be rejected as economically naive.

These reservations are not in essence dismissed by the introduction of the Community reserve. This is merely a step towards an improved utilization of quotas, though at the price of a further complication of the system and a further increase in its administrative costs.

A step forward, on the other hand, would be a product-specific calculation of the EC Member State breakdown under existing conditions, especially as all the statistical prerequisites exist. It is scarcely comprehensible that, instead of choosing this obvious solution, the institution of the Community reserve had to be resorted to. If such a realistic breakdown pattern were ascertained the way would be cleared for the total abolition of the quota arrangement since country-by-country breakdown and import structure would coincide. In this way all economic and legal objections would be taken care of, especially in view of justified doubts as to whether Member State shares do not violate the principle of a uniform customs area within the EC.

On the subject of the *maximum amount* arrangement it should be observed that, within the framework of ceiling-governed and quota-governed GSP imports, it represents an entirely reasonable instrument for the share-out of the market, one that operates as an effective corrective ensuring a certain equality of opportunity among supplying countries. Although past experience shows that maximum amounts undeniable have a restrictive effect, it cannot be denied that they also provide protection for lesser countries. The future existence of maximum amounts therefore seems justified with regard to quantitatively regulated GSP products.

2. Abolition of formal a-priori limitations

It has already been shown that the formal requirements for the granting of preferences may well have an obstructive effect on preferential trade. The question now arises as to whether and how these formal requirements might be liberalized in a way that would ensure a better utilization of the preference offer without at the same time jeopardizing the proper function of these limitations, i.e. abuse of the GSP.

The problem of notification—as a comparison of notified and eligible developing countries shows—has caused great difficulties to the developing countries in the past. The EC made allowance for this by operating the notification rules in a most generous way. But now that the GSP has been in existence for seven years it does not seem unreasonable to expect even the smaller countries with less experience in international trade to nominate their governmental authorities empowered to issue certificates of origin and to deposit the appropriate rubber stamps, especially as this is a once-and-for-all process. There does not therefore seem to be a need to liberalize the notification regulations.

A much more controversial feature of the a-priori limitations is represented by the rules of origin. Especially with regard to those products whose manufacture requires imported materials or products—and they account for approximately 30% of all products—the complicated rules of evidence of origin have a detrimental effect on the development of GSP trade. The determination of when a tariff leap has taken place under the BTN —remembering the lists of exception with their numerous annual amendments—faces the smaller supplier countries, in particular, with problems which the more competitive developing countries are better able to cope with because of their greater experience. Surely that is not a result in line with the objectives of the GSP.

A particularly aggravating feature is the fact that the procedure of determining origin differs very considerably among the eleven western systems of preferences. Comprehension of the various methods—processing criterion, value added criterion, bilateral origin, cumulative origin—not to mention differential formulations of detail, is difficult enough for an expert; the task would almost certainly be too much for an exporter in a developing country. Harmonization of the rules of origin among the different preferential systems is therefore urgently necessary, especially as their present complexity puts those very countries at a disadvantage whose advancement is one of the priority aims of the GSP.

A further shortcoming of the present rules of origin is the fact that the EC has so far been slow to decide in favour of acknowledging cumulative origin. The result is that the majority of developing countries is therefore being discriminated against in comparison with the members of the three preferential free trade areas, the ACP countries to whom cumulative origin was granted under the Lomé Convention, and the Maghrib countries. The existing arrangement fails to answer the question of why the advantages of cumulative origin might not also be granted at least

196

to other integration areas (such as CARICOM/LAFTA).

It is not clear in what way the general concession of cumulative origin could impair the objectives of the GSP: indeed such a liberalization would benefit the very countries to which the GSP is addressed and result in an increase of GSP potential.

Refusal to concede cumulative origin so far has had a developmentally negative effect in that it has impeded the otherwise positively assessed division of labour among the developing countries. Recognition of cumulative origin, on the other hand, might provide a stimulus to their increased economic integration.

That a consistent and prompt introduction of cumulative origin need not run into any technical or organizational difficulties is shown by the example of Australia which has practised this method for years. Besides, cumulative origin has already proved itself to be practicable in GSP trade with the free trade zones already enjoying that benefit and in trade with the ACP countries.

3. Broadening of the product spectrum

In the field of semi-finished and finished industrial products the opportunities for extending GSP trade are not so much in an increase of the number of eligible products as in the liberalization of the qualitative and quantitative limitations laid down in the GSP. Nevertheless the fact should not be overlooked that even chapters 25 to 99 still include dutiable goods which are not included in the scheme of preferences. Which of these products are of particular importance to the developing countries is shown by a "shopping list" compiled by UNCTAD on the basis of a survey of the developing countries.

The major interest of the developing countries [10], however, in line with their actual supply capabilities, is in the area of agricultural products of chapters 1 to 24. In spite of a continuous extension over the past few years these are still markedly under-

10. See UNCTAD: *Generalized System of Preferences. Replies from Preference-receiving Countries*, Geneva 1977, TD/B/C. 5/54 and Add. 1.

represented in the GSP. This applies more particularly to the least developed countries whose exports are concentrated on the agricultural sector and which are unlikely in the foreseeable future to become competitive in industrial products.

A major reason for the EC's reserve in granting preferences for agricultural products is the Common Agricultural Policy. This complex and highly sensitive institution permits the granting of preferences with regard to competitive products only on a limited scale. The common agricultural market has to be accepted at present as something untouchable—at least until the repeated demands for its general revision become more than stereotype political declarations. In consequence its effects on the product spectrum of the EC's GSP are not a realistic subject of discussion at the moment.

Another reason for the EC's limited GSP offer in the agricultural sector seems less inevitable: consideration of the interests of developing countries linked with the EC by special preferential agreements. The striking differences between the concessions granted under the GSP and, for instance, under the Lomé Convention with regard to the volume of eligible products and the size of preferential margins are bound to be seen from an economic point of view as discrimination against those countries which are solely dependent on the GSP. Nor does such a special position of the ACP countries seem indispensable from a developmental point of view: although this group includes a particularly large number of least developed countries, it does not comprise all the least developed countries. Deliberate support for the LLDCs within the framework of the GSP would be a more consistent procedure.

In the longer term, therefore, the aim, especially in the agricultural area which is so important to the developing countries, should be to place the ACP countries on the same footing as those countries which solely enjoy GSP benefits by way of broadening of the preferential offer and in increase in the preferential margin.

4. Modifications of the list of beneficiaries

The EC's endeavours to make allowance for the different state of development and the resultant great divergencies in the competitive strength of the developing countries has resulted in an increasing differentiation in the structure of the GSP. To name but one example, the regulations on preferential imports of sensitive textile products show the degree of complication that results from an attempt to limit preferential imports from competitive developing countries at the same time as promoting the opportunities for expansion of less competitive countries and, again at the same time, checking the competitive threat to domestic producers. The road chosen—however sensible the objectives it pursues—cannot, because of its opacity and the associated administrative effort, be regarded as showing the way towards the future development of the GSP.

If one is looking for an effective way of checking the one-sided utilization of preferential opportunities by a small number of countries—which, as a rule, would be competitive even under most-favoured-nation conditions—then the most consistent way that suggests itself is a fundamental revision of the lists of beneficiary countries. A further contribution to the simplification of the GSP would be the exclusion of those developing countries which, by comparison with the great bulk of Members of the Group of 77, would have to be denied developing country status. There can be no doubt that, from the economic and developmental point of view, such a decision would be the best way of increasing the efficacy of the system. At the same time, of course, one cannot disregard the fact that weighty political reasons may militate against a very much narrower definition of the "developing country" concept under the GSP. Weighing up of the economic against the political aspects must be left to the responsible politicians. But at least in the acceptance of further developing countries into the circle of GSP beneficiaries—as in the case of Bulgaria which has applied for inclusion—the problem of a country's state of development should receive greater attention from the outset.

Even the exclusion of certain competitive countries would not guarantee complete equality of opportunity among the developing countries. That is why the measures included in the GSP over the past two years for the special advancement of the least developed countries represent an important step towards a more equitable share-out of the opportunities inherent in the GSP. However, the contribution which the GSP—and trade-promoting measures generally—can make to the acceleration of the growth rate of particularly disadvantaged developing countries should not be overestimated in view of the fact that the primary problems of those countries are mostly of a domestic-economy nature.

ANNEXES

Annex 1

LIST OF DEVELOPING COUNTRIES AND TERRITORIES ENJOYING GENERALIZED TARIFF PREFERENCES (AS AT BEGINNING OF 1978)

I. Independent Countries

Afghanistan
Algeria
Angola
Argentina
Bahamas
Bahrain
Bangladesh
Barbados*
Benin*
Bhutan
Bolivia
Botswana
Brazil
Burma
Burundi*
Cameroon
Cape Verde Islands
Central African Republic
Chad*
Chile
Colombia
Comoros*
Congo, People's Republic of
Costa Rica
Cuba
Cyprus
Djibouti*
Dominican Republic
Ecuador
Egypt, Arab Republic of
El Salvador
Equatorial Guinea*
Ethiopia
Fiji
Gabon

Gambia*
Ghana
Grenada
Guatemala
Guinea*
Guinea Bissau
Guyana
Haiti
Honduras
India
Indonesia
Iran
Iraq
Ivory Coast
Jamaica
Jordan*
Kenya
Khmer Republic*
Korea (South)
Kuwait
Laos*
Lebanon
Lesotho
Liberia
Libya*
Malagasy Republic
Malawi
Malaysia
Maldive Islands
Mali*
Mauritania
Mauritius
Mexico
Morocco
Mozambique

203

Nauru *
Nepal
Nicaragua
Niger *
Nigeria
Oman *
Pakistan
Panama
Papua New Guinea
Paraguay
Peru
Philippines
Qatar
Romania *
Rwanda *
Sao Tomé and Principe
Saudi Arabia *
Senegal
Seychelles *
Sierra Leone
Singapore
Somalia *
Sri Lanka
Sudan

Surinam
Swaziland
Syria
Tanzania
Thailand
Togo *
Tonga
Trinidad and Tobago
Tunisia
Uganda *
United Arab Emirates *
Upper Volta
Uruguay
Venezuela
Vietnam
Western Samoa
Yemen, People's Democratic
   Republic of
Yemen Arab Republic *
Yugoslavia
Zaire
Zambia *

II. Countries and Territories Dependent or Administered, or for whose External Relations Member States of the Community or Third Countries are Wholly or Partly Responsible

Australian Antarctic Territory *
Belize
Bermuda *
British Antarctic Territory *
British Indian Ocean Territory (Aldabra, Farquhar, Chagos Archipel-
   ago, Desroches) *
British Pacific Ocean
Brunei *
Cayman Islands and Dependencies *
Christmas Island
Cocos (Keeling) Islands *
Corn Islands and Swan Islands *
Falkland Islands and Dependencies *
French Polynesia *
French Southern and Antarctic Territories *
Gibraltar
Heard Island and McDonald Islands *

Hong Kong
Leeward Islands
Macao
Netherlands Antilles
*New Caledonia and Dependencies**
Norfolk Island*
Pacific Islands administered by the United States of America or under
   United States trusteeship
Portuguese Timor
St Helena (including Ascension, Gough Island, and Tristan da Cunha)
Spanish territories in Africa
Territories for which New Zealand is responsible (Cook Islands, Niue
   Island, Tokelau Islands and Ross Dependency)*
Turks and Caicos Islands
Virgin Islands of the United States (St Croix, St Thomas, St John,
   etc.)*

Notes: The countries and territories in italics have special preferential agreements with
the EC.
The countries and territories marked with * had not met the prescribed notification
requirements by 1976.
Source: Own presentation based on: "Council Regulation (EEC) No. 2705/1977 of 28
November 1977 Opening Tariff Preferences for Certain Products Originating in Developing Countries", in: *Official Journal of the European Communities*, Legislation, Vol.
20, No. L. 234 of 19 December 1977, p. 23 ff.; Commission of the European Communities: *List of Main EEC Agreements with Other Countries*, Europe Information, External
Relations (1978) No. 6, as well as data of the EC Commission.

Annex 2

EXPLANATION OF THE REGULATION AND CPG PRODUCT CLASSIFICATION UNDER THE GSP

1. For the purpose of the statistical coverage of GSP imports the SOEC has developed a product code upon which the present study is based.
2. The so-called CPG code consists of
— a two-digit number of regulation,
— a four-digit tariff heading number and
— a four-digit current number (for instance 10.4102.0010).
3. The number of regulation is largely based on the individual EC regulations concerning the GSP. Its first digit represents the degree of sensitivity of the regulation unless the products in question are agricultural products (1 = sensitive; 2 = semi-sensitive; 3 = non-sensitive; 4 = agricultural products).

The second digit of the number of regulation assigns the GSP product to specific product and/or problem groups in accordance with EC regulations (e.g. 2 = ECSC products; 4 + 6 = textiles). Assignment of GSP products to the various regulations may change in the course of time, for instance if their degree of sensitivity changes.
4. The four-digit tariff heading number represents the Common Customs Tariff of the EC (CCT).
5. The four-digit current CPG number results from a current enumeration of CPG products within a regulation.
6. The CPG code represents a *statistical* classification of goods. Although it is largely based—as we have shown—on the Common Customs Tariff (CCT) it groups a few tariff items together with the result that the number of CPG codes is less than that of customs tariff items.
7. The tabulation below presents a picture of the regulations for the preferential years 1971 to 1976:

CCT chapters	1971	1972	1973	1974	1975g	1976
Sensitive Products (SEN)						
10 SEN products	×	×	×	×	×	×
12 SEN products ECSC	×	×	×	×	×	×
14 SEN products/cotton and textiles[a]	×	×	×	×	×	×
16 SEN products/textiles/cotton	×[f]	×[f]	×[f]	×[f]	×	×
18 SEN products/textiles/ Yugoslavia			×	×	×	×
Semi-Sensitive + Hybrid						
Products (SSEN + HYBR)						
20 SSEN products	×	×	×	×	×	×
21 HYBR products (SEN + SSEN)[h]					×	×
22 SSEN products ECSC	×	×	×	×	×	×
23 HYBR products (SEN + SSEN)[i]					×	×
24 SSEN products/cotton and textiles[a]	×	×	×	×	×	×
26 SSEN products/text./cotton	×	×	×	×	×	×
28 SSEN products/text./Yugoslavia			×	×	×	×
29 SSEN products/Romania				×	×	×
Non-Sensitive Products (NSEN)						
30 NSEN products	×	×	×	×	×	×
31 Jute + coir articles				d	d	×
32 NSEN products/ECSC	×	×	×	×	×	×
33 Jute + coir mats				e	e	×
34 NSEN products/cotton and textiles[a]	×	×	×	×	×	×
36 NSEN products/text./cotton	×[f]	×[f]	×[f]	×[f]	×	×
Agricultural Products						
40 Agricultural products (NSEN)	×	×	×	×	×	×
42 Coffee and cocoa butter (SEN)				×	×	×
43 Virginia Tobacco (SEN)				×	×	×
44 Pineapples (other than in slices or spirals) (SEN)				×	×	×
45 Pineapples (in slices and spirals (SEN)						×
46 Jute and coir articles (NSEN)				×	×	_b
47 Jute and coir mats (NSEN)				×	×	_c

a Excluding Yugoslavia.	f Including footwear, since 1975: in Reg. 10 + 30.
b See Reg. 31.	g Reg. 25: Slide projectors only in 1975.
c See Reg. 33.	h Excluding Romania.
d See Reg. 46.	i Including Romania.
e See Reg. 47.	

Source: Own presentation based on SOEC data.

Annex 3

NOTES ON THE METHOD USED FOR REDUCING EC IMPORTS FROM DEVELOPING COUNTRIES TO THE GSP POTENTIAL

1. The calculations are based on the import data of the SOEC's NIMEXE statistics for 1973 and 1976.
2. Reduction of the EC imports follows a method of calculation developed by UNCTAD,[1] though this has been revised for the purpose of this study.
3. The following reduction steps were performed:

A. EC imports from all countries;
B. of these: from third countries;
C. of these: from beneficiary developing countries;
D. of these: GSP products;
E. of these: from eligible developing countries;
F. of these: excluding developing countries with special preferences;
G. of these: excluding duty-free GSP products.

4. Notes:
a. Beneficiary developing countries:
   Developing countries able, within the framework of the GSP, to import into the EC all or certain GSP products on preferential terms (see the list of beneficiary developing countries for 1976 in Annex 1. 1973 *excluding* Romania (sic) since that country did not become a beneficiary until 1974).
b. GSP products:
   All products included in the EC's offer of preferences (including duty-free GSP products). A number of products are defined in greater detail in the GSP than in the SOEC's six-digit product classification of the NIMEXE statistics upon which the calculations are based. These "ex-items" cannot therefore be isolated and thus enter into the calculations together with *all other* products existing below the sixth digit. The result—especially in respect of agricultural products—is therefore a little magnified.
c. Eligible developing countries:
   Eligibility of developing countries is laid down in the country lists of

---

1. See UNCTAD: *Review of the Schemes of Generalized Preferences of Developed Market-Economy Countries, Operation and Effect of the Scheme of Generalized Preferences of the European Economic Community: Study of the Operation of the Scheme in 1972*, Geneva 1975, TD/B/C. 5/34/Add. 1, p. 7 ff.

the individual EC regulations. Exclusion of countries occurred during the period under review especially

— in respect of textiles which may be imported on preferential terms only from such countries as have signed the Multi-Fibre Agreement;
— in respect of jute and coir products and
— in respect of Romania which has been entitled since 1974 to supply an increasing number of products on preferential terms.

d. Developing countries with special preferences:
The EC has concluded special association, co-operation and preferential agreements with a number of extra-European developing countries (see § 10). These agreements, during the period from 1973 to 1976, included

— the Yaoundé Agreement,
— the Arusha Agreement,
— the Lomé Convention,
— separate agreements with Algeria, Morocco, Tunisia, Egypt, Cyprus and Lebanon as well as
— the regulation concerning imports from so-called overseas countries and territories (OCT).

The above-listed agreements, by comparison with the GSP, contain, or contained, more advantageous, equivalent or sometimes less advantageous trade preferences.
Imports in respect of which the developing countries enjoyed more advantageous or equivalent customs treatment on the grounds of their special agreements with the EC have been deducted in the calculations.
In the absence of monthly statistics the co-operation agreement with Algeria, which came into force on 1 July 1976, had to be regarded as effective for the whole of 1976.

e. Duty-free GSP products:
The GSP "comprises" a number of duty-free tariff items. Some of these constitute a preferential product in association with other dutiable items. Sometimes, however, an entire tariff heading number is listed as a GSP product (e.g. 27.06.00, 49.01.00 to 49.06.00).

f. Developing countries without notification:
Developing countries which have failed to meet the GSP's formal requirement concerning the deposition of stamps, etc., were nevertheless, as a general rule, not denied preferences prior to 1975. Since then, however, the EC's practice has been a little more strict (for the state of notification see Annex 1).

g. Duty-free imports from beneficiary developing countries:
In order to demonstrate the extraordinarily large share of duty-*free*

209

imports the reduction step C ("from beneficiary developing countries") was supplemented by the corresponding import data. For the agricultural imports of the years 1973 and 1976 as well as for industrial imports in 1973 the 1972 figures were uniformly used for the whole of the EC.[2] The data for industrial imports in 1976, into EC-6 and EC-9, on the other hand, were individually calculated.

2. See UNCTAD: TD/B/C. 5/34/Add. 1, p. 9.

NOTES ON THE METHOD USED FOR DETERMINING EXHAUSTED MEMBER STATE SHARES

1. In contrast to the practice applying to maximum amounts, Community tariff quotas and ceilings, whose exhaustion is published in the Official Journal of the European Community, there is no official source of reference at present for fully utilized Member State shares within the GSP framework.

2. In order to make it possible nevertheless to analyse Member State shares, their frequency, structure and effects, the target figures published in the EC Regulations on the GSP were compared with the actual GSP imports of the individual EC countries. On the realistic assumption that the limitations were strictly applied the frequency of Member State shares being reached was ascertained in respect of the individual EC countries for different GSP products by means of the coefficient of utilization.

3. As there are sensitive goods in respect of which the Member States shares are automatically applied without the need for a special application procedure or individual decisions, it may be assumed that the frequency of Member State share cases thus calculated comes very close to the actual number.

NOTES ON THE METHOD USED FOR DETERMINING MAXIMUM IMPORT LIMITS OF GSP TRADE UNDER SURVEILLANCE

1. The purpose of this calculation is the allotment of GSP trade to the different types of limitations involved (Community tariff quotas, Member State shares, ceilings and maximum amounts).

2. Wherever a single limitation applies the assignment presents no problem; in the case of a maximum amount the GSP imports of the supplier country concerned are assigned to it, in the case of national quotas the GSP imports of the EC country concerned are assigned to it. Community tariff quotas and ceilings account for the total GSP trade in the product concerned.

3. Difficulties arise in those cases in which different import limits have been reached.

a. Maximum amounts and ceilings/Community quotas:
   In this case Community tariff quotas and/or ceilings are assigned the entire GSP trade less the imports of the maximum amount countries that are recorded as maximum-amount-controlled.

b. Maximum amount and Member State shares:
   Here the trade was determined between EC countries and developing countries which had reached their upper limits and, for simplification, this was ascribed in equal parts to maximum-amount-controlled and Member-State-share-controlled trade.

Annex 6

BENEFICIARY DEVELOPING COUNTRIES UNDER THE PREFERENTIAL SYSTEMS OF THE INDUSTRIALIZED COUNTRIES (AS ON 1 MARCH 1977)

Preference-giving country	AUSTRALIA	AUSTRIA	CANADA	ČSSR	EEC	FINLAND	HUNGARY	JAPAN	NEW ZEALAND	NORWAY	SWEDEN	SWITZERLAND	USA	USSR
Beneficiary (1)	(2)	(3)	(4)	(5)	(6)	(7)	(8)	(9)	(10)	(11)	(12)	(13)	(14)	(15)

A. *Members of the Group of 77*

Beneficiary (1)	(2)	(3)	(4)	(5)	(6)	(7)	(8)	(9)	(10)	(11)	(12)	(13)	(14)	(15)
Afghanistan (LLDC)	×	×	×	×	×	×	×	×	×	×	×	×	×	×
Algeria (MED)	×	×	×	×	×	×	×	×	×	×	×	×		×
Angola	×	×a	×			×a	×			×	×	×	×a	×
Argentina	×	×	×	×	×	×	×	×	×	×	×	×	×	×
Bahamas (ACP) (CP)	×	×	×		×			×	×	×	×	×	×	
Bahrain	×	×	×	×	×	×			×	×	×	×	×	
Bangladesh (CP (LLDC)	×	×	×	×	×	×	×	×	×	×	×	×	×	×
Barbados (ACP) (CP)	×	×	×	×	×	×	×	×	×	×	×	×	×	
Benin (ACP) (LLDC)	×	×	×	×	×	×	×	×	×	×	×	×	×	×
Bhutan (LLDC)	×	×	×	×	×	×			×	×	×	×	×	
Bolivia	×	×	×	×	×	×	×	×	×	×	×	×	×	×
Botswana (ACP) (LLDC) (CP)	×	×	×	×	×	×	×	×	×	×	×	×	×	
Brazil	×	×	×	×	×	×	×	×	×	×	×	×	×	×
Burma (CP)	×	×	×	×	×	×	×	×	×	×	×	×	×	×
Burundi (ACP) (LLDC)	×	×	×	×	×	×	×	×	×	×	×	×	×	×
Cape Verde (ACP)	×	×	×		×	×		×	×	×	×	×	×	
Central African Emp. (ACP) (LLDC)	×	×	×	×	×	×	×	×	×	×	×	×	×	×
Chad (ACP) (LLDC)	×	×	×	×	×	×	×	×	×	×	×	×	×	×
Chile	×	×	×	×	×	×	×	×	×	×	×	×	×	
Colombia	×	×	×	×	×	×	×	×	×	×	×	×	×	×
Comoros (ACP)	×	×			×	×	×		×	×	×	×	×	
Congo (ACP)	×	×	×	×	×	×	×	×	×	×	×	×	×	×

213

Beneficiary (1)	(2)	(3)	(4)	(5)	(6)	(7)	(8)	(9)	(10)	(11)	(12)	(13)	(14)	(15)
Costa Rica	×	×	×	×	×	×	×	×	×	×	×	×	×	×
Cuba	×	×	×	×	×	×	×	×	×	×	×	×		
Cyprus (CP) (MED)	×	×	×	×	×	×			×	×	×	×	×	×
Democratic Kampuchea	×	×	×	×	×	×	×	×	×	×	×	×		
Democratic People's Republic of Korea	×				×						×	×		
Democratic Yemen (LLDC)	×	×	×	×	×	×	×	×	×	×	×	×		×
Dominican Republic	×	×	×	×	×	×	×	×	×	×	×	×	×	
Ecuador	×	×	×	×	×	×	×	×	×	×	×	×		×
Egypt (MED)	×	×	×	×	×	×	×	×	×	×	×	×	×	×
El Salvador	×	×	×	×	×	×			×	×	×	×	×	×
Equatorial Guinea (ACP)	×	×	×	×	×	×	×	×	×	×	×	×	×	×
Ethiopia (ACP) (LLDC)	×	×	×	×	×	×	×	×	×	×	×	×	×	×
Fiji (ACP) (CP)	×	×	×	×	×	×			×	×	×	×	×	
Gabon (ACP)	×	×	×	×	×	×	×	×	×	×	×	×		
Gambia (ACP) (CP) (LLDC)	×	×	×	×	×	×	×	×	×	×	×	×	×	×
Ghana (ACP) (CP)	×	×	×	×	×	×	×	×	×	×	×	×	×	×
Grenada (ACP) (CP)	×	×	×		×		×	×	×				×	×
Guatemala	×	×	×	×	×	×	×	×	×	×	×	×		
Guinea (ACP) (LLDC)	×	×	×	×	×	×	×	×	×	×	×	×	×	
Guinea-Bissau (ACP)	×	×	×		×	×		×	×	×	×	×	×	×
Guyana (ACP) (CP)	×	×	×	×	×	×	×	×	×	×	×	×	×	×
Haiti (LLDC)	×	×	×	×	×	×	×	×	×	×	×	×		
Honduras	×	×	×	×	×	×	×	×	×	×	×	×		
India (CP)	×	×	×	×	×	×	×	×	×	×	×	×c	×	×
Indonesia	×	×	×	×	×	×	×	×	×	×	×	×		×
Iran	×	×	×	×	×	×	×	×	×	×	×	×		×
Iraq	×	×	×	×	×	×	×	×	×	×	×	×		×
Ivory Coast (ACP)	×	×	×	×	×	×	×	×	×	×	×	×	×	×
Jamaica (ACP) (CP)	×	×	×	×	×	×	×	×	×	×	×	×	×	×
Jordan (MED)	×	×		×	×	×	×	×	×	×	×	×	×	×
Kenya (ACP) (CP)	×	×	×	×	×	×	×	×	×	×	×	×	×	×
Kuwait	×	×	×	×	×	×			×	×	×	×		×
Lao People's Democratic Republic (LLDC)	×	×	×	×	×	×	×	×	×	×	×	×		×
Lebanon (MED)	×	×	×	×	×	×	×	×	×	×	×	×	×	×
Lesotho (ACP) (LLDC)	×	×	×		×	×	×	×	×	×	×	×		
Liberia (ACP)	×	×	×	×	×	×	×	×	×	×	×	×	×	×
Libyan Arab Jamahiriya	×	×		×	×	×		×	×	×	×	×		×
Madagascar (ACP)	×	×	×	×	×	×	×	×	×	×	×	×	×	×
Malawi (ACP) (LLDC) (CP)	×	×	×		×	×	×	×	×	×	×	×		
Malaysia (CP)	×	×	×	×	×	×	×	×	×	×	×	×	×	×

Beneficiary (1)	(2)	(3)	(4)	(5)	(6)	(7)	(8)	(9)	(10)	(11)	(12)	(13)	(14)	(15)
Maldives (LLDC)	×	×	×	×	×	×	×	×	×	×	×	×	×	
Mali (ACP) (LLDC)	×	×	×	×	×	×	×	×	×	×	×	×	×	×
Malta (CP) (MED)	×	×	×	×					×	×	×	×	×	×
Mauritania (ACP)	×	×	×	×	×	×	×	×	×	×	×	×	×	×
Mauritius (ACP) (CP)	×	×	×	×	×	×	×	×	×	×	×	×	×	×
Mexico	×	×	×	×	×	×	×	×	×	×	×	×	×	×
Morocco (MED)	×	×	×	×	×	×	×	×	×	×	×	×	×	×
Mozambique	×	×	×		×	×			×	×	×	×		
Nepal (LLDC)	×	×	×	×	×	×	×	×	×	×	×	×	×	×
Nicaragua	×	×	×	×	×	×	×	×	×	×	×	×	×	
Niger (ACP) (LLDC)	×	×	×	×	×	×	×	×	×	×	×	×	×	
Nigeria (ACP) (CP)	×	×	×	×	×	×	×	×	×	×	×			×
Oman	×	×		×	×	×			×	×		×	×	
Pakistan (CP)	×	×	×	×	×	×	×	×	×	×	×	×	×	
Panama	×	×	×	×	×	×			×	×	×	×	×	×
Papua New Guinea (ACP)	×	×	×		×	×	×	×	×	×	×	×	×	
Paraguay	×	×	×	×	×	×			×	×	×	×	×	
Peru	×	×	×	×	×	×	×	×	×	×	×	×	×	×
Philippines	×	×	×	×	×	×	×	×	×	×	×	×	×	×
Qatar	×	×	×	×	×	×			×	×	×	×		
Republic of Korea	×	×	×		×	×			×	×	×	×	×	
Romania	×	×	×		×	×			×	×	×	×		
Rwanda (ACP) (LLDC)	×	×	×	×	×	×	×	×	×	×	×	×	×	×
Sao Tomé and Principe (ACP)	×	×	×		×	×			×	×	×	×	×	
Saudi Arabia	×	×		×	×	×			×	×	×	×		×
Senegal (ACP)	×	×	×	×	×	×	×	×	×	×	×	×	×	
Seychelles (ACP) (CP)	×	×	×		×	×		×	×	×	×	×	×	
Sierra Leone (ACP) (CP)	×	×	×	×	×	×	×	×	×	×	×	×	×	
Singapore (CP)	×	×	×	×	×	×	×	×	×	×	×	×	×	×
Socialist Republic of Viet Nam	×					×	×			×	×	×		
Somalia (ACP) (LLDC)	×	×	×	×	×	×	×	×	×	×	×	×	×	×
Sri Lanka	×	×	×	×	×	×	×	×	×	×	×	×	×	×
Sudan (ACP) (LLDC)	×	×	×	×	×	×	×	×	×	×	×	×	×	×
Surinam (CP) (ACP)	×	×	×		×	×			×	×	×	×	×	×
Swaziland (ACP) (CP)	×	×	×	×	×	×	×	×	×	×	×	×		
Syrian Arab Republic (MED)	×	×	×	×	×	×	×	×	×	×	×	×	×	×
Thailand	×	×	×	×	×	×			×	×	×	×	×	×
Togo (ACP)	×	×	×	×	×	×	×	×	×	×	×	×	×	×
Trinidad and Tobago (ACP) (CP)	×	×	×	×	×	×	×	×	×	×	×	×		
Tunisia (MED)	×	×	×	×	×	×	×	×	×	×	×	×	×	×

Beneficiary (1)	(2)	(3)	(4)	(5)	(6)	(7)	(8)	(9)	(10)	(11)	(12)	(13)	(14)	(15)
Uganda (ACP) (LLDC) (CP)	×	×	×	×	×	×	×	×	×	×	×	×		×
United Arab Emirates	×	×	×	×	×	×		×	×	×	×	×		×
Abu Dhabi	×			×								×	×	
Dubai	×			×								×	×	
Ras-al-Khaimah	×	×		×								×	×	
Fujairah	×			×								×	×	
Ajman	×			×								×	×	
Sharjah	×			×								×	×	
Umm Al Qaiwan	×			×								×	×	
United Rep. of Cameroon (ACP)	×	×	×	×	×	×	×	×	×	×	×	×	×	×
United Rep. of Tanzania (ACP) (LLDC) (CP)	×	×	×	×	×	×	×	×	×	×	×	×	×	×
Upper Volta (ACP) (LLDC)	×	×	×	×	×	×	×	×	×	×	×	×	×	×
Uruguay	×	×	×	×	×	×	×	×	×	×	×	×	×	×
Venezuela	×	×	×	×	×	×		×	×	×	×	×		×
Yemen (LLDC)	×	×	×	×	×	×	×	×	×	×	×	×	×	×
Yugoslavia	×	×	×	×	×	×		×	×	×	×	×		
Zaire (ACP)	×	×	×	×	×	×	×	×	×	×	×	×		×
Zambia (ACP) (CP)	×	×	×	×	×	×	×	×	×	×	×	×	×	×

B. *Other countries*

Beneficiary (1)	(2)	(3)	(4)	(5)	(6)	(7)	(8)	(9)	(10)	(11)	(12)	(13)	(14)	(15)
Albania	×								×					
Bulgaria	×	×	×		×		×	×			×	×		
Greece (MED)	×	×	×				×	×			×			
Israel (MED)	×	×	×		×		×	×	×	×	×	×		
Mongolia	×				×		×	×						
Muscat		×									×			
Nauru (CP)	×	×	×	×	×	×		×	×	×	×	×		
Portugal	×	×					×	×						×
Samoa (ACP) (LLDC) (CP)	×	×	×	×	×	×		×	×	×	×	×	×	
Spain (MED)		×					×	×			×			
Tonga (ACP) (CP)	×	×	×		×		×	×	×	×	×	×		
Turkey (MED)	×	×	×	×		×		×	×	×		×	×	

C. Territories[b]

A. EEC Member States

(1) France and Netherlands

Beneficiary (1)	(2)	(3)	(4)	(5)	(6)	(7)	(8)	(9)	(10)	(11)	(12)	(13)	(14)	(15)
French Territory of the Afars and Issas	×	×	×	×					×	×	×	×	×	×
Mayotte				×										
French Southern and Antarctic Territories:		×	×	×							×	×d		
Adelie Land												×		
Crozet												×		
Kerguelen												×		
New Amsterdam												×		
New Hebrides Condominium	×	×		×					×	×	×	×	×	×
French Oceania (Polynesia):	×	×	×	×					×	×	×	×	×	
Alofi												×		
Clipperton												×		
Futuna	×	×		×					×	×	×	×	×	
Horn												×		
Loyauté												×		
Marotiri												×		
Marquesas												×		
New Caledonia	×	×	×	×e					×	×	×	×	×	
Rapa												×		
Société (Tahiti)												×		
Tubai												×		
Tuamotu												×		
Uvéa												×		
Wallis	×	×		×					×	×	×	×	×	
St. Pierre and Miquelon	×	×	×							×	×	×		
Netherlands Antilles:	×	×	×	×					×	×	×	×	×	×
Aruba												×		
Bonaire												×		
Curaçao												×		
Saba												×		
St. Eustache												×		
St. Martin												×		

217

(2) *United Kingdom*

Beneficiary (1)	(2)	(3)	(4)	(5)	(6)	(7)	(8)	(9)	(10)	(11)	(12)	(13)	(14)	(15)
Belize	×	×	×		×			×	×	×	×	×	×	
Bermuda	×	×	×		×			×	×	×	×	×	×	
Brunei	×	×	×		×			×	×	×	×	×	×	
Cayman Islands	×	×	×		×			×	×	×	×	×	×	
Caicos Islands	×	×	×		×			×	×	×	×	×	×	
Gibraltar	×	×	×		×			×	×	×		×	×	
Hong Kong	×	×	×		×			×	×		×	×	×	×
West Indies					×									
Windward Islands:	×				×					×		×		
Dominica		×	×		×			×	×	×	×	×	×	
Grenadines										×		×		
St. Lucia		×	×		×			×	×	×	×	×	×	
St. Vincent		×	×		×			×	×	×	×	×	×	
Leeward Islands:	×				×							×		
Anguilla		×	×		×			×	×	×	×	×	×	
Antigua		×	×		×			×	×	×	×	×	×	
Montserrat		×	×		×			×	×	×	×	×	×	
Nevis		×	×		×			×	×	×	×	×	×	
St. Kitts		×	×		×			×	×	×	×	×	×	
Virgin Islands	×	×	×		×			×	×	×	×	×	×	
British Pacific Ocean:					×			×f	×			×		
Ducie												×		
Tuvalu	×	×	×		×			×	×	×	×	×	×	
Fanning									×	×		×		
Gilbert	×	×	×					×	×	×	×	×	×	
Henderson												×		
Ocean								×						
Oeno												×		
Phoenix								×						
Canton & Bury											×			
Pitcairn	×	×	×		×				×	×	×	×	×	
Solomon	×	×	×		×			×	×	×	×	×	×	
Santa Cruz								×				×		
Washington								×				×		
British Territories in the Indian Ocean and the South Atlantic:	×	×	×		×				×	×	×	×	×	
Aldabra					×						×			
Amirantes					×							×		
Chagos Archipelago					×						×	×		
Ascension			×		×							×		
Desroches					×						×	×		
Diego Alvarez (Gough)					×						×	×		

Beneficiary (1)	(2)	(3)	(4)	(5)	(6)	(7)	(8)	(9)	(10)	(11)	(12)	(13)	(14)	(15)
Falkland Islands (Malvinas) and dependencies	×	×	×		×		×	×	×	×	×g	×		
Farquhar					×			×						
St. Helena	×	×	×		×		×	×	×	×	×	×		
Tristan da Cunha			×		×			×		×				
Turks Islands	×	×	×		×		×	×	×	×	×	×		
British Antarctic territory					×			×						
B. *Australia*														
Australian Antarctic Territories					×			×						
Australian Islands:									×					
Cocos (Keeling) Islands			×		×			×			×	×		
Corn and Swan Islands					×			×	×		×	×		
Christmas Island			×		×			×				×		
Heard and McDonald Islands					×			×	×			×		
New Guinea		×	×		×		×		×	×	×h		×	×
New Ireland								×			×			
Norfolk Island			×		×			×	×		×	×		
C. *New Zealand*														
Overseas territories of New Zealand:		×			×			×		×				
Cook	×	×	×		×		×		×	×	×	×		
Niue	×	×			×		×		×	×	×	×		
Ross Dependencies, Tokelau (Union)	×	×			×		×		×	×	×	×		
D. *Portugal*														
Macao	×	×			×			×		×	×	×		
Timor	×	×			×						×	×		
West Africa:											×			
Cabinda			×		×						×			

Beneficiary (1)	(2)	(3)	(4)	(5)	(6)	(7)	(8)	(9)	(10)	(11)	(12)	(13)	(14)	(15)
E. *Spain*														
Spanish territory in Africa (Sahara):		×			×									
Ceuta		×										×		
Melilla		×										×		
Ifni		×										×		
Sahara (Rio de Oro, Sekia el Hamra and others	×	×							×			×	×	×[i]
Spanish North Africa			×											
F. *United States of America*														
Territories and dependencies in Oceania:		×			×					×	×	×		
Baker												×		
Carolines					×				×[j]	×		×		
Guam	×	×	×		×				×	×	×	×		
Howland										×		×		
Jarvis												×		
Johnston	×	×			×					×	×	×		
Manua												×		
Marianas					×				×	×		×		
Marshalls					×				×	×		×		
Midways	×	×			×					×	×	×		
Palau												×		
Palmyra									×			×		
Rose												×		
Samoa	×	×	×		×[k]				×[l]	×	×	×		
Sand	×	×			×					×	×	×		
Sporades of Central Polynesia												×		
Swain's Island		×			×				×	×	×	×		
Tutuila									×			×		
Wake	×	×			×					×				
Trust territory of the Pacific Islands	×	×			×				×	×	×		×	
Virgin Islands	×	×	×		×[m]				×	×[m]				
G. *Other*														
Kuria—Muria Islands Dependencies of Mauritius	×													

a Austria, EEC and Switzerland show separately Cabinda as beneficiary territory (see below).
b Classified according to the country of which the territory is a dependency, by which it is administered or which is responsible for its external relations.
c Including Sikkim.
d Including Austral Islands.
e And dependencies.
f Including - Flint; Caroline; Vostock; Malden; Starbuck.
g Falklands (Malvinas) only.
h Eastern part, including Papua and the Entrecasteaux and Lousiade Archipelago; Admiralty Islands; Bougainville, New Britain.
i Indicated as Western Sahara.
j Including Palau; Yap; Ponape and Truk Districts.
k Including Swain's Island.
l Including Manua group.
m Including St. Croix; St. Thomas; St. John; etc.

Notes:
— ACP signifies an African, Caribbean of Pacific country member of the Lomé Convention.
— CP signifies a Commonwealth country which enjoys special preferences in both the United Kingdom and the Canadian markets, with the exception of Burma, which enjoys special preferences only in the Canadian market.
— LLDC signifies one of the least developed among the developing countries.
— MED signifies a Mediterranean country which enjoys also special preferences of special tariff treatment under an Association or other preferential agreement with EEC.
— Bulgaria: Beneficiaries are not specified in the scheme. It has been stated, however, that Bulgaria "will accord preferential treatment to products originating in interested developed countries, irrespective of their economic and social system" (TD/B/378/Add. 1, p. 2).
— USSR: Beneficiaries are not specified in the scheme. The developing countries and territories listed refer to those with which the USSR maintains trade relations (see TD/B/C. 5/30/Add. 3, Annex II).

Source: UNCTAD: *Fourth General Report on the Implementation of the Generalized System of Preferences*, TD/B/C. 5/53 of 27 May 1977, Annex II.

Annex 7

PREFERENTIAL SYSTEMS FROM A THEORETICAL POINT OF VIEW

Purpose and premises of a theoretical analysis

Comparative statistical analysis[1] as a rule proceeds from a three-country-model: let country A be the preference-giving country, B the beneficiary country and C the non-beneficiary third country. Examination is confined to one product; the findings, however, are readily transferable to a multiplicity of products and countries. The market considered is characterized by perfect competition[2] so that the effects of the granting of preferences may be viewed "as if in a single market" (and represented graphically in a system of coordinates).

The main effects of preferences: trade creation, trade diversion and trade expansion

The starting point of the effects of preferences is the reduction of the price, directly linked with preference (in the theoretical model), of the preferential product $\times$ by the amount of the former customs duty, i.e. by the preferential margin. The reaction of trade flows to the change in the absolute price of $\times$ and in the relative prices of different suppliers

---

1. From the extensive literature on the granting of preferences only a few selected items can be quoted here: Klaus Poser: *Die Wirkungen internationaler Präferenzsysteme auf Preise und Handelsströme*, Berlin 1964; R. Pickel: *Handelspräferenzen als Mittel der Entwicklungspolitik unter besonderer Berücksichtigung des EWG- und des neuen australischen Präferenzsystems*, Diss. Cologne 1969; M. Feldsieper: *Zollpräferenzen für Entwicklungsländer*, Tübingen and Basle 1975; F. W. Meyer: "Über die Auswirkungen von Zollpräferenzen", in: E. v. Beckerath, F. W. Meyer and A. Müller-Armack (Ed.): *Wirtschaftsfragen der freien Welt*, Frankfurt Main 1957, p. 608 ff. The principal English publications to be quoted are J. Viner: *The Customs Union Issue*, New York, London 1950; J. E. Meade: *The Theory of Customs Unions*, Amsterdam 1955; H. G. Johnson: *Economic Policies Toward Less Developed Countries*, Washington 1967.
2. In particular the following conditions must be met:

— complete homogeneity of the product considered,
— no regional, time or national preferences,
— perfect knowledge of the market,
— normal price reaction of supply and demand,
— operation of the law of diminishing returns,
— constant technological level on the supplier side.

It is moreover assumed that the inputs are totally immovable internationally but highly mobile nationally. See K. Poser: *Die Wirkungen internationaler Präferenzsysteme auf Preise und Handelsströme*, loc. cit., p. 20 f. (hereinafter quoted as: *Die Wirkungen*).

222

may, in accordance with Viner's theoretical model, be represented in a simple graphic manner[3] as shown in Diagram 2.

Diagram 2. *Static Trade Effects of Preferential Tariff Cuts Given Totally Price-Elastic Supply and Rigid Demand*

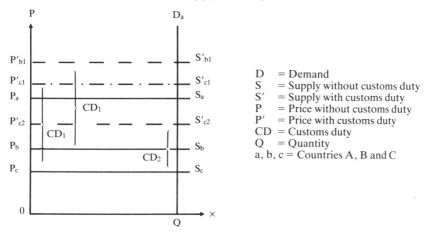

Let us start from the cost situation represented in the diagram (in accordance with the ratio of relative prices, disregarding customs duty): The product × is produced most expensively in country A (P_a) and most cheaply in country C (P_c). The effect of any preferential treatment of country B depends on the tariff policy in the starting situation:

— Given a prohibitive tariff policy the duty (CD_1) would be so high that the potential gross price[4] would lie above the prices of country A (IIS'_{c1}, IIS'_{b1}). There would be no foreign trade; country A would supply itself to the amount OQ. Granting preferences to country B would therefore mean that × can be offered more favourably by country B and that domestic production in A would be replaced by imports: *trade creation* would occur.

— If the duty in the starting situation was not prohibitive then granting preferences to B would result in A's previous foreign trade with C being wholly taken over by country B to the amount OQ—thus *trade diversion* would occur. However, an important reservation has to be made here, one applying in particular to trade with developing countries: the customs advantage enjoyed by country B as a result of preference results in trade diversion only if it offsets possible cost dis-

3. See J. Viner: *The Customs Union Issue*, loc. cit., p. 43-46. Graphic representation after K. Poser: *Die Wirkungen*, loc. cit. p. 23 ff.
4. P'_{b1} and P'_{c1}.

advantages compared with the third country C.[5] If this is not the case then the granting of preferences produces no effect.

The assumption in the diagram of a totally elastic supply and a totally inelastic demand is of course unrealistic.[6] If one therefore follows Meade[7] in including in the analysis the demand reaction to a price reduction of product × then the effect of the granting of preferences may be represented as in Diagram 3.

Diagram 3. *Static Trade Effects of Preferential Tariff Cuts Given Totally Price-Elastic Supply and Elastic Demand*

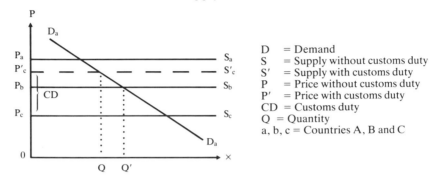

D = Demand
S = Supply without customs duty
S' = Supply with customs duty
P = Price without customs duty
P' = Price with customs duty
CD = Customs duty
Q = Quantity
a, b, c = Countries A, B and C

Assume not that a non-prohibitive duty applied in the starting situation, so that the quantity OQ was imported from country C. The granting of preferences, in addition to diverting trade from C to B, now leads to an increase in total trade by OQ' at the lower price P_b. This effect is called *trade expansion* by Meade.

The simultaneous occurrence of all three above effects may be represented very clearly within the framework of a model developed by Ferguson and Humphrey[8] (Diagram 4).

5. P_b must be less than P'_{c2}.
6. Strictly speaking this assumption represents a deviation from the premises of the model.
7. See J. E. Meade: *The Theory of Customs Union*, Amsterdam 1955, p. 37 ff.
8. See C. E. Ferguson and D. D. Humphrey: "The Domestic and World Benefits of a Customs Union", in: *Economia Internazionale*, Vol. XIII, 1960, p. 197-216. Representation again follows K. Poser: *Die Wirkungen*, loc. cit., p. 25 ff.

Diagram 4. *Static Trade Effects of Preferential Tariff Cuts Given Price-Elastic Supply and Demand*

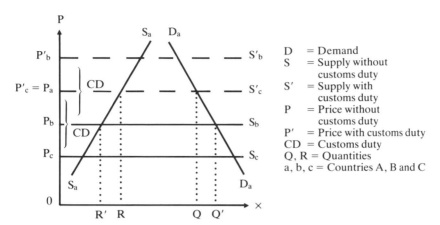

In this model it is assumed that both supply and demand in country A are price-elastic. In the starting situation the duty is so fixed that the price of products ×, including its duty burden, is at least equal to the domestic price P_a. Country A now satisfies its own demand to the amount OR from its own production and to the amount RQ by imports from country C. As a result of the granting of tariff preferences the price now drops from P_a to P_b: Country A now only produces the amount OR' itself and imports the amount R'Q' from country B. There has therefore been trade creation (R'R) as well as trade diversion (from country C to country B), as well as trade expansion (R'Q' - RQ).

The result would be modified if not only the supply in country A but also the supply in the beneficiary country B were regarded as elastic. This would then mean that, following an adjustment phase, the newly created price would be slightly higher than P_b because production costs would rise in B in connection with an expansion of the supply.

Scholars in the theory of the effects of preferences have varied the premises of these models in a multiplicity of ways and brought them closer to real conditions. To describe them in detail would exceed the scope of this study, especially as the above-mentioned principal effects of preferences would remain the same. The additional assumptions will therefore only be outlined in brief:

— Meyer[9] assumes that price-elastic supply conditions exist in country B as well as in country C. As a result of exports to A prices would drop in country C but rise in country B.

9. See F. W. Meyer: "Über die Auswirkungen von Zollpräferenzen", in: E. v. Beckerath (Ed.): *Wirtschaftsfragen der freien Welt*, Frankfurt/Main 1957, p. 608-618.

— Meyer additionally takes into account that both in country B and in country C there is a domestic demand for the preferential product: in country C the domestic demand will expand whereas in country B it will be forced back in favour of increasing exports.

— Poser[10], while following Meade, moreover points out that the beneficiary country B can have additional export partners (D). The increase in the price of product ×, resulting from the increased costs due to increasing exports to A, might now induce country D to direct its demand increasingly towards country C so that a further trade-diverting effect emerges. This effect, however, is feasible only in the presence of special assumptions concerning the capacity of supply of country B and country C.

Determinants of the effects of preferences

To sum up, the factors determining the nature and scale of the effects of preferences will be listed again.

The *preferential margin*—i.e. the difference between the original duty and the rate of duty following preference granting—must be large enough for possible cost disadvantages of the beneficiary country vis-à-vis third countries to be offset. If this is not the case and if third countries, in spite of tariff burdens, are still able to supply more cheaply than the beneficiary country then preference granting will have no effect whatever. If the duty in the starting situation was prohibitive and if the preferential margin is large enough to allow the import price to drop below the costs of domestic production in the preference-giving country, the granting of preferences will invariably lead to trade creation; in the case of non-prohibitive initial duty and—as mentioned above—appropriate cost relations it will result in trade diversion. It should be mentioned that the literature on the effects of the granting of preferences assesses trade creation as positive from the point of view of maximization of worldwide prosperity; trade diversion, on the other hand—since it implies the direction of inputs toward less efficient (because less cost-effective) areas—is assessed negatively.[11] Such a welfare-theoretical argumentation, however, should be, at most, a secondary criterion in the granting of preferences to developing countries.

Price elasticity of demand in the preference-giving country determines the extent of trade expansion. The more elastic the demand the more strongly will it react to the price reductions brought about by preference granting.

Price elasticity of the supply plays a part both in the beneficiary and in the preference-giving countries. The more elastic the supply in the

10. See K. Poser: *Die Wirkungen*, loc. cit.
11. See inter alia M. Feldsieper: *Zollpräferenzen für Entwicklungsländer*, loc. cit., p. 33; R. Pickel: *Handelspräferenzen als Mittel der Entwicklungspolitik unter besonderer Berücksichtigung des EWG- und des neuen australischen Präferenzsystems*, loc. cit., p. 73; J. Viner: *The Customs Union Issue*, loc. cit., p. 43.

beneficiary country, the less will be the price increase due to costs resulting from an expansion of the supply and the greater will be the benefit-of-scale effect of preference. On the other hand, the steeper the supply graph in the preference-giving country,[12] the sooner will the price cut result in a decline of domestic production and thus, for a given demand function, in increased trade expansion.

The trade structure, and more particularly the trade of the beneficiary country with third countries, likewise—as emerges from Meade's above-mentioned model—exerts a marked influence on the kind and scale of the effects of preference granting.

Critical consideration of the model premises

Nearly all the premises assumed in the model are more or less unrealistic.[13] The assumption of a perfect market is realized only for a small part of internationally traded products, mainly raw materials and primary foodstuffs. Semi-finished and finished products, however, which are of prime relevance to the granting of preferences to developing countries, are as a rule subject to a multiplicity of factual, regional, national and personal preferences, further reinforced by variety of quality, type and finish. Added to this is the fact that complete knowledge of the market, as presumed in the model, becomes an illusion under these conditions. All these factors may result in a situation in which the supply and demand reactions deduced from the model do not occur, or occur only on a reduced scale. The same result may be produced by the fact that the perfect-competition market is now only found in a very few areas. In reality suppliers do not only adjust to quantities but also enjoy a more or less wide scope for price fixing. In an imperfect market, therefore, many factors determine the price level of a product—duty, in consequence, is only one of several determinants of price variations. This means that the basic condition of the model, i.e. that a tariff cut will automatically—at least as a primary effect—result in a price reduction to the amount of the preferential margin, becomes questionable. This formula applies unreservedly only if the ultimate consumer from the preference-giving country obtains the preferential product direct from the foreign market—an exceedingly rare occurrence under realistic conditions. The moment that importers and/or exporters interpose themselves between the foreign producer and the ultimate consumer it depends on their market position and on their assessment of the competition and of demand elasticity whether the tariff cut results in a price cut for the purchaser, and thereby can result in the above-described benefit-of-scale effects, or whether it evaporates in the intermediate transaction in the form of

12. See the model of Humphrey and Ferguson on p. 225.
13. For a critique of the model see in particular K. Poser: *Die Wirkungen*, loc. cit., p. 89 ff. and R. Pickel: *Handelspräferenzen als Mittel der Entwicklungspolitik*, loc. cit., p. 76 ff.

higher profits or whether, at best, at a given total import volume, it leads to a regional shift of imports in favour of the beneficiary country. But even if the price reduction expected in the model does materialize this is no guarantee that the improved marketing opportunities associated with it will in fact be perceived by the beneficiary country, considering the imperfect knowledge of the market, and whether, for another thing, they can be fully utilized in view of the less than efficient marketing organization of the developing countries. Poser points out that, especially in the event of trade creation and trade diversion, additional measures are necessary, such as intensified publicity, establishment of a servicing network and of a distribution organization, or indeed the creation of a more flexible credit system, in order effectively to counter traditional trade relations, contractual obligations and national preferences.[14]

Dynamic effects

The inadequacies of comparative-static analysis have led general customs union theory[15]—on which the derivation of the effects of preferences is essentially based—increasingly to turn towards the dynamic effects. This was the more necessary in the case of the developing countries as traditional integration and customs union theory was tailored to the special conditions of the industrialized countries. However, the trade and allocation mechanisms, or the global welfare benefits to be gained from them, cannot be of prime importance to the developing countries if only because their prime interest is the creation and extension of their own productive capacities. That is why from their point of view dynamic effects are far more important than pure structural shifts in production and foreign trade.[16]

Recourse to dynamic integration theories, in particular to customs union theories, reveals that it is far less easy to derive or represent the dynamic effects of preferential systems in any concrete or model form. As a rule one confines oneself to an isolated enumeration of individual effects with emphasis on their hoped-for positive overall effect.[17] Feldsieper believes that this is due to the lack of a satisfactory growth theory and of more accurate knowledge of the scarcely quantifiable

14. See K. Poser: *Die Wirkungen*, loc. cit., p. 95 f.
15. See inter alia J. Viner: *The Customs Union Issue*, New York, London 1950; J. E. Meade: *The Theory of Customs Unions*, Amsterdam 1955. F. Gehrels: "Customs Unions from a Single-Country Viewpoint", in: *The Review of Economic Studies*, Vol. XXIV (1956/57), No. 63, p. 61-64.
16. See B. Balassa: "Toward a Theory of Economic Integration", in: M. S. Wionczek (Ed.): *Latin American Economic Integration*, New York, Washington, London 1966, p. 21-31.
17. See K. Keferstein: *Förderung des Aussenhandels unter Entwicklungsländern - eine entwicklungspolitische Alternative?*, Frankfurt 1978, p. 181.

dynamic effects.[18] In view of all this the dynamic effects which the systems of preferences may produce can therefore only be shown in general outline.

The "classical" argument in justification of tariff policy concessions to developing countries is the "infant industry" argument. Because the emergent industries of the developing countries are not yet internationally competitive, their competitiveness is to be "artificially" improved by preferential tariffs for a temporary period. In the long run, it is suggested, this preferential tariff granted to the developing countries will become dispensable because of the expected lowering of the manufacturing costs of industrial products.

Closely related to the above approach is the so-called "scale argument". Because the market in the developing countries is too small—owing to their low population figures and, even more so, their low per capita income—any extension of production and hence the achievement of "economies of scale" can be achieved only by exports. The need for the granting of preferences, therefore, is—in this view too, only a temporary one. It should be borne in mind, however, that the desired effect of preferential systems can be achieved in full only if the primary cause of the unfavourable cost situation in the developing countries is in fact due to insufficient demand. If, on the other hand, other production-impeding factors predominate—as, for instance, shortage of input factors or a mistaken economic policy—then the effect of preferences would not be an increase in output but merely a diversion of production from the domestic market to exports.

An additional long-term effect is the increased readiness to make investments, promoted by an improved profit situation, and hence an increase in the production potential of the developing countries. If these additional investments are direct investments by the industrialized countries then, in certain circumstances, a beneficial effect may be expected also on the balance of payments situation.

In addition to the direct effects on the preference-receiving sector, benefits from an increase in exports and/or production are reaped also by the adjoining production areas preceding and following the benefiting sector. This may in turn lead to the more cost-effective production of input factors and hence to an improvement in the competitive position of the export products (backward linkage effects).

The combined operation of the above-listed dynamic effects has a bearing on the long-term trend of the supply of preferential products from the developing countries. A system of preferences would, at best, produce short-term and medium-term effects if the graph of long-term supply for the preferential products in the developing countries is steeper than in the industrialized countries and if the tariff advantage is over-compensated by cost disadvantages. The dynamic effects discussed result in a flattening of the supply graph and thus lead to an improvement of the long-term prospects of preferential systems.

18. On this and the following see M. Feldsieper: *Zollpräferenzen für Entwicklungsländer*, Tübingen and Basle 1975, p. 51 f.

ANNEX TABLES

Table A1. *Preferential Trade by CCT Sections 1973 to 1976*
(in 1,000 UA)

CCT section		1973	1974	1975	1976
I.	Live animals; animal products	13,135	8,622	28,754	50,473
II.	Vegetable products	4,535	36,130	41,636	72,390
III.	Fats and oils	769	15,800	20,099	207,741
IV.	Foodstuffs, tobacco	11,312	204,855	204,263	400,866
V.	Mineral products	16,268	194,593	227,747	570,486
VI.	Chemical products	49,230	132,146	128,746	146,256
VII.	Plastics, rubber	16,047	52,937	44,629	68,652
VIII.	Hides, furskins and articles thereof	41,005	83,912	89,076	138,097
IX.	Wood, cork and articles thereof	41,020	122,753	65,801	100,195
X.	Paper and articles thereof	16,533	30,049	28,784	39,776
XI.	Textiles and textile articles	112,630	210,533	273,331	325,492
XII.	Footwear, umbrellas	15,432	101,701	46,828	62,043
XIII.	Stone, glass, ceramic products	10,903	20,783	19,545	29,518
XIV.	Pearls, coin, precious stones	3,147	11,137	9,767	17,092
XV.	Base metals	64,069	129,533	112,039	197,658
XVI.	Machinery, electrical equipment	101,804	223,449	200,667	302,997
XVII.	Vehicles	45,265	50,507	61,924	77,136
XVIII.	Precision instruments and apparatus	20,769	41,761	58,367	120,484
XIX.	Arms and ammunition	532	637	584	633
XX.	Miscellaneous articles	27,713	81,318	67,210	107,797
XXI.	Works of art	—	55	144	68
Total GSP trade		612,118	1,753,211	1,729,945	3,035,852

Source: Own calculations based on SOEC and German Federal Ministry of Economic Affairs data.

232

Table A2. *GSP Imports as Proportions of the Gross Domestic Product (GDP) of the EC Countries 1976* (in Million EUA and as a Percentage)

EC country	GDP in mill. EUA	GSP imports in mill. EUA	Percentage share
France	310,100	275	0.09
Benelux	139,800	426	0.30
Federal Republic of Germany	398,800	1,173	0.29
Italy	152,800	309	0.20
United Kingdom	194,700	642	0.33
Ireland	7,200	13	0.18
Denmark	34,700	83	0.24
EC total	1,238,100	2,921	0.24

Source: Own calculations based on SOEC and German Federal Ministry of Economic Affairs data.

Table A3. GSP Imports of the EC Countries by Degree of Sensitivity in the Agricultural and Industrial Areas, 1973 to 1976 (in Million UA)

EC country	Year	Chapters 1-24			Chapters 25-99					Chapters 1-99 [a]				
		SEN	NSEN	Total[a]	SEN	HYBR	SSEN	NSEN	Total[a]	SEN	HYBR	SSEN	NSEN	Total
France	1973	—	12	12	28	—	9	51	88	28	—	9	62	100
	1974	2	28	29	60	—	24	96	179	61	—	24	123	208
	1975	1	34	35	30	10	15	58	113	31	10	15	91	148
	1976	2	62	64	41	10	58	93	202	43	10	58	155	265
Benelux	1973	—	5	5	29	—	21	39	89	29	—	21	44	94
	1974	6	17	24	45	—	45	66	156	51	—	45	83	179
	1975	6	19	24	23	—	57	78	159	29	—	57	97	183
	1976	9	68	77	28	12	132	109	281	37	12	132	177	358
Federal Republic of Germany	1973	—	11	10	83	—	42	161	287	84	—	42	171	297
	1974	6	57	63	92	—	189	198	479	98	—	189	255	542
	1975	7	71	77	60	44	148	273	526	67	44	148	344	604
	1976	15	119	134	76	46	26	382	768	92	46	264	500	902

Table A3 (continued)

	Year													
Italy	1973	—	3	3	42	—	15	62	119	42	—	15	65	122
	1974	0	18	19	52	—	111	105	268	52	—	111	124	287
	1975	3	13	16	20	16	191	43	270	23	16	191	55	286
	1976	8	25	33	33	20	295	78	427	41	20	295	104	460
United Kingdom	1974	82	45	127	124	—	51	150	325	206	—	51	195	451
	1975	55	79	134	50	26	68	159	303	106	26	68	238	437
	1976	143	262	405	59	29	217	245	550	202	29	217	507	956
Ireland	1974	0	1	1	2	—	2	9	13	2	—	2	10	14
	1975	3	0	3	1	1	1	4	6	3	1	1	4	9
	1976	3	3	6	1	2	2	8	14	5	2	2	11	20
Denmark	1974	1	3	4	26	—	30	12	68	27	—	30	15	71
	1975	1	4	5	14	4	27	13	58	15	4	27	17	63
	1976	3	9	12	19	4	19	21	63	21	4	19	30	75
Total[a]	1973	—	31	30	182	—	87	313	582	183	—	87	342	612
	1974	97	169	265	400	—	452	637	1,488	496	—	452	805	1,753
	1975	76	219	295	199	101	507	628	1,435	274	101	507	847	1,730
	1976	183	548	731	258	124	987	936	2,304	441	124	987	1,484	3,036

[a] Slight discrepancies due to rounding errors.
Note: GSP imports less than 500,000 UA : 0; no GSP imports : –.
Source: Own calculations based on SOEC and German Federal Ministry of Economic Affairs data.

Table A4. *GSP Imports of the EC by Degree of Sensitivity, 1973 to 1976*
(as a Percentage)

EC country	Year	SEN	HYBR	SSEN	NSEN	Total[a]
France	1973	28.3	—	9.1	62.6	100
	1974	29.3	—	11.5	59.1	100
	1975	21.1	6.8	10.2	61.9	100
	1976	16.2	3.8	21.8	58.3	100
Benelux	1973	30.9	—	22.3	46.8	100
	1974	28.5	—	25.1	46.4	100
	1975	15.8	—	31.1	53.0	100
	1976	10.3	3.4	36.9	49.4	100
Federal Republic of Germany	1973	28.2	—	14.1	57.7	100
	1974	18.1	—	34.9	47.0	100
	1975	11.1	7.3	24.5	57.0	100
	1976	10.2	5.1	29.3	55.4	100
Italy	1973	34.4	—	12.3	53.3	100
	1974	18.1	—	38.7	43.2	100
	1975	8.1	5.6	67.0	19.3	100
	1976	8.9	4.3	64.1	22.6	100
United Kingdom	1973	—	—	—	—	—
	1974	45.6	—	11.3	43.1	100
	1975	24.2	5.9	15.5	54.3	100
	1976	21.2	3.0	22.7	53.1	100
Ireland	1973	—	—	—	—	—
	1974	14.3	—	14.3	71.4	100
	1975	33.3	11.1	11.1	44.4	100
	1976	25.0	10.0	10.0	55.0	100
Denmark	1973	—	—	—	—	—
	1974	37.5	—	41.7	20.8	100
	1975	23.8	6.3	42.9	27.0	100
	1976	28.4	5.4	25.7	40.5	100
EC total[a]	1973	29.9	—	14.2	35.9	100
	1974	28.3	—	25.8	45.9	100
	1975	15.9	5.8	29.3	49.0	100
	1976	14.5	4.1	32.5	48.9	100

[a] Slight discrepancies due to rounding errors.
Source: Own calculations based on SOEC and German Federal Ministry of Economic Affairs data.

Table A5. *Dutiable Non-GSP Goods of Chapters 25-99 by CCT Sections, 1976*[a]
(in Million UA)

CCT section		Imports	Percentage share
V.	Mineral products	107	17.7
VI.	Chemical products	41	6.8
VIII.	Hides, furskins and articles thereof	148	24.5
IX.	Wood, cork and articles thereof	1	0.2
XI.	Textiles and textile articles	81	13.4
XV.	Base metals	225	37.3
		603	100[b]

[a] Excluding developing countries with special preferences.
[b] Slight discrepancies due to rounding errors.
Source: Own calculations based on SOEC and German Federal Ministry of Economic Affairs data.

Part 1. Descriptions of Chapters

CCT chapter	Description
02	Meat and edible meat offals
03	Fish, crustaceans and molluscs
04	Dairy produce, birds' eggs, natural honey, edible products of animal origin, not elsewhere specified or included
05	Products of animal origin, not elsewhere specified or included
07	Edible vegetables and certain roots and tubers
08	Edible fruit and nuts; peel of melons or citrus fruit
09	Coffee, tea, maté and spices
11	Products of the milling industry; malt and starches; gluten; inulin
12	Oil seeds and oleaginous fruit; miscellaneous grains, seeds and fruit; industrial and medical plants; straw and fodder
13	Raw vegetable materials of a kind suitable for use in dyeing or in tanning; lacs; gums, resins and other vegetable saps and extracts
14	Vegetable plaiting and carving materials; vegetable products not elsewhere specified or included
15	Animal and vegetable fats and oils and their cleavage products; prepared edible fats; animal and vegetable waxes
16	Preparations of meat, of fish, of crustaceans or molluscs
17	Sugars and sugar confectionery
18	Cocoa and cocoa preparations
19	Preparations of cereals, flour or starch; pastry-cooks' products
20	Preparations of vegetables, fruit or other parts of plants
21	Miscellaneous edible preparations
22	Beverages, spirits and vinegar
23	Residues and waste from the food industries; prepared animal fodder
24	Tobacco
25	Salt; sulphur; earths and stone; plastering materials, lime and cement
27	Mineral fuels, mineral oils and products of their distillation; bituminous substances; mineral waxes

CCT chapter	Description
28	Inorganic chemicals; organic and inorganic compounds of precious metals, or rare earth metals, of radio-active elements and of isotopes
29	Organic chemicals
30	Pharmaceutical products
31	Fertilisers
32	Tanning and dyeing extracts; tannins and their derivatives; dyes, colours, paints and varnishes; putty, fillers and stopping; inks
33	Essential oils and resinoids; perfumery, cosmetics and toilet preparations
34	Soap, organic surface-active agents, washing preparations, lubricating preparations, artificial waxes, prepared waxes, polishing and scouring preparations, candles and similar articles, modelling pastes and "dental waxes"
35	Albuminoidal substances; glues
36	Explosives; Pyrotechnic products; matches; pyrophoric alloys; certain combustible preparations
37	Photographic and cinematographic goods
38	Miscellaneous chemical products
39	Artificial resins and plastic materials, cellulose esters and ethers; articles thereof
40	Rubber, synthetic rubber, factice, and articles thereof
41	Raw hides and skins (other than fur skins) and leather
42	Articles of leather; saddlery and harness; travel goods, handbags and similar containers; articles of animal gut (other than silk-worm gut)
43	Furskins and artificial fur; manufactures thereof
44	Wood and articles of wood; wood charcoal;
45	Cork and articles of cork
46	Manufactures of straw, of esparto and of other plaiting materials; basketware and wickerwork
47	Paper-making material
48	Paper and paperboard; articles of paper pulp, of paper or of paperboard
49	Printed books, newspapers, pictures and other products of the printing industry; manuscripts, type-scripts and plans
50	Silk and waste silk
51	Man-made fibres (continuous)
52	Metallised textiles

CCT chapter	Description
53	Wool and other animal hair
54	Flax and ramie
55	Cotton
56	Man-made fibres (discontinuous)
57	Other vegetable textile materials; paper yarn and woven fabrics of paper yarn
58	Carpets, mats, matting and tapestries; pile and chenille fabrics; narrow fabrics; trimmings; tulle and other net fabrics; lace; embroidery
59	Wadding and felt; twine, cordage, ropes and cables; special fabrics; impregnated and coated fabrics; textile articles of a kind suitable for industrial use
60	Knitted and crocheted goods
61	Articles of apparel and clothing accessories of textile fabric, other than knitted or crocheted goods
62	Other made up textile articles
63	Old clothing and other textile articles; rags
64	Footwear, gaiters and the like; parts of such articles
65	Headgear and parts thereof
66	Umbrellas, sunshades, walking-sticks, whips, riding-crops and parts thereof
67	Prepared feathers and down and articles made of feathers or of down; artificial flowers; articles of human hair; fans
68	Articles of stone, of plaster, of cement, of asbestos, of mica and of similar materials
69	Ceramic products
70	Glass and glassware
71	Pearls, precious and semi-precious stones, precious metals, rolled precious metals, and articles thereof; imitation jewellery;
73	Iron and steel and articles thereof
74	Copper and articles thereof
75	Nickel and articles thereof
76	Aluminium and articles thereof
78	Lead and articles thereof
79	Zinc and articles thereof
80	Tin and articles thereof
81	Other base metals employed in metallurgy and articles thereof
82	Tools, implements, cutlery, spoons and forks, of base metal; parts thereof

CCT chapter	Description
83	Miscellaneous articles of base metal
84	Boilers, machinery and mechanical appliances; parts thereof
85	Electrical machinery and equipment; parts thereof
86	Railway and tramway locomotives, rolling-stock and parts thereof; railway and tramway track fixtures and fittings; traffic signalling equipment of all kinds (not electrically powered)
87	Vehicles, other than railway or tramway rolling-stock, and parts thereof
88	Aircraft and parts thereof; parachutes; catapults and similar aircraft launching gear; ground flying trainers
89	Ships, boats and floating structures
90	Optical, photographic, cinematographic, measuring, checking, precision, medical and surgical instruments and apparatus; parts thereof
91	Clocks and watches and parts thereof
92	Musical instruments; sound recorders and reproducers; television image and sound recorders and reproducers, magnetic; parts and accessories of such articles
93	Arms and ammunition; parts thereof
94	Furniture and parts thereof; bedding, mattresses, mattress supports, cushions and similar stuffed furnishings
95	Articles and manufactures of carving or moulding material
96	Brooms, brushes, feather dusters, powder-puffs and sieves
97	Toys, games and sports requisites; parts thereof
98	Miscellaneous manufactured articles
99	Works of art, collectors' pieces, and antiques

Table A6. Part 2. *Imports by Chapters*

CCT chapter	GSP Imports Total EC			
	1973	1974	1975	1976
02	13,135,323	8,213,373	12,250,856	20,933,529
03	—	106,096	4,316,146	10,308,843
04	—	—	12,152,964	19,171,161
05	—	302,299	34,211	59,824
07	3,110,698	6,581,791	8,102,392	6,117,608
08	380,685	22,426,999	22,885,372	26,461,997
09	—	1,803,391	6,153,837	34,326,848
11	126,726	171,664	158,487	244,027
12	589,162	3,415,478	1,647,384	1,656,559
13	327,376	1,730,488	2,688,159	3,551,166
14	—	—	0,858	31,984
15	769,126	15,799,737	20,098,676	207,740,688
16	6,018,487	33,050,653	31,515,785	48,491,162
17	88,197	512,131	493,000	1,048,422
18	—	19,087,920	2,798,986	4,734,517
19	441,788	1,284,490	2,206,110	3,713,292
20	3,514,598	19,968,895	9,194,270	39,451,965
21	1,159,552	48,111,190	97,641,293	184,167,216
22	89,140	263,566	275,106	511,829
23	—	53,091,726	41,623,018	50,079,352
24	—	29,484,677	18,515,666	68,668,285
25	851,691	3,119,955	493,233	1,419,300
27	15,415,961	191,473,122	227,253,378	569,066,436
28	7,143,687	31,277,589	20,321,921	29,281,416
29	22,592,012	63,124,180	76,120,166	79,378,256
30	4,705,903	9,410,004	7,262,228	6,642,536
31	151,404	648,553	508,257	3,862,260
32	293,927	510,089	2,236,043	4,139,521
33	3,073,405	11,277,692	4,744,834	7,648,881
34	4,218,565	6,878,112	5,315,162	6,983,715
35	313,300	672,714	1,230,549	1,421,385
36	1,709,206	1,551,247	847,173	1,229,620
37	314,822	1,026,743	1,859,750	722,575
38	4,713,715	5,769,362	8,300,384	4,945,336
39	10,309,877	38,692,976	28,812,211	44,061,475
40	5,736,740	14,243,545	15,816,479	24,590,290
41	8,924,104	25,910,772	25,563,735	38,129,075
42	6,542,210	25,633,157	30,248,320	40,366,529
43	25,538,875	32,368,070	33,264,872	59,601,739
44	37,041,286	110,595,058	57,498,710	79,815,574

CCT chapter	GSP Imports Total EC			
	1973	1974	1975	1976
45	546,634	968,079	937,766	1,732,146
46	3,432,284	11,189,885	7,364,722	18,647,779
47	5,132,372	1,706,353	2,965,785	349,572
48	10,466,481	26,347,108	25,013,759	38,344,666
49	934,073	1,995,797	804,238	1,081,943
50	1,928,320	4,161,408	3,483,544	7,721,605
51	569,004	1,512,753	2,669,924	3,816,243
52	—	—	20,958	2,556
53	2,537,998	2,088,994	4,991,796	8,468,201
54	317,252	343,803	606,496	1,040,664
55	13,924,526	33,112,628	32,009,543	41,701,765
56	3,432,280	7,503,082	36,174,067	8,748,631
57	302,139	3,581,093	15,558,534	7,601,510
58	56,636,807	103,335,475	117,126,635	172,926,249
59	2,027,114	5,958,132	3,804,607	4,717,861
60	7,865,612	18,486,032	19,972,337	21,529,437
61	22,170,421	23,578,697	30,602,399	33,214,964
62	878,546	6,870,435	6,308,132	13,994,399
63	39,604	—	2,435	7,419
64	7,602,707	80,509,548	26,570,895	32,783,330
65	899,887	3,741,268	3,174,759	6,677,582
66	1,739,130	4,404,517	4,050,418	6,491,027
67	5,189,994	13,046,655	13,031,686	16,091,546
68	4,003,219	7,575,159	6,905,061	8,162,517
69	3,024,206	6,271,711	6,296,837	11,066,168
70	3,876,833	6,936,032	6,343,452	10,289,644
71	3,146,881	11,136,519	9,766,599	17,092,087
73	37,521,562	65,194,359	53,362,516	102,475,806
74	5,178,005	9,506,324	9,735,246	18,058,677
75	4,722	831,665	1,898,670	1,390,866
76	2,848,187	9,510,750	7,982,049	17,067,131
78	424,122	636,498	206,248	422,732
79	1,117,903	943,634	1,015,186	1,147,863
80	180,335	435,440	389,116	393,322
81	7,121	—	60,216	551,835
82	9,963,248	26,993,822	23,957,456	37,575,650
83	6,824,118	15,480,523	13,432,759	18,574,557
84	51,428,981	123,397,965	111,200,684	162,778,207
85	50,375,773	100,051,016	89,466,643	140,219,155
86	10,671,720	887,745	466,560	90,063

Table A6 (continued)

CCT chapter	GSP Imports Total EC			
	1973	1974	1975	1976
87	32,142,354	47,289,850	60,015,803	76,073,123
88	1,623	4,322	733,104	236,812
89	2,449,266	2,325,049	708,835	736,260
90	17,234,986	30,263,957	35,725,852	50,402,460
91	412,510	4,761,066	11,609,414	43,487,213
92	3,121,713	6,736,350	11,032,061	26,594,522
93	531,508	637,018	584,482	633,152
94	10,065,452	19,692,005	16,591,320	22,846,282
95	2,245,703	5,128,121	5,843,758	9,265,371
96	547,319	2,275,772	1,950,633	2,929,162
97	13,184,313	47,074,183	38,189,714	65,419,166
98	1,669,924	7,147,912	4,634,952	7,336,991
99	—	55,254	144,442	67,790
Total	612,118,340	1,753,211,265	1,729,945,084	3,035,851,869

Note:

EC-countries: France
Benelux
Federal Republic of Germany
Italy
United Kingdom
Ireland
Denmark

CCT chapters: For description see Table A6, part 1.

CCT chapter	GSP-Imports France			
	1973	1974	1975	1976
02	5,813,818	2,317,453	3,762,141	8,426,489
03	—	19,945	2,047,730	2,795,682
04	—	—	369,422	362,349
05	—	19,163	—	6,794
07	968,268	2,019,038	3,197,530	3,368,436
08	149,303	2,208,913	2,596,527	3,165,967
09	—	710,025	2,849,876	8,696,250
11	59,978	13,846	6,888	—
12	211,402	342,909	713,750	765,141
13	160,110	530,969	550,048	742,462
15	114,398	866,258	1,165,478	2,761,551
16	2,156,518	5,376,319	6,227,902	13,878,941
17	14,644	47,754	4,079	38,926
19	96,817	161,622	198,455	524,851
20	1,053,956	2,598,615	401,323	484,235
21	635,774	6,665,913	6,750,353	13,206,067
22	75,077	58,324	72,990	129,072
23	—	3,579,085	2,080,561	2,695
24	—	1,565,130	2,069,552	4,597,609
27	1,843,723	495,854	14,970	31,008,955
28	583,894	9,014,742	163,654	413,193
29	4,196,381	7,205,071	6,720,053	8,511,149
30	168,447	565,837	176,108	127,088
31	—	—	—	601,690
32	4,496	12,216	2,071	316,252
33	2,137,303	4,941,177	1,011,162	1,689,910

Table A7 (continued)

CCT chapter	GSP-Imports France			
	1973	1974	1975	1976
34	1,032,998	1,327,216	705,850	994,946
35	15,010	90,458	278,456	134,117
36	19,069	38,089	46,916	265,388
37	27,589	136,684	121,141	138,094
38	469,646	1,260,126	967,490	360,989
39	2,527,541	4,676,388	3,042,595	3,793,833
40	235,639	442,490	693,289	341,322
41	1,464,202	3,227,987	3,908,693	4,591,121
42	970,339	3,493,101	3,375,753	4,077,421
43	3,045,465	4,373,143	2,049,784	5,060,519
44	2,892,159	4,449,930	1,449,935	2,722,446
45	15,681	40,829	75,513	90,932
46	565,465	1,905,047	1,041,561	2,957,860
47	80,839	112,497	—	—
48	977,144	2,417,365	3,363,753	4,038,590
49	128,232	259,542	29,103	145,552
50	260,514	710,373	285,094	452,361
51	224,899	346,094	139,605	170,042
53	28,952	121,651	213,867	208,875
54	173,716	182,503	263,882	55,826
55	3,645,884	6,127,439	5,041,453	6,806,926
56	1,330,774	1,102,967	224,860	810,880
57	—	97,156	7,519	383,370
58	6,693,928	15,766,809	9,331,475	16,732,474
59	401,119	690,062	497,614	1,005,217
60	2,757,254	5,943,525	5,304,908	6,422,584
61	1,859,946	3,119,741	3,487,915	5,838,745
62	88,412	942,809	242,065	1,837,862
63	27,007	—	1,194	0,828
64	1,749,447	10,890,138	4,742,037	5,166,986
65	146,301	236,131	184,224	238,591
66	377,029	881,964	476,165	934,089
67	958,519	996,005	752,014	807,701
68	496,801	806,027	441,772	803,059
69	239,042	699,016	287,578	982,603
70	253,350	525,910	225,831	472,349
71	1,005,487	2,422,094	1,699,950	2,265,464
73	1,606,104	3,307,162	2,319,241	6,510,535
74	2,009,068	2,836,596	1,610,917	1,195,053
75	0,775	8,331	4,092	2,457
76	247,691	405,685	249,764	339,722

Table A7 (continued)

CCT chapter	GSP-Imports France			
	1973	1974	1975	1976
78	—	—	5,949	13,463
79	41,549	—	3,329	—
80	60,483	72,404	2,893	30,958
81	—	—	—	0,449
82	1,345,867	2,806,094	2,499,574	5,536,001
83	843,779	1,056,917	836,940	1,089,748
84	11,986,751	24,098,210	8,776,843	12,765,985
85	6,542,377	11,409,549	8,585,664	12,998,053
86	197,809	50,401	61,069	79,734
87	9,005,483	15,929,622	11,409,862	11,625,036
88	—	—	730,250	233,481
89	404,295	187,094	52,261	28,362
90	2,429,789	2,555,513	2,548,555	3,758,594
91	27,574	215,079	381,219	3,710,624
92	563,239	1,313,394	900,775	1,920,906
93	54,753	227,713	84,555	16,261
94	1,102,003	2,731,233	1,842,412	2,457,967
95	1,298,099	2,953,689	3,217,766	5,063,486
96	152,694	159,663	150,354	210,828
97	2,117,427	2,988,260	2,947,879	6,388,936
98	320,811	997,699	431,733	719,083
99	—	5,776	122,526	63,871
Total	100,008,127	208,511,577	147,929,899	265,482,309

Table A7 (continued)

CCT chapter	GSP-Imports Benelux			
	1973	1974	1975	1976
02	1,027,301	781,022	1,474,653	3,381,491
03	—	8,507	863,975	2,990,098
04	—	—	457,908	1,874,710
05	—	31,805	10,836	3,882
07	106,494	411,728	94,759	581,538
08	54,287	2,866,786	2,842,624	4,277,122
09	—	110,278	967,467	4,510,965
11	—	40,177	14,226	3,089
12	46,587	232,777	151,727	99,163
13	59,718	167,314	28,265	180,988
15	527,486	1,419,186	3,172,716	39,677,163
16	2,177,450	5,177,233	5,404,853	6,294,635
17	22,006	160,566	62,838	120,305
18	—	84,163	—	—
19	326,190	192,379	524,100	1,228,571
20	573,160	1,380,817	900,111	2,897,673
21	236,564	4,447,482	1,724,118	2,673,750
22	—	3,084	—	0,961
23	—	4,329,549	1,271,442	1,386,243
24	—	1,704,174	4,438,107	4,830,694
25	—	—	0,404	—
27	1,543,520	14,424,734	31,158,234	96,800,941
28	1,321,530	1,558,640	3,548,790	2,728,738
29	6,038,993	9,522,274	28,191,285	27,911,187
30	509,689	2,610,290	310,025	602,995
31	19,025	26,226	61,154	213,576
32	129,737	148,774	557,040	1,261,949
33	149,231	866,290	200,837	298,425
34	1,451,402	2,080,247	1,596,735	1,661,801
35	23,559	17,987	120,600	130,091
36	1,483	5,839	11,716	15,946
37	33,268	82,316	1,262,938	42,670
38	960,459	1,114,413	900,500	440,454
39	2,257,675	4,686,834	4,503,390	7,969,868
40	235,444	981,553	337,692	1,250,156
41	1,457,228	2,339,037	2,768,373	3,029,181
42	1,554,968	3,220,252	3,221,329	4,864,757
43	866,969	2,318,731	2,232,380	3,704,743
44	6,543,579	11,465,249	5,812,403	6,253,532
45	75,946	199,330	96,725	97,685

Table A7 (continued)

CCT chapter	GSP-Imports Benelux			
	1973	1974	1975	1976
46	565,778	1,199,584	247,667	1,792,565
47	—	47,307	—	—
48	1,912,270	3,916,690	5,146,203	5,978,982
49	144,656	366,995	126,456	190,627
50	65,745	211,710	63,892	205,592
51	104,555	101,538	94,835	153,532
52	—	—	4,965	—
53	81,215	28,046	21,922	128,421
54	2,254	19,195	18,672	96,761
55	2,065,287	3,401,760	2,515,962	3,121,729
56	189,193	298,282	230,069	325,067
57	—	362,863	—	4,616,196
58	9,250,894	13,271,847	10,705,459	13,887,889
59	108,492	561,167	576,000	695,444
60	2,194,054	3,032,842	2,943,954	3,098,080
61	8,094,358	1,966,783	2,757,281	2,924,342
62	183,178	1,967,818	791,020	3,241,286
63	1,149	—	0,445	—
64	1,533,249	11,333,251	3,718,830	5,013,813
65	165,365	208,334	245,267	387,921
66	224,419	575,675	15,957	539,841
67	950,088	1,428,133	431,201	1,696,281
68	142,448	257,760	397,161	266,976
69	196,364	526,171	730,574	1,757,862
70	427,081	492,309	1,001,583	1,512,976
71	346,537	901,163	266,396	1,261,366
73	5,039,548	5,184,293	2,343,204	5,650,264
74	301,820	727,818	765,964	1,432,662
75	1,616	25,868	6,679	2,674
76	252,108	200,594	277,561	1,615,077
79	0,782	0,893	0,087	3,426
80	3,624	9,348	8,864	2,626
81	1,657	—	—	—
82	1,991,564	3,277,951	2,868,639	3,462,275
83	1,594,876	2,115,513	1,826,096	2,191,326
84	4,369,414	9,145,759	5,173,370	9,719,837
85	9,535,397	14,212,322	11,269,705	14,959,603
86	586,164	—	330,741	—
87	3,319,202	4,085,977	5,941,677	7,970,493
88	—	—	1,406	—

Table A7 (continued)

CCT chapter	GSP-Imports Benelux			
	1973	1974	1975	1976
89	191,255	88,904	284,344	302,042
90	1,280,864	2,663,185	1,428,307	2,375,391
91	70,437	357,153	713,935	3,304,598
92	574,227	639,921	448,593	5,034,715
93	6,486	13,961	88,059	184,207
94	1,965,030	2,683,625	2,704,053	3,390,284
95	258,506	268,301	466,690	896,445
96	95,972	248,092	93,245	228,561
97	2,585,361	4,678,815	1,275,556	5,792,321
98	401,148	762,955	401,383	721,101
99	—	3,299	—	—
Total	93,706,635	179,089,813	183,067,204	358,425,213

CCT chapter	GSP-Imports Federal Republic of Germany			
	1973	1974	1975	1976
02	5,596,429	3,822,411	6,647,191	8,747,254
03	—	4,215	243,513	1,231,569
04	—	—	11,141,567	14,044,550
05	—	76,634	22,645	44,704
07	670,583	635,451	416,752	36,917
08	142,293	4,121,803	4,176,885	4,022,078
09	—	480,139	1,646,862	10,879,970
11	66,748	92,311	120,134	210,744
12	33,247	621,474	319,070	409,170
13	105,843	407,912	626,340	632,165
14	—	—	0,858	31,984
15	85,357	5,687,845	6,443,749	36,635,510
16	1,671,965	4,143,990	5,162,162	5,930,699
17	51,547	97,901	257,219	395,497
18	—	—	178,202	61,857
19	18,781	106,099	112,634	119,276
20	1,597,273	2,945,400	4,665,855	10,525,686
21	256,867	2,682,500	1,787,210	6,710,911
22	0,273	73,976	139,922	236,138
23	—	34,624,266	29,630,436	26,457,131
24	—	2,057,020	3,658,619	6,611,508
25	104,641	188,919	224,490	831,023
27	8,788,366	97,594,002	40,685,439	86,132,594
28	1,960,225	1,253,803	3,084,914	7,435,292
29	8,762,029	16,353,669	18,751,900	18,029,114
30	1,071,147	1,373,606	2,128,707	4,109,240
31	122,970	—	—	665,537
32	89,530	10,375	677,785	418,184
33	745,790	1,258,342	585,152	688,463
34	1,551,385	1,706,012	1,610,600	1,935,567
35	232,379	229,818	400,706	228,311
36	1,260,282	1,122,908	639,358	651,470
37	229,389	159,299	227,885	278,430
38	2,582,936	892,578	2,553,567	2,089,602
39	3,639,162	4,861,370	6,448,087	8,025,169
40	3,801,510	5,990,476	7,937,867	10,694,095
41	4,255,011	6,664,123	6,713,689	11,072,877
42	3,397,368	7,995,943	13,057,341	16,775,902
43	16,955,955	15,861,149	24,453,038	43,146,848
44	21,227,214	20,884,767	19,099,410	21,134,063

Table A7 (continued)

CCT chapter	GSP-Imports Federal Republic of Germany			
	1973	1974	1975	1976
45	415,470	514,639	646,450	1,161,425
46	1,692,118	4,690,552	3,510,744	8,087,474
47	121,585	378,406	684,922	—
48	2,496,653	4,941,261	5,949,330	12,724,388
49	569,211	683,843	414,173	408,121
50	1,355,493	1,820,028	1,592,237	2,457,171
51	216,877	158,275	334,958	473,988
53	1,109,759	814,289	1,776,730	4,836,708
54	78,586	16,267	112,667	281,254
55	4,514,188	6,895,594	5,099,237	7,579,409
56	1,382,878	1,985,250	808,233	897,684
57	247,987	399,256	585,343	938,367
58	28,576,654	39,926,439	74,320,278	86,818,346
59	895,668	1,739,435	1,345,055	1,317,042
60	2,246,798	3,360,378	4,538,064	10,602,725
61	11,351,317	6,238,055	7,008,617	9,726,395
62	398,138	1,699,334	1,965,487	3,096,880
63	0,273	—	0,444	—
64	4,038,183	22,738,204	8,649,956	8,899,322
65	546,612	806,305	930,291	2,085,666
66	689,027	937,760	1,273,332	1,706,387
67	2,911,141	4,697,982	5,711,278	5,727,577
68	2,089,244	3,024,285	3,119,238	4,227,270
69	2,405,443	3,745,104	3,970,319	5,136,340
70	1,817,702	2,999,241	3,161,587	4,189,956
71	1,386,033	2,608,532	3,021,844	5,358,758
73	15,620,956	16,396,190	15,730,007	36,155,472
74	2,440,426	2,896,850	3,448,631	5,204,056
75	2,331	11,006	19,082	10,801
76	2,048,635	3,250,234	3,176,883	6,234,003
78	218,543	289,205	59,086	188,230
79	1,027,880	898,436	858,112	889,209
80	115,515	284,680	352,808	344,621
81	5,464	—	1,839	67,354
82	5,727,493	7,230,948	8,373,315	13,466,541
83	3,560,225	4,957,310	5,561,218	7,209,499
84	29,866,245	51,942,566	75,059,088	95,545,511
85	19,279,350	31,002,897	36,483,468	54,070,179
86	9,542,211	116,458	22,912	10,329
87	17,462,942	19,968,881	32,982,507	42,522,963

Table A7 (continued)

CCT chapter	GSP-Imports Federal Republic of Germany			
	1973	1974	1975	1976
88	1,619	1,759	1,050	1,137
89	1,593,814	532,119	63,713	58,976
90	10,959,583	14,326,534	21,575,136	26,677,749
91	203,024	1,151,718	3,937,692	14,586,241
92	885,184	842,219	5,078,744	9,857,362
93	341,841	204,102	349,386	326,967
94	4,811,741	5,657,984	5,587,403	6,690,125
95	467,979	582,890	923,372	1,289,480
96	226,014	411,660	697,420	780,457
97	5,375,973	12,038,856	13,972,891	19,802,630
98	704,443	1,988,056	2,064,974	2,624,588
99	—	6,079	18,174	—
Total	297,116,964	541,890,857	603,607,485	901,670,232

CCT chapter	GSP-Imports Italy			
	1973	1974	1975	1976
02	697,775	1,157,919	306,528	305,878
03	—	5,016	1,052,506	2,225,138
04	—	—	28,409	113,419
05	—	34,058	—	—
07	1,365,353	3,439,873	4,393,037	877,431
08	34,802	88,666	20,000	191,918
09	—	79,997	70,748	1,974,922
11	—	8,951	4,619	7,142
12	297,926	1,632,108	415,386	199,850
13	1,705	67,720	81,305	6,224
15	41,885	1,374,994	633,396	9,496,604
16	12,554	285,335	218,740	227,310
19	—	27,104	3,336	—
20	290,209	780,675	271,556	788,869
21	30,347	126,666	77,766	94,859
22	13,790	65,824	61,125	95,734
23	—	9,325,708	5,281,145	9,436,480
24	—	60,000	2,855,095	6,806,400
25	747,050	2,931,036	266,768	587,713
27	3,240,352	62,772,758	131,426,775	217,153,316
28	3,278,038	11,998,605	3,142,349	10,051,330
29	3,594,609	11,108,781	4,337,837	5,938,668
30	2,956,620	4,086,507	4,085,293	660,502
31	9,409	401,700	268,000	268,000
32	70,164	271,559	445,170	889,153
33	41,081	349,092	94,285	173,705
34	182,780	262,872	70,936	398,159
35	42,352	40,779	0,512	122,171
36	428,372	384,411	146,176	277,352
37	24,576	57,931	5,670	50,496
38	700,674	2,190,080	535,945	394,466
39	1,885,499	4,064,380	1,781,184	3,926,559
40	1,464,147	2,510,307	1,097,151	2,537,935
41	1,747,663	6,394,455	4,921,945	10,411,690
42	619,535	2,323,694	1,728,860	2,152,362
43	4,670,486	7,070,922	1,597,987	1,563,408
44	6,378,334	11,690,815	6,130,568	17,570,303
45	39,537	—	86,189	231,679
46	608,923	2,421,704	1,825,841	4,360,143
47	4,929,948	1,013,347	2,219,218	343,430

Table A7 (continued)

CCT chapter	GSP-Imports Italy			
	1973	1974	1975	1976
48	5,060,414	11,626,080	3,981,423	7,566,995
49	91,974	86,729	18,264	4,730
50	246,568	1,235,195	1,126,092	3,724,683
51	22,673	394,469	611,149	840,032
53	1,318,072	858,018	1,489,209	292,451
54	62,696	123,275	167,322	606,533
55	3,699,167	6,580,135	5,702,810	11,103,478
56	529,435	1,882,824	32,385,626	1,635,439
57	54,152	389,064	607,199	1,050,978
58	12,115,331	15,050,815	8,327,542	16,903,789
59	621,835	1,201,666	66,881	437,673
60	667,506	2,017,595	973,365	3,035,014
61	864,799	3,939,682	3,068,977	3,590,215
62	208,818	1,652,493	726,344	1,926,679
63	11,175	—	—	—
64	281,828	886,925	630,429	1,041,203
65	41,609	223,610	108,900	128,329
66	448,655	914,164	497,960	742,875
67	370,246	1,023,084	595,838	996,488
68	1,274,726	1,857,797	1,071,963	1,427,302
69	183,357	541,355	327,860	1,390,919
70	1,378,700	1,617,723	827,592	2,886,734
71	408,824	1,993,083	801,292	1,497,062
73	15,254,954	19,718,631	10,721,708	20,060,301
74	426,691	208,832	271,822	1,901,291
75	—	4,293	—	0,232
76	299,753	565,388	283,667	521,528
78	205,579	347,293	139,699	221,039
79	47,692	—	—	14,160
80	0,713	46,843	14,230	—
81	—	—	29,278	—
82	898,324	1,811,737	692,320	3,068,388
83	825,238	1,354,712	587,905	1,092,494
84	5,206,571	11,073,096	3,708,595	7,353,769
85	15,018,649	21,719,473	13,021,776	25,642,592
86	345,536	52,119	—	—
87	2,354,727	3,948,804	1,504,854	3,744,301
88	0,004	—	—	—
89	259,902	1,256,105	36,389	56,945
90	2,564,750	3,028,623	1,188,512	3,842,661

Table A7 (continued)

CCT chapter	GSP-Imports Italy			
	1973	1974	1975	1976
91	111,475	333,461	194,492	1,394,367
92	1,099,063	562,211	157,183	735,082
93	128,428	157,242	55,240	41,044
94	2,186,678	3,136,431	1,870,805	2,881,656
95	221,119	625,208	216,196	566,479
96	72,639	332,031	119,942	60,289
97	3,105,552	7,173,025	4,983,369	10,250,567
98	243,522	457,113	58,479	340,003
99	—	4,826	—	—
Total	121,286,614	286,919,627	285,959,854	459,529,507

Table A7 (continued)

CCT chapter	GSP-Imports United Kingdom			
	1973	1974	1975	1976
02	—	134,568	60,343	72,417
03	—	65,742	107,909	1,051,256
04	—	—	—	2,605,991
05	—	105,159	0,719	2,705
07	—	—	0,314	1,253,286
08	—	11,727,369	12,373,822	14,005,911
09	—	357,826	426,203	7,376,840
11	—	16,379	12,620	23,052
12	—	391,298	47,451	107,196
13	—	361,836	1,081,407	1,500,109
15	—	6,316,072	8,679,484	114,008,799
16	—	16,805,501	13,178,261	20,470,185
17	—	179,092	167,279	493,694
18	—	19,003,757	2,620,784	4,672,660
19	—	746,338	1,350,401	1,747,885
20	—	11,968,449	2,887,589	24,013,352
21	—	34,096,922	87,248,545	161,368,872
22	—	62,358	1,069	49,924
23	—	1,224,460	1,730,860	10,362,195
24	—	23,167,466	1,885,553	40,000,896
25	—	—	1,571	0,564
27	—	1,300,015	11,868,452	136,128,428
28	—	980,717	2,946,202	5,477,069
29	—	14,331,121	17,212,269	18,117,748
30	—	640,891	502,532	1,070,268
31	—	220,627	179,103	1,506,697
32	—	51,214	471,145	1,156,795
33	—	3,674,705	2,587,880	4,375,960
34	—	1,339,765	1,250,254	1,935,172
35	—	293,672	428,634	806,695
36	—	—	—	5,760
37	—	585,269	228,709	199,087
38	—	77,409	3,279,918	1,655,493
39	—	18,412,613	11,548,400	18,041,924
40	—	3,842,584	5,009,931	8,965,959
41	—	5,894,789	6,121,514	7,847,832
42	—	6,897,162	7,102,901	9,757,903
43	—	2,143,316	2,765,567	5,318,895
44	—	57,293,992	22,435,067	27,430,075
45	—	16,292	21,164	103,123

Table A7 (continued)

CCT chapter	GSP-Imports United Kingdom			
	1973	1974	1975	1976
46	—	682,869	632,090	1,175,845
47	—	152,474	61,645	6,142
48	—	3,253,556	6,088,414	7,490,834
49	—	560,960	190,357	278,631
50	—	105,439	322,936	802,753
51	—	481,820	1,466,530	2,089,361
52	—	—	15,993	2,556
53	—	251,748	1,453,902	2,868,036
54	—	2,563	43,953	0,290
55	—	4,827,676	7,241,549	4,872,093
56	—	749,254	1,682,208	2,902,408
57	—	2,179,817	13,974,076	19,908
58	—	12,136,159	7,487,919	26,855,794
59	—	1,237,779	1,058,342	959,425
60	—	3,160,384	5,373,132	3,608,354
61	—	5,754,436	13,173,591	8,992,299
62	—	355,648	1,879,013	3,345,915
63	—	—	0,352	6,591
64	—	28,101,976	6,736,650	9,629,437
65	—	1,944,832	1,421,063	3,258,957
66	—	990,920	1,720,051	2,449,227
67	—	4,563,194	5,072,305	6,165,068
68	—	1,569,503	1,811,917	1,395,097
69	—	523,759	811,523	1,569,625
70	—	1,069,149	912,155	966,342
71	—	3,067,731	3,839,668	6,459,392
73	—	19,195,475	21,311,500	30,962,418
74	—	2,641,093	3,502,572	8,039,708
75	—	609,305	1,821,233	1,337,774
76	—	4,929,552	3,783,948	7,817,210
78	—	—	1,514	—
79	—	27,716	152,891	236,769
80	—	20,177	5,904	11,174
81	—	—	29,099	484,032
82	—	10,870,165	8,676,679	10,834,578
83	—	4,649,719	3,702,785	5,690,811
84	—	23,260,708	15,879,526	33,118,114
85	—	20,213,390	19,035,618	30,731,153
86	—	668,767	51,838	—
87	—	2,272,459	4,668,168	7,234,685

Table A7 (continued)

CCT chapter	GSP-Imports United Kingdom			
	1973	1974	1975	1976
88	—	2,563	0,398	2,194
89	—	244,288	263,573	275,908
90	—	7,031,270	8,578,779	12,915,091
91	—	2,647,974	6,264,108	19,354,466
92	—	3,258,400	4,377,324	8,553,871
93	—	20,467	2,466	20,323
94	—	4,393,903	3,815,341	5,957,219
95	—	651,034	997,252	1,272,157
96	—	1,083,694	847,980	1,540,425
97	—	17,468,762	13,501,858	20,401,295
98	—	2,690,961	1,566,661	2,726,925
99	—	34,611	1,531	0,646
Total	—	451,336,844	437,133,706	955,561,290

Table A7 (continued)

CCT chapter	GSP-Imports Ireland			
	1973	1974	1975	1976
03	—	1,386	—	—
07	—	55,243	—	—
08	—	533,921	350,663	296,683
09	—	26,620	1,591	80,861
13	—	55,685	—	—
15	—	1,462	—	2,154,966
16	—	33,188	0,982	—
17	—	0,891	—	—
19	—	46,063	17,184	90,417
20	—	122,905	11,675	89,884
21	—	13,319	4,438	36,963
24	—	261,818	2,634,666	3,366,683
27	—	1,232,125	—	—
28	—	31,082	0,122	—
29	—	3,088,520	10,049	10,471
30	—	1,994	—	—
31	—	—	—	606,760
32	—	6,215	—	—
33	—	167,945	244,164	380,237
34	—	72,963	21,306	8,343
37	—	0,894	—	—
38	—	225,561	49,740	—
39	—	584,426	192,828	563,026
40	—	92,203	395,853	306,805
41	—	155,505	167,708	142,139
42	—	105,354	167,348	155,179
43	—	4,225	—	0,878
44	—	811,810	115,712	104,223
46	—	7,690	2,611	13,132
47	—	2,322	—	—
48	—	147,271	144,385	234,505
49	—	16,156	4,340	1,732
51	—	7,129	—	25,569
55	—	—	—	403,371
56	—	—	—	47,115
57	—	97,667	35,736	163,798
58	—	214,718	0,685	37,674
59	—	46,137	0,749	0,903
60	—	28,442	102,330	487,494
61	—	27,363	155,020	560,382

CCT chapter	GSP-Imports Ireland			
	1973	1974	1975	1976
62	—	2,563	5,216	22,129
64	—	110,757	27,610	312,816
65	—	19,013	24,914	93,463
66	—	—	8,818	69,770
67	—	130,293	121,854	172,340
68	—	8,023	—	0,375
69	—	1,622	—	13,520
70	—	49,388	5,754	6,796
71	—	39,364	6,808	15,673
73	—	810,336	423,143	2,455,140
74	—	30,614	22,214	70,179
75	—	172,862	47,584	36,928
76	—	15,749	54,477	191,425
82	—	143,757	200,835	467,199
83	—	242,352	55,164	168,323
84	—	1,769,769	1,282,311	2,415,656
85	—	811,280	374,174	738,856
87	—	399,568	881,474	899,367
90	—	136,859	92,554	277,724
91	—	46,755	98,536	132,044
92	—	26,871	11,861	182,360
94	—	21,182	16,443	18,158
95	—	4,650	0,336	10,591
96	—	9,544	29,023	77,351
97	—	735,943	483,360	969,974
98	—	132,918	26,412	54,243
99	—	0,186	—	—
Total	—	14,200,436	9,132,760	20,242,593

Table A7 (continued)

CCT chapter	GSP-Imports Denmark			
	1973	1974	1975	1976
03	—	1,285	0,513	15,100
04	—	—	155,658	170,142
05	—	35,480	0,011	1,739
07	—	20,458	—	—
08	—	879,541	524,851	502,318
09	—	38,506	191,090	807,040
12	—	194,912	—	76,039
13	—	139,052	320,794	489,218
15	—	133,920	3,853	3,006,095
16	—	1,229,087	1,322,885	1,689,392
17	—	25,927	1,585	—
19	—	4,885	—	2,292
20	—	172,034	56,161	652,266
21	—	78,388	48,863	75,794
23	—	8,658	1,628,574	2,434,608
24	—	669,069	974,074	2,454,495
27	—	13,653,634	12,099,508	1,842,202
28	—	6,440,000	7,435,890	3,175,794
29	—	1,514,744	896,773	859,919
30	—	130,879	59,563	72,443
32	—	9,736	82,832	97,188
33	—	20,141	21,354	42,181
34	—	89,037	59,481	49,727
35	—	—	1,641	—
36	—	—	3,007	13,704
37	—	4,350	13,407	13,798
38	—	9,195	13,224	4,332
39	—	1,406,965	1,295,727	1,741,096
40	—	383,932	344,696	494,018
41	—	1,234,876	961,813	1,034,235
42	—	1,597,651	1,594,788	2,583,005
43	—	596,584	166,116	806,448
44	—	3,998,495	2,455,615	4,600,932
45	—	196,989	11,725	47,302
46	—	282,439	104,208	260,760
48	—	44,885	340,251	310,372
49	—	21,572	21,545	52,550
50	—	78,663	93,293	79,045
51	—	23,428	22,847	63,719
53	—	15,242	36,166	133,710

CCT chapter	GSP-Imports Denmark			
	1973	1974	1975	1976
55	—	5,280,024	6,408,532	7,814,759
56	—	1,484,496	843,071	2,130,038
57	—	55,270	348,661	428,893
58	—	6,968,688	6,953,277	11,690,283
59	—	481,886	259,966	302,157
60	—	942,866	736,584	1,491,894
61	—	2,532,637	950,998	1,582,586
62	—	249,770	698,987	523,648
64	—	6,448,297	2,065,383	2,719,753
65	—	303,043	260,100	484,655
66	—	104,034	58,135	48,838
67	—	207,964	347,196	526,091
68	—	51,764	63,010	42,438
69	—	234,684	168,983	215,299
70	—	182,312	208,950	254,491
71	—	104,552	130,641	234,372
73	—	582,272	513,713	681,676
74	—	164,521	113,126	215,728
76	—	143,548	155,749	348,166
79	—	16,589	0,767	4,299
80	—	1,988	4,417	3,943
82	—	853,170	646,094	740,668
83	—	1,104,000	862,651	1,132,356
84	—	2,107,857	1,320,951	1,859,335
85	—	682,105	696,238	1,078,719
87	—	684,539	2,627,261	2,076,278
89	—	16,539	8,555	14,027
90	—	521,973	314,009	555,250
91	—	8,926	19,432	1,004,873
92	—	93,334	57,581	310,226
93	—	13,533	4,776	44,350
94	—	1,067,647	754,863	1,450,873
95	—	42,349	22,146	166,733
96	—	31,088	12,669	40,251
97	—	1,990,522	1,024,801	1,813,443
98	—	118,210	85,310	151,048
99	—	0,477	2,211	3,273
Total	—	71,262,113	63,114,176	74,940,728

BIBLIOGRAPHY

Anonymous, "Kluft zwischen Teheran und EG", in: *Handelsblatt* of 13 July 1978.

Balassa, B., "European Integration: Problems and Issues", in: *The American Economic Review, Papers and Proceedings*, Vol. 53 (1963), No. 2, p. 175-184.

"Tariff Protection in Industrial Countries: An Evaluation", in: The Journal of Political Economy, Vol. 73 (1965), No. 6, p. 573-594.

"Toward a Theory of Economic Integration", in: M. S. Wionczek (Ed.): *Latin American Economic Integration*, New York, Washington, London 1966, p. 21-31.

Baldwin, R. E., Murray, T., "MFN Tariff Reductions and Developing Country Trade Benefits under the GSP", in: *The Economic Journal*, Vol. 87 (1977), No. 345, p. 30-46.

Behnam, M. R., *Development and Structure of the Generalized System of Preferences*, in: Journal of World Trade Law, Vol. 9 (1975), No. 4, p. 442-458.

Blackhurst, R., "General Versus Preferential Tariff Reduction for LDC Exports: An Analysis of Welfare Effects", in: *The Southern Economic Journal*, Vol. 38 (1972), No. 3, p. 350-362.

Borrmann, A., Vogelsang, D., et al., *Zum Verhältnis von Außenwirtschafts- und Entwicklungspolitik*, Hamburg 1975.

Bundesminister der Finanzen (Ed.), *Deutscher Gebrauchs-Zolltarif (DGebrZT)*, Bonn 1973 and 1976.

Bundesstelle für Außenhandelsinformationen, "Allgemeine Zollpräferenzen gegenüber Entwicklungsländern", in: *BfA-Zollinformationen*, Zolldienst, No. 11, 1975, p. 9 ff.

Clague, K. C., "The Trade Effects of Tariff Preferences", in: *The Southern Economic Journal*, Vol. 38 (1972), No. 3, p. 379-389.

Cooper, R. N., *The European Community's System of Generalized Tariff Preferences: A Critique*, Yale University, Economic Growth Center, Center Paper No. 185, New Haven, Connecticut 1973.

Corden, W. M., *The Theory of Protection*, Oxford 1971.

Donges, J., Fels, G., Neu, A. D., et al., *Protektion und Branchenstruktur der westdeutschen Wirtschaft, Kieler Studien* No. 123, Tübingen 1973.

European Communities

The Community's Generalized Tariff Preferences Schemes

Schemes

1971 "Council Regulations (EEC) Nos. 1308/71 to 1314/71 inclusive, of 21 June 1971 (1971 scheme, except ECSC products)". OJ No. L 142 of 28 June 1971.
"Decisions of the Representatives of the Governments of the Member States of the European Coal and Steel Community, meeting in Council of 21 June 1971—71/232/ECSC and 71/233/ECSC (ECSC products)". OJ No. L 142 of 28 June 1971.

1972 "Council Regulations (EEC) Nos. 2794/71 to 2800/71 inclusive, of 20 December 1971 (1972 scheme, except ECSC products)". OJ No. L 287 of 30 December 1971.
"Decisions of the Representatives of the Governments of the Member States of the European Coal and Steel Community, meeting in Council of 20 December 1971—71/403/ECSC and 71/4041/ECSC (ECSC products)". OJ No. L 287 of 30 December 1971.

1973 "Council Regulations (EEC) Nos. 2761/72 to 2767/72 inclusive, of 19 December 1972 (1973 scheme, except ECSC products)". OJ No. L 296 of 30 December 1972.
"Decisions of the Representatives of the Governments of

the Member States of the European Coal and Steel Community, meeting in Council of 19 December 1972—72/432/ECSC and 72/433/ECSC (ECSC products)". OJ No. L 296 of 30 December 1972.

1974 "Council Regulations (EEC) Nos. 3500/73 to 3509/73 inclusive, of 18 December 1973 (1974 scheme, except ECSC products, textile products originating in Yugoslavia and raw or unmanufactured flue-cured Virginia type tobacco)". OJ No. L 358 of 28 December 1973.

"Decisions of the Representatives of the Governments of the Member States of the European Coal and Steel Community, meeting in Council of 18 December 1973—73/443/ECSC and 73/444/ECSC (ECSC products)". OJ No. L 358 of 28 December 1973.

"Council Regulations (EEC) Nos. 3577/73 and 3578/73 of 28 December 1973 (textile products originating in Yugoslavia)". OJ No. L 359 of 28 December 1973.

"Council Regulation (EEC) No. 166/74 of 21 January 1974 (raw flue-cured Virginia type tobacco)". OJ No. L 20 of 24 January 1974.

1975 "Council Regulations (EEC) Nos. 3045/74 to 3058/74 of 12 December 1974 (1975 scheme, except ECSC products, pepper, and vegetable oils)". OJ No. L 329 of 9 December 1974.

"Decisions of the Representatives of the Governments of the Member States of the European Coal and Steel Community, meeting in Council of 2 December 1974—74/596/ECSC and 74/597/ECSC (ECSC products)". OJ No. L 329 of 9 December 1974.

"Council Regulation (EEC) No. 1213/75 of 7 May 1975 (pepper, vegetable oils)". OJ No. L 124 of 15 May 1975.

"Corrigenda to Council Regulations (EEC) Nos. 3052/74 to 3055/74". OJ No. L 10 of 15 January 1975.

"Corrigenda to Council Regulations (EEC) Nos. 3045/74, 3047/74, 3048/74, 3052/74, 3054/74 and 3055/74". OJ No. L 121 of 14 May 1975.

1976 "Council Regulations (EEC) Nos. 3001/75 to 3015/75 inclusive, of 17 November 1975 (1976 scheme, except ECSC products)". OJ No. L 310 of 29 November 1975.

"Decisions of the Representatives of the Governments of the Member States of the European Coal and Steel Community, meeting in Council of 17 November 1975—75/694/ECSC and 75/695/ECSC (ECSC products)". OJ No. L 310 of 29 November 1975.

"Corrigenda to Council Regulations (EEC) Nos. 3003/75, 3004/75, 3008/75, 3009/75, 3010/75, 3011/75, 3012/75, 3013/75, 3014/75, 3015/75 and to the Decisions of the Representatives of the Governments of the Member States of the European Coal and Steel Community, meeting in Council of 17 November 1975—75/694/ECSC and 75/695/ECSC". OJ No. L 44 of 20 February 1976.

1977 "Council Regulations (EEC) Nos. 3019/76 to 3029/76 inclusive, of 13 December 1976 (1977 scheme, except ECSC products)". OJ No. L 349 of 20 December 1976.

"Decisions of the Representatives of the Governments of the Member States of the European Coal and Steel Community, meeting in Council of 13 December 1976—76/908/ECSC and 76/909/ECSC (ECSC products)". OJ No. L 349 of 20 December 1976.

"Council Regulations (EEC) Nos. 523/77 and 524/77 (repealing from 1 April 1977 Council Regulations (EEC) No. 3028/76 and 3029/76 regarding preserved pineapples)". OJ No. L 73 of 21 March 1977.

"Corrigenda to Council Regulation (EEC) No. 3022/76 of 13 December 1976 (textile articles)". OJ No. L 112 of 4 May 1977.

1978 "Council Regulations (EEC) Nos. 2703/77 to 2713/77 inclusive, of 28 November 1977 (1978 scheme, except ECSC products)". OJ No. L 324 of 19 December 1977.

"Decisions of the Representatives of the Governments of the Member States of the European Coal and Steel Community, meeting in Council of 28 November 1977—77/768/ECSC and 77/769/ECSC (ECSC products)". OJ No. L 324 of 19 December 1977.

Rules of origin

"Commission Regulation (EEC) No. 1371/71 of 30 June 1971 (general)". OJ No. L 146 of 1 July 1971.

"Commission Regulation (EEC) No. 2171/71 of 11 October 1971 (extension of the time limit for admission into the Community of products benefiting from the GSP, under certain conditions)". OJ No. L 229 of 12 October 1971.

"Commission Regulation (EEC) No. 2862/71 of 22 December 1971 (general)". OJ No. L 289 of 31 December 1971.

"Commission Regulation (EEC) No. 2818/72 of 22 December 1972 (general)". OJ No. L 297 of 24 December 1972.

"Commission Regulation (EEC) No. 3188/73 of 22 November 1973 (textile products)". OJ No. L 323 of 24 November 1973.

"Commission Regulations (EEC) No. 3614/73 of 20 December 1973 (general) and No. 3615/73 of 20 December 1973 (cumulative origin)". OJ No. L 358 of 28 December 1973.

"Commission Regulation (EEC) No. 460/74 of 21 February 1974 (extension of List A)". OJ No. L 55 of 26 February 1974.

"Commission Regulations (EEC) No. 3106/74 of 5 December 1974 (general), No. 3107/74 of 5 December 1974 (cumulative origin—ASEAN), No. 3108/74 of 5 December 1974 (cumulative origin—MCCA), No. 3109/74 of 5 December 1974 (cumulative origin—Andean group)," OJ No. L 336 of 16 December 1974.

"Commission Regulations (EEC) No. 3214/75 of 3 December 1975 (general), No. 3215/75 of 3 December 1975 (cumulative origin—ASEAN), No. 3216/75 of 3 December 1975 (cumulative origin—MCCA), No. 3217/75 of 3 December 1975 (cumulative origin—Andean group)." OJ No. L 323 of 15 December 1975.

"Commission Regulations (EEC) No. 3200/76 of 21 December 1976 (general), No. 3201/76 of 21 December 1976 (cumulative origin—ASEAN), No. 3202/76 of 21 December 1976 (cumulative origin—MCCA), No. 3203/76 of 21 December 1976 (cumulative origin—Andean group)." OJ No. L 361 of 30 December 1976.

"Commission Regulation (EEC) No. 230/77 of 2 February 1977 repealing Article 9 of Regulations (EEC) Nos. 3201/76, 3202/76 and 3203/76 of the Commission as regards the definition of the concept of originating products in connection with the generalized scheme of preferences". OJ No. L 31 of 3 February 1977.

"Commission Regulations (EEC) No. 2966/77 of 23 December 1977 (general), No. 2967/77 of 23 December 1977 (cumulative origin—ASEAN), No. 2968/77 of 23 December 1977 (cumulative origin—MCCA), No. 2969/77 of 23 December 1977 (cumulative origin—Andean group)." OJ No. L 351 of 31 December 1977.

Other EC publications

"Council Regulation (EEC) No. 1/73 of 19 December 1972 amending Regulation (EEC) No. 950/68 on the common customs tariff". OJ No. L 1 of 1 January 1973, p. 1ff.

"Council Regulation (EEC) No. 3000/75 of 17 November 1975 amending Regulation (EEC) No. 950/68 on the common customs tariff". OJ No. L 304 of 24 November 1975, p. 1 ff.

"Council Regulation (EEC) No. 3065/75 of 24 November 1975 amending Regulation (EEC) 1445/72 concerning the nomenclature of goods for the external trade statistics of the Communities and statistics of trade between Member States (NIMEXE)". OJ No. L 307 of 27 November 1975, p. 1 ff.

Commission of the European Communities

Practical Guide to the Use of the European Communities' Scheme of Generalized Tariff Preferences, Brussels and Luxemburg 1976, 1977 and 1978.

European Communities Generalized Tariff Preferences Scheme for 1977, COM (76) 303 final of 30 June 1976.

List of Main EEC Agreements with Other Countries. Europe Information, External Relations (1978) No. 6.

European Parliament

"Report drawn up on behalf of the Committee on Development and Co-operation on the Proposals from the Commission of the European Communities to the Council (Doc. 254/77) concerning regulations relating to the application for the year 1978 of the generalized tariff preferences of the European Community". *European Parliament, Working Documents 1977-1978*, Doc. 302/

77 of 10 October 1977.
"Written Question No. 52/77", OJ Vol. 20, No. C 162 of 11 July 1977.
"Proposals from the Commission of the European Communities to the Council concerning the application for the year 1978 of the generalized tariff preferences of the European Community", *European Parliament, Working Documents 1977-1978*, Doc. 245/ 77 of 9 September 1977.

Evans, C., *A Possible Solution to the Conflict Between the General Agreement and Preferential Arrangements in Favor of Developing Countries*, Geneva 1970.

Feldsieper, M., *Zollpräferenzen für Entwicklungsländer, Bochumer Schriften zur Entwicklungsforschung und Entwicklungspolitik*, Vol. 20, Tübingen and Basle 1975.

Ferguson, C. E.; Humphrey, D. D., "The Domestic and World Benefit of a Customs Union", in: *Economia Internazionale*, Vol. XIII, 1960, p. 197-216.

Finger, J. M., "The Generalized Scheme of Preferences—Impact on the Donor Countries", in: *Bulletin of Economic Research*, Vol. 25 (1973), No. 1, p. 43-54.

Fuhrmann, G., "Die Zukunft des Zollpräferenzsystems für Entwicklungsländer", in: *Außenwirtschaftsdienst des Betriebs-Beraters*, Vol. 17 (1971), No. 11, p. 515-518.

Gehrels, F., "Customs Union from a Single-Country Viewpoint", in: *The Review of Economic Studies*, Vol. 24 (1956-1957), No. 63, p. 61-64.

Hiemenz, H.; Hoffmann, L.; Rabenau, K. von, "Die Theorie der effektiven Protektion", in: *Weltwirtschaftliches Archiv*, Vol. 107, Part II, Tübingen 1971, p. 191-234.

Hörig, E. A., "Allgemeine Zollpräferenzen für Entwicklungsländer", in: *Nachrichten für Außenhandel*, No. 7 of 10 January 1974, No. 242 of 16 December 1974, No. 2 of 5 January 1976, No. 10 of 14 January 1977, No. 6 of 9 January 1978, No. 66 of 3 April 1979.

Iqbal, Z., "Uberprüfung der Präferenzsysteme", in: *Finanzierung und Entwicklung*, Vol. 12 (1975), No. 3, p. 34-39.

Johann, H., *Zollpräferenzen zugunsten von unterentwickelten Ländern*, Hamburg 1969.

Johnson, H. G., *Economic Policies Toward Less Developed Countries*, Washington 1967.

Keferstein, K., *Förderung des Außenhandels unter Entwicklungsländern - eine entwicklungspolitische Alternative?*, Frankfurt 1978.

Krämer, H. R., *"Zwei Jahre Zollpräferenzen der Europäischen Gemeinschaften zugunsten von Entwicklungsländern - Methoden und erste Ergebnisse"*, in: *Die Weltwirtschaft*, ed. by H. Giersch, 1973, No. 1, p. 196-212.

Kühn, J., *"Gemeinschaftliche Zollpräferenzen für Entwicklungsländer"*, in: *Presse- und Informationsamt der Bundesregierung*, Bulletin, No. 96 of 24 June 1971.
"Handelspolitik auf dem Prüfstand", in: *Handelsblatt*, No. 204 of 22 October 1973.

Lerche, D., *Grundlagen und Perspektiven des Euro-Arabischen Dialogs. Schriften des Deutschen Instituts für Entwicklungspolitik (DIE)*, Vol. 46, Berlin 1977.

Linder, St. B., "Customs, Unions and Economic Development", in: M. S. Wionczek (Ed.): *Latin American Economic Integration, Experiences and Prospects*, New York, etc. 1966, p. 32-41.

Meade, J. E., *The Theory of Customs Unions*, Amsterdam 1955.

Meier, G. M., *Problems of Cooperation for Development*, New York, London, Toronto 1974.

Meyer, F. W., *"Uber die Auswirkungen von Zollpräferenzen"*, in: E. v. Beckerath (Ed.): *Wirtschaftsfragen der freien Welt*, Frankfurt/Main 1957, p. 608-616.

Möbius, U., *"Gemeinschaftskontingente für gewerbliche Produkte aus Entwicklungsländern"*, in: *DIW-Wochenbericht*, Vol. 41 (1974), No. 29, p. 253-257.

Murray, T., *Trade Preferences for Developing Countries*, London and Basingstoke 1977.
"How Helpful is the Generalized System of Preferences to Developing Countries?", in: *The Economic Journal*, Vol. 83 (1973), p. 449-455.

Niemeier, E., *Zollpräferenzen für Entwicklungsländer*, Hamburg 1970.

OECD, *Development Co-operation*, 1977 Review, Paris 1977.

Pickel, R., *Handelspräferenzen als Mittel der Entwicklungspolitik unter besonderer Berücksichtigung des EWG- und des neuen australischen Präferenzsystems*, Diss., Cologne 1969.

Pitrone, A., *EEC GSP Scheme*, Rome, n.d.

Poser, K., *Die Wirkungen internationaler Präferenzsysteme auf Preise und Handelsströme - Eine preistheoretische Analyse, Volkswirtschaftliche Schriften*, No. 77, Berlin 1964.

Prebisch, R., *Towards a New Trade Policy for Development: Report by the Secretary General of the United Nations Conference on Trade and Development*, New York 1964.

Schumacher, D., "Beschäftigungswirkungen von Importen aus Entwicklungsländern nicht dramatisieren", in: *DIW-Wochenbericht*, Vol. 45 (1978), No. 1, p. 6-11.

800 Erwerbstätige für den Export in Entwicklungsländern beschäftigt, in: *DIW-Wochenbericht*, Vol. 45 (1978), No. 5, p. 58-61.

Sellekaerts, W., *"How Meaningful are Empirical Studies on Trade Creation and Diversion"*, in: *Weltwirtschaftliches Archiv*, Vol. 109 (1973), No. 4, p. 519-553.

Statistical Office of the European Communities, Geonomenclature 1975-1976, Luxemburg 1977.

Monthly External Trade Bulletin, Special Issue 1958-1976, Luxemburg 1978.

Nomenclature of goods for the external trade statistics of the Communities and statistics of the trade between Member States (NIMEXE), 1973 issue with substitution pages for 1974 and 1975, Luxemburg 1972, 1973 and 1974.

Statistisches Bundesamt, Wiesbaden, *Internationales Warenverzeichnis für den Außenhandel (SITC II), German translation of the Standard International Trade Classification, Rev. 2, of the United Nations*, 1975, Stuttgart, Mainz 1976.

Steinbach, U., *"Der Europäisch-Arabische Dialog - ein Beitrag zum Frieden im Nahen Osten"*, in: *Verbund Stiftung Deutsches Übersee-Institut, Mitteilungen, 1st Quarter 1978*, p. 23-38.

Tigani, E. I., "Die ökonomische Bedeutung der allgemeinen Zollpräferenzen für Halb- und Fertigwaren der Entwicklungsländer", in: Vierteljahresberichte, Forschungsinstitut der Friedrich-Ebert-Stiftung (1976), No. 64, p. 129-142.

Tulloch, P., The Politics of Preferences, London 1975.

UNCTAD

The Generalized System of Preferences: Effects of the Enlargement of the European Economic Community, Geneva 1973, TD/B/C.5/8.

General Report on the Implementation of the Generalized System of Preferences, Geneva 1973, TD/B/C.5/9.

Second General Report on the Implementation of the Generalized System of Preferences, Geneva 1974, TD/B/C.5/22.

Review of the Schemes of Generalized Preferences of Developed Market-Economy Countries, Scheme of Generalized Preferences of the United States of America, Geneva 1975, TD/B/C.5/38.

The Generalized System of Preferences and the Least Developed Among the Developing Countries. Effects of the GSP on the Least Developed Among the Developing Countries, Geneva 1975, TD/B./C.5/39.

Third General Report on the Implementation of the Generalized System of Preferences, Geneva 1975, TD/B/C.5/41.

Review of the Schemes of Generalized Preferences of Developed Market—Economy Countries, Operation and Effects of the Scheme of Generalized Preferences of the European Economic Community: Study of the Operation of the Scheme in 1972, Geneva 1975, TD/B/C.5/34/Add. 1.

Consultations on Concrete Proposals for Improvements in the Rules of Origin, Including Greater Harmonization and Simplification. Comparative Analysis of the Rules of Origin Applied by the Preference—Giving Market Economy Countries, Geneva 1977, TD/B/C.5/WG (VI)/4.

Review of the Schemes of Generalized Preferences of Developed Market—Economy Countries, Trade Implications of the United States Scheme of Generalized Preferences, Geneva 1977, TD/B/C.5/47.

Resolution 96 (IV) of the United Nations Conference on Trade and Development, Section I, A, paragraph (a), quoted from UNCTAD: *Effects of the Generalized System of Preferences on Developing Countries. Sharing their Special Tariff Advantages as a Result of the Implementation of the System Convention*, Geneva 1977, TD/B/C.5/49, Add. 1, p. 3.

Effects of the Generalized System of Preferences on Developing Countries Sharing their Special Tariff Advantages as a Result of the Implementation of the System: The GSP and the Lomé Convention, Geneva 1977, TD/B/C.5/49, Add. 1.

Effects of the Generalized System of Preferences on Developing Countries Sharing their Special Tariff Advantages as a Result of the Implementation of the System: The GSP and the EEC/ Maghrib Co-operation Agreements, Geneva 1977, TD/B/C.5/ 49, Add. 2.

Other Questions Related to the Operation of the Generalized System of Preferences: The Generalized System of Preferences and the Multilateral Trade Negotiations, Geneva 1977, TD/B/ C.5/52.

Fourth General Report on the Implementation of the Generalized System of Preferences, Geneva 1977, TD/B/C.5/53.

Generalized System of Preferences. Replies from Preference-receiving countries, Geneva 1977, TD/B/C.5/54 and Add. 1.

Generalized System of Preferences, Cumulative list of Documents, Geneva 1977, TD/B/GSP/DOC 5/2.

UNCTAD/UNDP

Generalized System of Preferences. Handbook on the Scheme of Japan, Geneva 1976, UNCTAD/TAP/81/Rev. 3.

Generalized System of Preferences. Handbook of the Scheme of the European Economic Community 1974, 1975, 1976, Geneva 1974, 1975, 1976, UNCTAD/TAP/104/Rev. 1, 2, 3.

Generalized System of Preferences. Digest of Rules of Origin, Geneva 1976, UNCTAD/TAP/133/Rev. 2.

Generalized System of Preferences. Handbook of the Scheme of the United States of America, Geneva 1976, UNCTAD/ TAP/163/Rev. 1.

Generalized System of Preferences. Handbook of the Scheme of Austria, Finland, Norway, Sweden and Switzerland, Geneva 1976, UNCTAD/TAP/177.

Viner, J., *The Customs Union Issue*, New York and London 1950.

Vogel, W., *"Abkommen der Europäischen Wirtschaftsgemeinschaft mit Algerien, Marokko und Tunesien"*, in: *Mitteilungen der Bundesstelle für Außenhandelsinformation, Beilage zu den NfA*, Vol. 26 (1976), No. 163.

Weintraub, S., *Trade Preferences for Undeveloped Countries*, New York, etc. 1976.

COLOPHON

letter: times 11/13, 10/10 and 8/10
setter: Loonzetterij Aalsmeer
printer: Samsom Sijthoff Grafische Bedrijven
binder: Callenbach
cover-design: Jan Jonkers